American Folk Music and Musicians Series

SERIES EDITOR: RALPH LEE SMITH
1. *Wasn't That a Time! Firsthand Accounts of the Folk Music Revival,* edited by Ronald D. Cohen. 1995, paperback edition, 2002.
2. *Appalachian Dulcimer Traditions,* by Ralph Lee Smith. 1997, paperback edition, 2001.

SERIES EDITORS: RALPH LEE SMITH AND RONALD D. COHEN
3. *Ballad of an American: The Autobiography of Earl Robinson,* by Earl Robinson with Eric A. Gordon. 1998.
4. *American Folk Music and Left-Wing Politics, 1927–1957,* by Richard A. Reuss with JoAnne C. Reuss. 2000.
5. *The Hammered Dulcimer: A History,* by Paul M. Gifford. 2001.

SERIES EDITORS: RONALD D. COHEN AND ED KAHN
6. *The Unbroken Circle: Tradition and Innovation in the Music of Ry Cooder and Taj Majal,* by Fred Metting. 2001.
7. *The Formative Dylan: Transmission and Stylistic Influences, 1961–1963,* by Todd Harvey. 2001.

SERIES EDITORS: RONALD D. COHEN
8. *Exploring Roots Music: Twenty Years of the JEMF Quarterly,* edited by Nolan Porterfield. 2004.
9. *Revolutionizing Children's Records: The Young People's Records and Children's Record Guild Series, 1946–1977,* by David Bonner. 2007.
10. *Paul Clayton and the Folksong Revival,* by Bob Coltman. 2008.
11. *A History of Folk Music Festivals in the United States: Feasts of Musical Celebration,* by Ronald D. Cohen. 2008.
12. *Ramblin' Jack Elliott: The Never-Ending Highway,* by Hank Reineke. 2010.
13. *Appalachian Dulcimer Traditions: Second Edition,* by Ralph Lee Smith. 2010.
14. *A Pete Seeger Discography: Seventy Years of Recordings,* by David King Dunaway. 2011.
15. *The Ballad Collectors of North America: How Gathering Folksongs Transformed Academic Thought and American Identity,* edited by Scott B. Spencer. 2012.

The Ballad Collectors of North America

How Gathering Folksongs Transformed Academic Thought and American Identity

Edited by Scott B. Spencer

American Folk Music and Musicians, No. 15

THE SCARECROW PRESS, INC.
Lanham • Toronto • Plymouth, UK
2012

Published by Scarecrow Press, Inc.
A wholly owned subsidiary of The Rowman & Littlefield Publishing Group, Inc.
4501 Forbes Boulevard, Suite 200, Lanham, Maryland 20706
http://www.scarecrowpress.com

Estover Road, Plymouth PL6 7PY, United Kingdom

Copyright © 2012 by Scott B. Spencer

All rights reserved. No part of this book may be reproduced in any form or by any electronic or mechanical means, including information storage and retrieval systems, without written permission from the publisher, except by a reviewer who may quote passages in a review.

British Library Cataloguing in Publication Information Available

Library of Congress Cataloging-in-Publication Data

The ballad collectors of North America : how gathering folksongs transformed academic thought and American identity / edited by Scott B. Spencer.
 p. cm. -- (American folk music and musicians series)
Includes bibliographical references and index.
ISBN 978-0-8108-8155-6 (cloth : alk. paper) -- ISBN 978-0-8108-8156-3 (ebook)
1. Folk music--Collectors and collecting--United States. 2. Ballads, English--United States--History and criticism. 3. Folk music--United States--History and criticism. I. Spencer, Scott B., 1970-
ML3551.B18 2012
782.42162'1300922--dc23
2011028986

™ The paper used in this publication meets the minimum requirements of American National Standard for Information Sciences Permanence of Paper for Printed Library Materials, ANSI/NISO Z39.48-1992.

Printed in the United States of America

Contents

	Series Foreword *Ronald Cohen*	vii
1	Ballad Collecting: Impetus and Impact *Scott B. Spencer*	1
2	Franz Boas, the Phonograph, and the Columbia School *Erika Brady*	17
3	Ballad Collectors in the Ozarks *Norm Cohen*	37
4	Songcatchers in the West: Cowboy Songs *Guy Logsdon*	51
5	Songcatchers in the West: Other Traditions *Guy Logsdon*	67
6	Folk Song Collectors in the Midwest *James P. Leary*	83
7	Ballad Collectors in the Northeast *Nancy-Jean Ballard Seigel*	103
8	Four Songcatchers in Eastern Canada *I. Sheldon Posen*	121
9	The Lomaxes *Matthew Barton*	151
10	Robert Winslow Gordon *Paul J. Stamler*	171
11	Collecting Occupational Songs *Dan Milner*	191
12	Commodification and Revival *Paul J. Stamler*	207
	Index	223
	About the Contributors	235

Series Foreword

Ronald Cohen

The American Folk Music and Musicians Series began in 2002 with a volume of essays focusing on the folk revival of the 1960s, mostly memories of the participants. We now add a compilation of fascinating scholarly explorations of the lives and work of a variety of ballad and folksong collectors in North America during the early decades of the twentieth century. Most folk music histories focus on the songs and their performers, with little thought given to where the songs have come from, except for the work of D. K. Wilgus. In his far-reaching *Anglo-American Folksong Scholarship Since 1898* (1959), Wilgus focused on hundreds of published collections, but with little information or analysis about the collectors themselves. Moreover, there has been much published since Wilgus's groundbreaking study. The authors in *The Ballad Collectors of North America* have covered much geographical and topical ground, with detailed information on the collectors' backgrounds and contributions. There is also one chapter on eastern Canada, the first attempt for the series to include territory north of the United States. Editor Scott Spencer's insightful introduction places the chapters into their larger scholarly framework. Of course, these essays only scratch the surface, and much more work needs to be done on who the multitude of ballad and folksong collectors were and what they were able to accomplish. The next book in the series will be an in-depth history of the Kingston Trio.

Ronald D. Cohen

ONE
Ballad Collecting: Impetus and Impact

Scott B. Spencer

Just as ballad collectors across North America in the first half of the twentieth century simply collected folk songs, in the same way this volume is simply a series of biographies of those intrepid researchers. With research and experience, one finds that neither undertaking can possibly be limited to such an essentialist study. While the songs they collected and the books they published have become instrumental in the collective consciousness of our ideas of "folk" or what it is to be American, the stories of those who did the untidy work of the actual collecting—their personal journeys, their stories, the larger social and technologic currents in which they operated, and the impact their efforts had on larger social movements—are mostly unsung.

An image on the cover of this book is very telling. In the Library of Congress photograph collection, the lower left cover image is listed as "Blackfoot Chief, Mountain Chief making phonographic record at Smithsonian, 2/9/1916." While today's collectors and researchers are delighted by the original inclusion of the name of the singer and surrounding metadata, no mention is made of the pictured recordist. This volume will shed some light on these often unmentioned collectors and the stories behind their efforts. In the image in question, Frances Densmore is recording Mountain Chief on wax cylinder in the Smithsonian as part of the larger Cylinder Project. The story of how she came to that moment, the larger research she was undertaking which included that moment, and the academic and social context in which she undertook her research will be found in a following chapter.

Some of the most glaring contextual gaps in the stories of the ballad collectors have recently been filled with major publications on some of the most immediately recognizable ballad collectors—such as Alan Lomax (1915–2002)[1] and Sidney Robertson Cowell (1903–1995).[2] Yet, as stated eloquently in many of the following chapters, the bulk of the lesser-known field collectors have left little information on themselves in their volumes of collected folklore. This volume is intended to fill in some of the missing biographical information—to detail the lives of the collectors and the stories of why they were drawn to such dusty and grueling work, to bring the reader behind the microphone or transcriptionist's pen and begin to know the collectors themselves and the reasons why they were driven to gather songs across North America.

In presenting such biographies, it is difficult to ignore the prevailing academic trends and social movements often passing thorough and paralleling the movements of these collectors. Often called "songcatchers," these brave souls ventured into areas of the continent known to be insular, inaccessible, and wary of outsiders with the tools of the trade: pen and paper, cylinder recorder, personality, and perseverance. They did so to document ways of life thought to be quickly vanishing with the impact of radio and phonograph, printed page and broadcast media.

Though songcatchers often came to the practice with the purest of intentions, many had agendas in their collection efforts and sought out certain tropes within the larger ballad traditions. Others were moved by personal experience to collect songs and melodies. Many were driven by teachers who pushed them to collect rapidly vanishing lore—often of a particular predetermined genre. Others saw academic worth in the texts of songs and used them to relate both to earlier archetypes of song and to schools of thought in academia. A few even jumped on the ballad bandwagon—trying to make a name for themselves and a quick buck by singing and publishing songs in a burgeoning folk revival, hoping to solidify their reputation as a holder of folk knowledge, or anchoring their place in academia by publishing collections and critiques as part of a professorship.

Most of the songcatchers detailed in this book faced unexpected paradigm shifts during their efforts: a shift in focus from text to melody, the advent and eventual portability of recording technology, changing gender roles in academia, and even changing conceptions of where meaning and import lay in balladry as cultural memory and art form. In chapter 2, Erika Brady catches the use of transient technology as she details Franz Boaz's use of the phonograph to capture songs while at Columbia University and traces the incorporation of recording technology in academic fields such as musicology and folklore. Finally, as these ballad collectors gathered folk culture from around North America, their efforts, publications, and public appearances helped to influence a continent undergoing self-examination and the shaping of a collective identity early in an era of mass media and folk revival. In essence, the collectors brought localized traditions to greater audiences, enabling people to access a body of folk knowledge and eventually drive a national folk consciousness and resulting folk revival, as detailed in Paul Stamler's final chapter on commodification and revival of folksong.

It is difficult to find a more salient example of popular identity-driven folklore than in the collection of western song—especially that of cowboy songs. In a continent defined by westward expansion and the idea of the wild frontier, cowboy culture became an important identity marker and an internationally identifiable cultural export. In Guy Logsdon's chapter on the collectors of cowboy songs, Austin E. and Alta S. Fife shine through as exponents of the avid collector searching for windows into a base North American experience, the pathos and freedom of the cowboy, and the most authentic songs to represent the frontier:

> The best of the cowboy songs came into being after 1870 and before 1930. Their real substance consists of the candid and dramatic way in which they reveal the human condition in those decades of frontier life when men lived, labored, loved, and died where laws, conventions, and tradition were lacking or ineffectual. To the present generation, which feels the omnipresence of law, moral codes, economic and social conformity, and the tyrannies of technology, the *ethnic* significance of cowboy and western songs may well reside in the singer's (and listener's) vicarious experience with a moment of freedom and high adventure that is no longer possible in real life.[3]

Logsdon continues his study of the collectors of western traditions in the following chapter, covering a vast geographic region populated by economic migrants, escapees of the Dust Bowl of the 1930s, miners, ranchers, and those seeking a new life and identity. He details the influences of collectors of lesser-known but equally important traditions in the West—especially those collecting commonly overlooked Mormon song traditions. So much of American identity is wrapped up in ideas of the frontier and legends of the cowboys that it is surprising to learn of the diversity of traditions found in the West.

Balladry is popularly connected to Appalachia, and as Norm Cohen brings out in his chapter, many of the settlers in the Ozark Mountains brought their traditions from Appalachia during America's early waves of migration. Academics searching for "authentic songs" came to the Ozarks relatively late in the ballad craze but found rich sources of songs, variants, and singers. In his piece, Cohen also investigates the often artificial divide between academic and amateur ballad collectors. Usually touted as an important distinction in collection styles and results (especially by academic collectors), Cohen discusses two songcatchers with parallel interests, yet each firmly planted on opposite sides of this perceptual divide.

To continue a regional focus, James P. Leary, Nancy-Jean Seigel, and Sheldon Posen each bring to this collection chapters on songcatchers in central and northern areas of the continent. Again spotlighting the vast differences between geographic locations, we find that some of the greatest disparities between song traditions come from differences in local industry and natural resources, immigration patterns, and even means of locomotion. Leary brings us intrepid collectors sweating and drinking through bawdy songs in the logging camps of the upper Midwest and others searching to find continuity in songs sung by recent immigrants from around the world residing across the lower Midwest. He also reminds us how diverse the people of the Midwest have been, as the area functioned as a crossroads for migrants moving west past the shores of the Great Lakes, interacting with other migrants and various native peoples. Parallels can be found between songs of these inland seas and those discussed by Seigel. Her chapter on ballad collection in the New England states brings us songs of the sea and shore, sailing, logging and fishing, and also uses the collectors of the northeast as a window into the particular challenges and advantages women collectors faced in both the field and academia. Sheldon Posen's chapter on four songcatchers in eastern Canada sheds light on the role of the collector in the field, and especially the role of personality and writing style in ethnography. It also traces intersecting lines of inquiry—both by means of geographic and temporal proximity, and by approach toward developing styles of ethnography in song collection.

Dan Milner's chapter on occupational songs brings our focus back from that of regionalism, showing universal themes in song across the continent. His chapter also demonstrates the actual function of song in the workplace, as teams of sailors used songs to keep time as they collectively hauled a bowline, pumped a bilge, or hoisted sail. He also brings us to the canals and rail lines that connected many of the industrial and shipping centers, detailing the rich singing traditions on these early national highways. One of the surprising aspects of occupational song that Milner returns to is not only the physical function of the songs but also the amount of vital information wrapped up in them—from clues on how to survive in the mines when things go wrong, to historic news of tragic events, geographic information, and even availability of work in certain areas.

Finally, Matt Barton and Paul Stamler detail three of the larger names in ballad collection and folksong revival: John A. and Alan Lomax and Robert Winslow Gordon. Spanning the height of the ballad collection era, these three effectively ushered in a folk revival through their collection efforts, publications, and performance in the popular realm. Barton's chapter spans the era, from John Lomax's early academic affiliations to Alan's personal and political identification with the singers as people rather than objects of study. Stamler's piece on Robert Winslow Gordon brings wonderful contradictions in a collector's use of songs—showing that Gordon acted as dusty academic, adventurous collector in the field, popular serial writer, recording artist, and tragic figure.

FRANCIS JAMES CHILD AND THE IMPETUS TO COLLECT BALLADS

As suggested above, a book dedicated to the collectors of ballads in North America must necessarily cast a wide net, bringing together an entire continent, multiple schools of academic thought, a variety of recording technologies and arenas of publication, and a seemingly endless string of songs. If there is one common antecedent governing the following chapters, it is this: most of the collectors, ideas, institutions, and general fervor for the collection, study, and publication of ballads began with the pursuits of Harvard professor Francis James Child.

Francis James Child was born in February 1, 1825, in Boston.[4] His father was a sailmaker and a well-respected member of the community. In his obituary for Francis Child in the *Proceedings of the American Academy of Arts and Sciences*, C. E. Norton lauded the family and described the senior Child as "one of that class of intelligent and independent mechanics which has had a large share in determining the character of our democratic community, as of old the same class had in Athens and Florence."[5] The youngest of five brothers and sisters, Child attended public schools in Boston, excelling in a variety of subjects in the English High School, earning respect from his peers and achieving "all the honors."[6] Catching the attention of Epes Sargent Dixwell, the master of the Latin School in Boston, the Child family was encouraged to send Francis there in preparation for college.[7] In typical style, he placed top in his class and was encouraged to attend Harvard.[8]

Harvard University was a perfect match for Child despite self-perceived class disparities, and he quickly proved himself as "the best writer, best speaker, best mathematician, the most accomplished person in knowledge of general literature."[9] He was also quite popular with his schoolmates, posthumously noted by C. E. Norton that "the sweetness of his disposition, the pleasant mingling in his nature of gay spirits and serious purpose, his high principles, his unaffected modesty won the affection of his teachers and of his comrades."[10] Child was chosen as class orator, and graduated in 1846—again at the top of his class of sixty students.[11]

After graduation, Child was offered a tutorship in mathematics at Harvard and two years later accepted a tutorship there in history, political economy, and English literature.[12] During his tutorships, Child published a few edited volumes of poetry, including *Four Old Plays* (1848).[13] As graduate schools were a distinctly European phenomenon, a loan from Jonathan I. Bowditch, to whom *Four Old Plays* was dedicated, allowed Child to take a leave of absence from Harvard and remove himself to Germany where he studied English drama and Germanic philology at the University of Göttingen and Berlin's Humboldt University, where he attended talks by the influential brothers Grimm. The University of Göttingen later awarded him an honorary doctorate—one of three he received during the course of his life.[14] At the end of his studies in Germany, and at the age of twenty-six, he was invited to return to Harvard to replace Edward T. Channing as the Boylston Professor of Rhetoric and Oratory.[15] In 1876, University of California President Daniel Gilman, who was developing a university based on the German Humboldt model of higher education, offered Child a research professorship at the new Johns Hopkins University. Harvard relaxed the demands of the Boylston professorship, allowing Child to adopt the inaugural title of Professor of English and devote much of his time to ballad research.

He was married to Elizabeth Ellery Sedgwick in 1860, and together they had four children.

CHILD AND ORAL LITERATURE

As Professor of Rhetoric and Oratory, Child produced a number of editions of English poetry and from 1853 edited a series dedicated to British poets. Of the 130 volumes contained in this series, 8 volumes were dedicated to ballads, entitled *English and Scottish Ballads* vol. 1–8 (1857–1858).[16] Child's interest in balladry originated from a fascination with the fundamental differences between the written and spoken word, and especially with oral remnants of common oratory that might have predated written forms. This "oral literature" represented to Child a window into conceptual forms, or "thoughtful expression," prior to class distinctions associated with printed literature. As the folklore scholar David E. Bynum has offered, "Concerned as he thus so greatly was with rhetoric, oratory, and the motives of those mental disciplines, Child was inevitably drawn into pondering the essential differences between speech and writing, and to searching for the origins of thoughtful expression in English."[17]

Dedicated to the rubric of poetic expression, and despite having produced many volumes of British poets through his extensive series, he found the works of Chaucer to be particularly challenging—mainly due to Chaucer's incorporation of both oral and written traditions in his dialogue. English balladry must have been a refreshing turn for Child, as a system for coding and analyzing the texts might have even acted as a vehicle for better dealing with Chaucer. He commented that such ballad texts represented

> a distinct and very important species of poetry. Its historical and natural place is anterior to the appearance of the poetry of art, to which it

has formed a step, and by which it has been regularly displaced, and, in some cases, all but extinguished. Whenever a people in the course of its development reaches a certain intellectual and moral stage, it will feel an impulse to express itself, and the form of expression to which it is first impelled is, as is well known, not prose, but verse, and in fact narrative verse. Such poetry . . . is in its essence an expression of our common human nature, and so of universal and indestructible interest.[18]

His intent to work with popular ballads was twofold. He endeavored first to find the most authentic, pure, and unadulterated version of each ballad—whether by folk utterance, transcription, or printed source; he then strove to publish the most perfect form of that text—an ur-text—for future use by researchers into such areas.

Child expanded his original 1857–1858 work—collecting, amassing, and eventually categorizing into distinct textual families (with the assistance of a colleague over the course of twenty-one years) the plethora of texts, variants, and fragments of each ballad.[19] The undertaking was unprecedented, and as his student and protégée, George Lyman Kittredge (1860–1941), described in the eventual introduction to Child's tome,

> The book [*English and Scottish Ballads*, 1857–1858] circulated widely, and was at once admitted to supersede all previous attempts in the same field. To Mr. Child, however, it was but the starting-point for further researches. He soon formed the plan of a much more extensive collection on an altogether different model. This was to include every obtainable version of every extant English or Scottish ballad, with the fullest possible discussion of related songs or stories in the "popular" literature of all nations. To this enterprise be resolved, if need were, to devote the rest of his life. His first care was to secure trustworthy texts. In his earlier collection he had been forced to depend almost entirely on printed books. No progress, he was convinced, could be made till recourse could be had to manuscripts. . . . It was clear to Mr. Child that he could not safely take anything at second hand, and he determined not to print a line of his projected work till he had exhausted every effort to get hold of whatever manuscript material might be in existence. . . . A number of manuscripts were in private hands; of others the existence was not suspected. But Mr. Child was untiring.[20]

The resulting monumental work, *The English and Scottish Popular Ballads* (1882–1898), detailed 350 Child ur-ballads and came to be viewed as the crowning achievement of folklore at that time.[21] Child died after completing the bulk of the work, and Kittredge completed the introduction and bibliography to fulfill the project. The respect the work was awarded quickly canonized both publication and contents, leaving scarce theoretical room for the addition of further texts or an author with whom to debate. Of course, as with any canonization, there quickly came challenges to the completeness and veracity of the work.

Kittredge carried on the work of Child, presiding over the collection at Harvard and trebling its *collectanae*. He also dutifully trained the following generation of graduate students, including Phillips Barry (1880–1937), Samuel Preston Bayard (1908–1997), Bertrand Harris Bronson (1902–1986), Fannie Hardy Eckstorm (1865–1946), Helen Hartness Flanders (1890–1972), John Avery Lomax (1867–1948), and William Wells Newell (1839–1907). Kittredge often gets short shrift in the story of ballad collectors, though his impact over the course of generations was unparalleled.[22] One of Child's and Kittredge's lasting influences is the association between academic institution and ballad collection. As D. K. Wilgus has written,

> The most important single fact of American collection has been its close relationship to educational institutions. The institutions themselves have not always officially approved and supported folksong collection; but academic folklore interest encouraged teachers to take advantage of the American emphasis on universal education, which brought into the classroom informants and contacts with traditional culture. In the early years of the century the work of Professors Child and Kittredge had made Harvard University an unofficial center of folksong study. . . . The direct and indirect influence of Harvard University produced results which, when archives and theses are eventually surveyed, will be truly staggering.[23]

The turn of the century found many devotees of Child and the Harvard school battling over the texts of the Child ballads, debating ideas of authenticity in the texts, the singers, and the academic and publishing process. Kittredge himself went on to study and publish on witchcraft trials, Arthurian legends, and other areas, firmly planting himself in the field of folklore and eventually serving for a few years as president of the American Folklore Society. As scholars such as Bertrand Harris Bronson, Cecil J. Sharp (1859–1924), and Olive Dame Campbell (1882–1954) began to find other variants of Child ballads, and indeed other ballads throughout England and especially the Appalachian mountains of America, a steamy battle erupted over the validity of many of the new discoveries. With such battles also came fragmentation, as scholars turned to the melodies of the ballads, trying to find other approaches to the problems of authenticity and definitions of oral traditions.

As a result (and here I'll begin to paint with a broad academic brush), Kittredge's line of inquiry into remnants of English balladry surviving through migration led to Cecil Sharp's work on the melodies of the Child ballads, which led to Bronson's expanded view of ballad scholarship and Mieczyslaw Kolinski's (1901–1981) reanalyses of regional migration, transmission, and the relative impermanence of melody and text. Child and Kittredge's devotees and their strident work on the ballad tradition produced some of the most detailed and vibrant work on the idea of an oral tradition. Some of those working on oral traditions helped to pave the way for a wider acceptance of ballad forms in academic thought. Others challenged the fundamental principles behind Child's impetus to collect and the institutions dedicated to perpetuating the collections, marking the end of the ballad wars and the start of engagement with balladry by multiple academic fields of thought. Walter Ong (1912–2003) was one of those who challenged. A pioneer in the media ecology movement and professor of English literature, he attacked Child's fundamental premise:

> Scholarship in the past has generated such monstrous concepts as "oral literature." This strictly preposterous term remains in circulation today even among scholars now more and more acutely aware how embarrassingly it reveals our inability to represent to our own minds a heritage of verbally organized materials except as some variant of writing, even when they have nothing to do with writing at all. The title of the great Milman Parry Collection of Oral Literature at Harvard University monumentalizes the state of awareness of an earlier generation of scholars rather than that of its recent curators.[24]

In the decades before this final attack on Child's fundamental hypothesis for the study of balladry, a number of researchers influenced by Child's work opened lines of thought through unexplored academic paradigms.

POST-CHILD RESEARCHERS AND THE INVOLVEMENT OF OTHER DISCIPLINES

With the explosion of interpretations of the Child ballads, challenges to their organization, and demands for redefinitions of fundamental ideas of orality and literacy came adaptation of the ballad genre by multiple academic fields. The varied uses of these texts by diverse fields can be seen in some of the influential publications offered by Child and Kittredge's students.

In his work *The Traditional Tunes of the Child Ballads* (1959), Bertram Harris Bronson offers an abridged version of the Child ballads, including simple melodies along with the texts.[25] In this way, he opens the folkloric study of ballads to the musical realm, hastening the adoption of balladry by the field of ethnomusicology. Bronson notes that his collection has been somewhat limited by its constraint within Child's collected ballads, and hints that other ballad collectors were questioning the authority of Child himself: "It is very noticeable that of late students are becoming increasingly restive under Child's authority, more and more unwilling to grant a mere second-class citizenship to the ballads in their own collections which missed of his royal accolade."[26]

He also postulates that the focus of ballad research should be on the primacy of tune over the text. It should be noted that his inclusion of specific tune ballads reflects his perception of how well he thought the evidence worked. Because of this approach, many of the original Child ballads, especially obscure and rare variants, were eliminated from his study. Bronson uses the selected melodic variations in the tunes to study concepts of melodic tradition and transmission: "It is in the variants alone that we can study the process of melodic tradition and transmission; and through them alone can we hope to arrive at sound generalizations as to the laws and forces that find expression in these forms."[27] Through his paring down of the Child material and his primary focus on the melodies, it seems that Bronson attempted to remake the definitive collection of ballads for future studies, and to influence subsequent studies of ballad material toward the melodic rather than the textual.

One important distinction in Bronson's approach toward ballad study was his belief that variations by the same singer on the same tune relate to a larger musical conception of that tune, one that would permit variation and still retain its identity. His theory of tune perception suggests that a reduction of all versions and variants of a particular singer would let us know what the singer "had in mind." In many ways, this concept relates to Saussure's ideas of *langue* and *parole* in linguistics: a ballad could have many different instances or performances, but would still adhere to an overarching idea of the ur-ballad, as Child had assumed.[28]

D. K. Wilgus, in his *Anglo-American Folksong Scholarship Since 1898* (1959), suggests that any modern study of ballad or folksong should also turn to collected recordings.[29] In particular, his work focuses on the study of extant Anglo-American folk song collections, yet he manages to contextualize this area of study within the larger trends in Scandinavia, Europe, and Canada. One of the more important aspects of Wilgus's work is his discussion of the role of American archives and collections. Wilgus describes the current holdings in American archives, noting the predominance of textual transcriptions over melodic transcriptions and recorded materials. Writing from the perspective of 1959, he argues that the current approach toward folksong scholarship demands a reinvestigation of the interrelationship between melody and text. As the early collectors tended to oversimplify their transcriptions, Wilgus suggests that their documents would benefit from support from concurrent recordings.

As an extension of this discussion, Wilgus wrote that the field should look beyond the standard studies of text and tune into the context of the songs and their performance (opening such research to field of ethnomusicology). He noted that the early collectors focused their studies exclusively on ballad text, only turning to melodic material after the Child ballads had been canonized and closed to further additions. He also suggests that the students of Child, including Cecil Sharp and Tristram Coffin (1892–1955) — in using only the ballads collected by their predecessor — inadvertently acted to further isolate and canonize the Child ballads.

With his call for contextual analysis, Wilgus suggests that the recordings collected in the field might have substantial impact on the study of ballads. From this position, Wilgus discusses the quality of different recording formats for the preservation of folksong, chronicling the use of wax cylinders and wire and disc recorders — leaning heavily on the recording efforts of Alan Lomax and espousing the creation of the Archive of American Folksong in the Library of Congress.

Bertrand Harris Bronson, in his insightful collection of essays, *The Ballad as Song* (1969), presents his thoughts on ballad collection and scholarship surrounding the Child ballads.[30] With a predominant focus on transmission and variation, the essays function to reinterpret much of Bronson's previous work in the face of changing academic perspectives on ballad study. Bronson himself suggests that the book reflects "the author's persistent efforts to control the material collected and to gain a better understanding of various aspects of an inexhaustible field."[31] In a particularly important chapter, titled "The Morphology of the Ballad Tunes," he debates Sharp's tripartite model of Continuity, Selection, and Variation as applied to Child ballads. Bronson argues that Selection should be removed from the discussion as is too closely related to the other concepts and suggests that the model should be reworked to incorporate a "norm of traditional variation" in folk song. In doing so, he encourages the field to drop the previous "evolutionary" ideas surrounding the variations in ballads as proposed by Sharp and many of his students in favor of a current anthropological approach, allowing for change in performance and transmission as an important facet of culture.

Another of Bronson's effective chapters, "Folk-Song and Live Recording" serves as a tirade against the death of Folk-Song by the recording industry. Bronson suggests that any tendency by a singer toward individuality in interpretation will be wiped out through repeated exposure to a recording of the same piece. He also mentions that recordings shape the performance of Folk-Songs, since the media of the record demands variety and number of songs, and both recording media and radio insist on precise timing. He also comments on the impact that recordings were having on the learning process, stating that "when it has become easier for a singer to sit in his own room in California and learn a song from an Orkney Islander than to go across the street and learn one from a descendant of the forty-niners, it is folly to waste time any longer over questions of who learned what from where."[32] Bronson also puts on his musicologist's hat to write briefly on modality, the interrelationship of text and melody, melodic variation, and melodic cataloguing practices. He also explores the area of variation between modes within particular ballads and within particular regions — an area relatively unexplored, yet a plausible vehicle for further investigations by scholars into his theories on "norms of traditional variation."

With a new perspective gained from hindsight, Bronson's *The Singing Tradition of the Child Ballads* (1976) again attacks the Child ballads, trying to further reinterpret the monumental work for a new academic audience.[33] He offers a brief history of the post-Child attempts to gather melodies to the Child texts and comments that the return to the field by Child's followers reunited the study of printed music with its social and musical living tradition. Bronson links this historic return to the field by ballad collectors to the modern realm of the cultural anthropologists and ethnomusicologists in the following line: "Here, surprisingly, was uncovered a vast treasury of fresh oral versions, which in effect transformed the subject from an antiquarian study to a socio-musicological inquiry grounded in contemporary evidence."[34]

Bronson frequently comments on the role of variation in folksong scholarship, writing that ballad variants can rarely be found without substantial change over more than two or three generations, yet he argues that, in general, these tunes "cling to some sort of quintessential core of identity," and thus can be classified in families.[35] Legendary ethnomusicologist Bruno Nettl has taken this line of thought and discounted the need for classification. Writing on the importance of studying ballads in the development of the field of ethnomusicology, he suggests instead that the nature of musical change should be the object of study:

> I believe we should study change, record it, and preserve it. Change is, after all, a basic phenomenon of human culture. Its prevalence reminds us that we cannot look at culture as a stagnant group of "things." I would suggest that we abandon the musical artifact, the piece, the song, the individual situation as the focus of our study and begin to concentrate on the process of change itself.[36]

In sum, Bronson offers reinterpretations of the Child ballads, making them more current and palatable for modern scholars, while opening the subject matter to researchers from more musical subfields.

Seen as a movement, the aforementioned academic scattering, reinterpretation, and redefinition of the Child ballads by his acolytes came to be known as "the Ballad Wars." From it emerged a solidified theoretic concept of "the authentic" which assumed that authenticity was located in places beyond the text or melody. As scholars fetishized the work of particular folklorists and ballad collectors, an assumption arose that the inherent musical authenticity might be partly tied to the stature of the collector himself (and it usually was a him). Similarly, as Olive Dame Campbell proved through her ballad collecting efforts in Appalachia, authenticity could also be associated with region or even era. With so many academics involved in studying various aspects of balladry, a variety of academic fields other than English came to be involved. Folklorists were drawn to the individuals singing ballads and the stories told in them; musicologists came to see the melodies of the ballads as virtually tantamount to the texts themselves; ethnomusicologists embraced the nature of change and cultural context in song utterances; anthropologists used the ballads as a window into social structure and societal function. Such was the use of ballads by the academic set.

FOLK REVIVALS

Paul Stamler's chapter on Loraine Wyman (1885–1937) and Carl Sandburg (1878–1967) details an important shift in the use of ballads by the collectors themselves. His chapter explores the adroit blending of academic and popular work by two important collectors and brings us to the advent of commodification and an important folk revival. A number of studies have been presented on the topic of folk revivals, usually through the fields of ethnomusicology, folklore, or history, and often involving in-depth studies of the American folk music revival of the 1960s. Most of the relevant studies have been viewed through the popular academic lens of a political movement or labor struggle, as has been common in the fields of folklore and labor history. The influential essays in Neil Rosenberg's *Transforming Tradition: Folk Music Revivals Examined* (1993) largely stem from the academic view that the American postwar generation had developed a collective consciousness and embraced music as a tool for social and political change.[37] Serge Denisoff's masterful work, *Great Day Coming: Folk Music and the American Left* (1971) documents the early folksingers of the generation as they engaged with the labor movement and the Communist Party, and brought songs and songwriting skills to those attempting to organize labor unions or broadcast their views in political protests from the post-Depression era to the late 1960s.[38] Many of the ballads, movements, and documents of the time were brought to the politically engaged (especially of the Left) through popular publications such as *Sing Out!*; *Hootenanny*; *Little Sandy Review* (American); *Hoot!* (Canadian); and *Broadside* (which dealt with both American and British political struggles).

With the publication of such books as Whisnant's *All That Is Native and Fine* (1983),[39] Bogart's *Sense of Place* (1990),[40] McKay's *The Quest of the Folk* (1994),[41] and Filene's *Romancing the Folk* (2000),[42] this collective consciousness was conceptually subdivided into distinct yet interrelated geographic regions, as the subject matter is further subdivided into musical genre and political leanings. With the publication of (our series editor) Ronald D. Cohen's *Wasn't That a Time!: Firsthand Accounts of the Folk Music Revival* (1995), the accepted academic treatment of the folk revival shifted from the impartial academic treatise to that of involved informant.[43] Many of the authors represented in Cohen's work had been personally involved in the movement and were able to impart their own stories and academic training to the treatment of the subject. This new direction has influenced many of the works that have followed and seems to have shifted the academic standpoint of the folk revival scholar from casual observer to that of participant/observer—mirroring a parallel shift in much of the academic social sciences world.

This new academic approach is also reflected in the aforementioned *Transforming Tradition*, in which the authors bring to their writings an ongoing engagement with ideas of authenticity and "cultural borrowing" as performers wear the identities of the music they perform and shift between musical styles. In addition, Robert S. Cantwell's *When We Were Good: The Folk Revival* (1996)[44] and series editor Ronald Cohen's *Rainbow Quest: The Folk Revival and American Society 1940–1970* (2002) reflect this new approach, mixing narrative and scholarly approaches with personal experiences and solid historical research.[45]

Despite the strict interpretations of these works on the political nature of the folk revival, such studies have tended to break down in the post-revival era. As Gillian Mitchell mentions in her work on the North American folk movement (2007), the revival (and I would argue any study on the revival) breaks down with the protests surrounding the Chicago Democratic National Convention in 1968 and the impending invention of the World Music genre.[46]

A FINAL NOTE

Writing almost a century and a half after Child's groundbreaking *English and Scottish Ballads* and merely pages ahead of a series of fascinating stories surrounding the intervening years of collection and publication efforts, a few words must be said about longevity. First, the songs and memories of ballad singers long dead—entrusted to page, scratched into wax, printed in musty collections—are still singular sources of fascination, regardless of what has been done with them in the ensuing centuries. Second, I must mention that as a product of educational systems and student of professors so profoundly shaped by the Ballad Wars, I am honored to turn my attention back to the subject matter that brought me to my graduate studies and influenced me throughout my studies. In conversations with the other authors in this volume, we have collectively realized that despite our varied musical backgrounds and wide range of academic fields, we have all been profoundly influenced by those collectors of songs before us and would wish to thank them for their work. Personally, I owe debts of gratitude to many noted in this volume and feel (as many here do) that we are merely standing on the shoulders of the collectors who have come before us. That a handful of these deserving individuals finally have their stories told is all ample reward for this undertaking.

Longevity takes many forms, and the various authors and editors surrounding this project know this well. Originally developed by Ed Cray, this project has been slowly shaped by series editor Ronald Cohen, rekindled by Dan Milner during a chance conversation on Child after a rehearsal in New York City, reshaped again by Ronald Cohen, and finally steeped in the patience and wisdom of Scarecrow's own Bennett Graff. Thanks should also be said to the digital prowess of Fergus Fahey at the National University of Ireland, Galway, who turned paper-based straw into digital gold with his magical scanner.

NOTES

1. Ronald D. Cohen, ed., *Alan Lomax, Assistant in Charge: The Library of Congress Letters, 1935–1945* (Jackson: University Press of Mississippi, 2011); John Szwed, *Alan Lomax: The Man Who Recorded the World* (New York: Viking Press, 2010); Ronald D. Cohen, ed., *Alan Lomax: Selected Writings, 1934–1997* (New York: Routledge, 2005). This volume includes introductory essays by Gage Averill, Matthew Barton, Ronald D. Cohen, Ed Kahn, and Andrew L. Kaye.

2. Deirdre Ní Chonghaile, *'ag teacht le cuan': Irish traditional music and the Aran Islands* (unpublished PhD dissertation, University College Cork, Ireland, 2010); and a forthcoming article for the *Journal of American Folklore*.

3. Austin E. and Alta S. Fife, eds. *Cowboy and Western Songs: A Comprehensive Anthology* (New York: Clarkson N. Potter, Inc., 1960), xi.

4. C. E. Norton, "Francis James Child," *Proceedings of the American Academy of Arts and Sciences* 32:17 (July 1897), 333–339.

5. Norton, *Proceedings*, 333.

6. Norton, *Proceedings*, 333.

7. Norton, *Proceedings*, 333; Sigrid Rieuwerts, "In Memoriam: Francis James Child (1825–1896)," in Tom Cheesman and Sigrid Rieuwerts, eds., *Ballads into Books: The Legacies of Francis James Child: Selected Papers from the 26th International Ballad Conference, Swansea, Wales, 19–24 July 1996* (Berne: Peter Lang, European Academic Publishers, 1977), 20.

8. Norton, *Proceedings*, 333.

9. James C. Turner, *The Liberal Education of Charles Eliot Norton* (Baltimore: Johns Hopkins University Press, 2002), 50.

10. Norton, *Proceedings*, 333.

11. Norton, *Proceedings*, 333; Turner, *Liberal Education*, 54.

12. Rieuwerts, "In Memoriam," 20.

13. Francis James Child, *Four Old Plays: Three Interludes: Thersytes, Jack Jugler and Heywood's Pardoner and Frere: and Jocasta, a Tragedy by Gascoigne and Kinwelmarsh, with an Introduction and Notes* (Cambridge, MA: G. Nichols, 1848).

14. Rieuwerts, "In Memoriam," 20. The others include Columbia and Harvard.

15. Rieuwerts, "In Memoriam," 20.

16. Francis James Child, *English and Scottish Ballads* vol. 1–8 (Boston: Little, Brown, 1857–1858); G. L. Kittredge "Preface," in Francis James Child, *English and Scottish Popular Ballads*, xxvi.

17. David E. Bynum, *Child's Legacy Enlarged: Four Generations of Oral Literary Studies at Harvard University Since 1856* (Cambridge, MA: Center for the Study of Oral Literature, 1974).

18. Walter Morris Hart, "Professor Child and the Ballad," *PMLA* 21 (1906), 756.
19. Tom Cheesman and Sigrid Rieuwerts, eds., *Ballads into Books: The Legacies of Francis James Child: Selected Papers from the 26th International Ballad Conference, Swansea, Wales, 19–24 July 1996* (Berne: Peter Lang, European Academic Publishers, 1977), 12.
20. G. L. Kittredge, "Francis James Child," in F. J. Child, *The English and Scottish Popular Ballads*, vol. 10 (Boston: Houghton Mifflin, 1898), xxvii–xxviii.
21. Francis James Child, *The English and Scottish Popular Ballads*, vols. 1–10 (Boston: Houghton Mifflin, 1882–1898).
22. Sadly, Kittredge will get short shrift in this chapter as well. For more information, please see his biography, Clyde Kenneth Hyder, *George Lyman Kittredge: Teacher and Scholar* (Lawrence: University of Kansas Press, 1962).
23. D. K. Wilgus, *Anglo-American Folksong Scholarship Since 1898* (New Brunswick: Rutgers University Press, 1959), 173–174.
24. Walter Ong, *Orality and Literacy: The Technologizing of the Word* (London and New York: Methuen, 1982), 11–12.
25. Bertrand Harris Bronson, *The Traditional Tunes of the Child Ballads: With Their Texts, According to the Extant Records of Great Britain and America* vols. 1–4 (Princeton: Princeton University Press, 1959).
26. Bronson, *Traditional Tunes*, xiii.
27. Bronson, *Traditional Tunes*, xxiii.
28. See Ferdinand de Saussure, *Course in General Linguistics*, translated by Roy Harris (LaSalle, IL: Open Court Publishing Company, 1972).
29. Wilgus, *Anglo-American*.
30. Bertrand Harris Bronson, *The Ballad as Song* (Berkeley: University of California Press, 1969).
31. Bronson, *Ballad as Song*, vii.
32. Bronson, *Ballad as Song*, 147.
33. Bertrand Harris Bronson, ed., *The Singing Tradition of Child's Popular Ballads* (Princeton: Princeton University Press, 1976).
34. Bronson, *Singing Tradition*, xxii.
35. Bronson, *Singing Tradition*, xxx.
36. Bruno Nettl, "The Concept of Preservation in Ethnomusicology," in Irene V. Jackson, ed., *More Than Drumming: Essays on African and Afro-Latin American Music and Musicians* (Westport, CT: Greenwood Press, 1985), 18.
37. Neil Rosenberg, ed., *Transforming Tradition: Folk Music Revivals Examined* (Bloomington: University of Illinois Press, 1993).
38. R. Serge Denisoff, *Great Day Coming: Folk Music and the American Left* (Bloomington: University of Illinois Press, 1971).
39. David Whisnant, *All That Is Native and Fine: The Politics of Culture in an American Region* (Chapel Hill: University of North Carolina Press, 1983).
40. Barbara Allen Bogart, *Sense of Place: American Regional Cultures* (Louisville: University Press of Kentucky, 1990).
41. Ian McKay, *The Quest of the Folk: Antimodernism and Cultural Selection in Twentieth-Century Nova Scotia* (Montreal: McGill–Queens University Press, 1994).
42. Benjamin Filene, *Romancing the Folk: Public Memory and American Roots Music* (Chapel Hill: University of North Carolina Press, 2000).
43. Ronald D. Cohen, *Wasn't That a Time!: Firsthand Accounts of the Folk Music Revival*, (Lanham, MD: Scarecrow Press, 1995).
44. Robert S. Cantwell, *When We Were Good: The Folk Revival* (Cambridge, MA: Harvard University Press, 1996).
45. Ronald D. Cohen, *Rainbow Quest: The Folk Revival and American Society 1940–1970* (Boston: University of Massachusetts Press, 2002).
46. Gillian Mitchell, *The North American Folk Music Revival: Nation and Identity in the United States and Canada, 1945–1980* (Surrey, England: Ashgate Publishing, 2007).

TWO

Franz Boas, the Phonograph, and the Columbia School

Erika Brady

> Give not, give not the yawning grave its plunder,
> Save, save the lore for future ages' joy:
> The stories full of beauty and of wonder
> The songs more pristine than the songs of Troy,
> The ancient speech forever to be banished—
> Lore that tomorrow to the grave goes down!
> All other thoughts from our horizons banish,
> Let any sacrifice our labor crown.
> —John Peabody Harrington[1]

Although not best known of the many ethnologists employed by the Bureau of American Ethnology (BAE) over its eighty-six–year span, John Peabody Harrington might stand as an exemplar of the agency's field staff in its heyday. His devoted documentation of the languages, mythology, and other lore of the native people of California remains a source of astonishment in equal measure for its extent and its disorganization. His anthem to the task, composed in 1922 to honor his colleague C. Hart Merriam, suggests the urgency felt by Harrington and his cohort in their efforts to "save, save the lore" and tidy up the collections later. The stanza quoted above represents a catalog of endangered cultural materials, emphasizing songs, stories, and language, all of which could be reduced to the collectors' category of "sound events."

Like their contemporaries—those "songcatchers" primarily in pursuit of Anglo-American ballad—ethnologists such as Harrington placed particular value on oral texts and understood their particular challenge to be the documentation of such "lore," often in tongues and musical modalities poorly served by conventional means of notation. Only by an almost obsessive amassing of particulars of expressive culture, directly observed and recorded, could any general understanding of the larger patterns with a group be understood. Like many of his colleagues at the BAE, as well as at academic centers for the developing field of cultural anthropology, Harrington's priorities and methods might be traced directly to the influence of Franz Boas—in Harrington's case by way of his teacher at Berkeley, Alfred L. Kroeber. In its curious amalgam of romantic and scientific impulse "Save, Save the Lore" might almost be an intentional summary of the Boasian enterprise—an enterprise with influence that extended well beyond the realm of ethnology to include folklorists and collectors of the more literary schools.

During the period in which the conventions of realist ethnography emerged, no ethnographer was more engaged by the dilemma of the paradigmatic versus the particular in presentation of fieldwork and the issue of experiential authority than Franz Boas, whose paternal relationship to the nascent discipline of anthropology is summarized affectionately in the nickname given to him by his students: "Papa Franz." Like collector Jesse Walter Fewkes, a scientist by training, with [Frank Hamilton] Cushing he shared a deeply humanistic worldview.[2] The comprehension of these apparent oppositions in one individual is perhaps understood in light of the German tradition of a scientific training not necessarily divorced from expressive, aesthetic, and even Romantic concerns. Boas's work and teaching was characterized by a naturalist's attraction to text-based fieldwork collection; the body of work has been criticized by subsequent generations of scholars as more accumulative than evaluative: driven as a field-worker, he was deeply reluctant to theorize in advance of his data, and that mountain of data never achieved the critical mass he seems to have required to pronounce beyond his firm conviction in favor of diffusion as the dominant factor in cross-cultural expressive forms.

From the turn of the century through the early thirties, most of the professional folklorists using the phonograph as a fieldwork tool were directly influenced in doing so by Franz Boas. Their use of the machine effectively fulfilled Boas's mandate to pursue "folklore"—that is, "people['s] records of themselves in their own words."[3] The results of their investigations in this area were most frequently published in the *Journal of American Folk-Lore,* which by 1908 the "Boasians" had effectively commandeered and would control for almost thirty years, edited by Boas himself (1908–1924), Ruth Benedict (1925–1939), and Gladys Reichard (1940).[4] Such a mandate led many of Boas's colleagues and students, folklorists and anthropologists, to supplement their notebook and pencil with a phonograph in the field; Gladys Reichard, Paul Radin, Ruth Underhill, Clark Wissler, Robert H. Lowie, Helen Heffron Roberts, Martha Beckwith, Elsie Clews Parsons, and Alfred Kroeber among others all made significant cylinder recordings of field data. The reasons for this consistent methodological *patternare* were rooted in the emergent culture of anthropology at Columbia, including elements of ideology and an intellectual zeitgeist as well as more practical persuasions.

Use of the phonograph satisfied the passionate urgency conveyed by Boas to his colleagues and students. Total immersion in a culture as a technique demands expertise, time, and interpersonal skills of a high order. Although Boas's fieldwork did tend at times toward what would later be called "participant observation" of general social patterns, the basis for his fieldwork was emphatically on collection of *texts*.[5] Verbatim textual transcription is exhausting for ethnographer, translator, and informant. With a phonograph, a collector could gather many times the quantity of linguistic and musical material possible using other means. Theodora Kroeber described her husband Alfred's experience with Boas as a teacher at Columbia at the turn of the century in terms he himself must have provided, since it was long before their meeting and marriage:

> Virgin but fleeting—this was the urgency and the poetry of Boas' message. Everywhere over the land were virgin languages, brought to their polished and idiosyncratic perfection of grammar and syntax without benefit of a single recording scratch of stylus on papyrus or stone; living languages orally learned and transmitted and about to die with their last speakers. Everywhere there were to be discovered Ways of Life, many many ways. There were gods and created worlds unlike other gods and worlds, with extended relationships and values and ideals and dreams unlike anything known or imagined elsewhere, all soon to be forever lost—part of the human condition, part of the beautiful heartbreaking history of man. The time was late, the dark forces of invasion had almost done their ignorant work of annihilation. To the field then! With notebook and pencil, record, record, record.[6]

One might add "the phonograph" to "notebook and pencil." The importance of efficiency in field collecting and the usefulness of the phonograph in boosting productivity emerges with special clarity when one considers that, by today's standards, field trips were normally quite short during most of the cylinder era, seldom lasting longer than a couple of months at a time, and sometimes as brief as a mere day or two. Boas and his students, though considered quintessential field-workers, did not spend extended periods in the field in general—certainly not on the scale of later British anthropologists following the Malinowskian tradition. Rosalie H. Wax has pointed out that the nature of funding of early ethnographic work did not allow for long periods in the field, and in fact the nature of their data did not require it. They seldom achieved full fluency in the native languages, relying heavily on bilingual interpreters and informants. Boas himself made thirteen trips to the Northwest Coast, seldom spending more than two months at a time, and seems to have "worked" at least forty culture areas.[7] The phonograph, for all its limitation, was a valuable tool in responding to the evangelical call to "record."

There might have been an ideological, even theoretical appeal to the use of the phonograph as well. Although Boas himself did not go as far as influential physicist Ernst Mach in adopting a pragmatic view of scientific laws as purely heuristic and potentially temporary constructs, there is nonetheless in his anthropological work and teachings more than a whiff of Mach's radical sensationalist epistemology—the notion that knowledge must be rooted not in speculation but in experience, unimpeded by externally imposed paradigms and categories.[8] The Machian epistemological revolution and the accompanying redefinition of knowledge in the wake of Charles Sanders Peirce's pragmaticism (especially the more diffuse interpretation and application found in William James's construct) can be seen in Boas's insistence on fieldwork incorporating direct observation and documentation of specific expressive forms; perhaps as well these intellectual trends exerted a negative influence affecting Boas's notorious reluctance to move beyond collection of texts to more expansive and theoretical works synthesizing the materials collected.[9]

There is a clear relationship between the critical positivism espoused by followers of Mach in many disciplines and the anthropological notion of cultural relativism pursued by Boas and his colleagues with missionary zeal:

> We learn from the data of ethnology that not only our ability and knowledge but also the manner and ways of our feeling and thinking is the result of our upbringing as individuals and our history as a people. To draw conclusions about the development of mankind as a whole we must try to divest ourselves of these influences, and this is only possible by immersing ourselves in the spirit of primitive peoples whose perspectives and development have almost nothing in common with our own.[10]

The relationship with Mach is largely implicit in Boas's writing and teaching but becomes explicit in the work and activity of students and coworkers such as Robert Lowie, Paul Radin, and Elsie Clews Parsons.[11]

But the very process of "immersion in the spirit" of peoples whose perspectives and development are utterly foreign is fraught with the risk of unconscious superimposition of the investigator's own native categories and constructs. The risk is greatest when the attempt is made at the most abstract and inclusive levels, as in the willy-nilly categorization of societies along an evolutionary continuum from "savagery" to "civilization" against which Boas campaigned so vigorously. The risk persists in the process of recording the most basic expressive forms, even inhering in the cross-cultural perception of as irreducible a form as linguistic phonemes. In an 1889 essay titled "On Alternating Sounds," Boas observes that field notes even of scientists trained in supposedly objective systems for recording language demonstrate patterns of error—"mishearing"—consistent with their native tongue: "the nationality even of well-trained observers may readily be recognized."[12]

The spirit of critical positivism energizing the American anthropologists clustered around Boas—the so-called Columbia school—supported the extensive use of the phonograph among the members of the group. It provided a form of documentation directly apprehensible to the senses, presumably uncontaminated by the observer's inevitable categorical and perceptual biases. Boas himself had experimented extensively with the phonograph in 1893 and 1895, recording Kwakiutl and Thompson River Indian material;[13] while not effusive concerning the experience, he continued to use the device intermittently throughout his career.[14]

Finally, there might be a practical and human reason for the attraction of the device for this group. "Critical positivism" was a thrilling approach to ethnology for neophyte Columbia anthropologists when the topic was on the agenda in the familiar intellectual give-and-take of Alexander Goldenweiser's discussion group, the now-celebrated Pearson Circle.[15] It was in this stimulating and urbane setting that Lowie and Radin in particular first grappled with the implications of the "new science" for anthropology. But the implementation of these insights in fieldwork represented a challenge of a different order. The "how-to" component in anthropological education at Columbia in the early years of the century was notably lacking. Papa Franz was a vigorous supporter of his students, but his pedagogy was notoriously unspecific; Boas's teaching style in this regard has been generously described by Herskovits as "subtle" and more bluntly by Lowie as "odd."[16] Use of the phonograph created a body of data supposedly pure in Machian terms; it also supplied a welcome degree of practical concreteness to the methodological problems posed by implementation of Boas's anthropological agenda. For insecure beginners in the field, armed only with the memory of Boas's lectures on linguistics and statistics, the phonograph provided a welcome focus and distraction as they found their feet.

They used the machine, but most of the Columbia ethnographers never overcame a certain ambivalence, even hostility, toward it, even after some of the technical shortcomings of the machine had been resolved and its price brought within their range. Granted, the phonograph was only suitable for the documentation of certain kinds of cultural phenomena: it was blind to nonverbal aspects of ritual and manifestations of material culture, as well as to intangible behavioral patterns such as kinship and social structure. The use of the phonograph automatically framed information as a presentation or performance, something set aside and special: brief, powerful, and permanent. As such it was best suited to record materials that were naturally and intrinsically "performances," formulaically defined and set off in the normal course of events from the usual flow of social expression—that is, songs, religious ceremonies, and narratives. But it was precisely these expressive forms that were of particular interest to ethnologists of the Boasian tribe; the source of their ambivalence must be sought elsewhere.

Folklorist Simon Bronner has characterized the late nineteenth and early twentieth centuries as a period in American intellectual history in the course of which examination of "time" and "space" in the sciences became professionalized: "Geographers and naturalists offered more exact descriptions of space, historians and geologists gave them for time."[17] Ethnologists faced a more difficult dilemma: quantification of space and time in the arena of culture and tradition posed a challenge to both method and theory—a challenge to both scientific accuracy and humanistic values. The phonograph seemingly represented a useful, if not ideal, tool in this process of professionalization: it captured sound events objectively and with some degree of fidelity. Although cumbersome to pack into remote areas, it was not a significant burden in an era when even those travelers "roughing it" thought nothing of carrying with them an extraordinary amount of gear by today's standards. More burdensome than the literal encumbrance of the phonograph was the symbolic baggage that accompanied its use. Though it could be seen as a gleaming modern emblem of professionalization of ethnology—Fewkes certainly regarded it as such—its presence in the fieldwork encounter could also imply a deficit on the part of the ethnographer: lack of full linguistic fluency, lack of training enabling swift and accurate linguistic or musical transcription, or, most damning of all, lack of the easy and full identification with the subjects that would lend fullest possible authority to the ethnographer's accounts. Its mechanical nature, at first glance an asset in the "measurement" of data representing cultural time and space, might have seemed uncomfortably reminiscent of inappropriate tools such as the calipers used for measurement of cranial capacity early in the careers of ethnographers such as Boas, Wissler, Lowie, and Kroeber, later to be recalled by some with regret. As a result, the relatively few evaluations of the usefulness of the phonograph surviving from the period suggest an ambivalence on the part of field-workers toward its usefulness that cannot be fully explained by its technical limitations or practicality.

Similarly, ethnomusicologist Helen Heffron Roberts, a later student of Boas, made superbly effective use of the cylinder phonograph, notably in her collection of Northern California Karok and Konomihu music. These recordings represent possibly the finest single cylinder collection in the Archive of Folk Culture, technically high in quality and supported by splendidly accurate transcriptions and documentation. Her commitment to the cylinder phonograph as a tool led her to investigate the technical side of recording as well, consulting with Edison himself concerning problems of preservation and rerecording cylinders.[18] Yet she too expressed reservations concerning the use of the phonograph:

> Longhand notation is, of course, very much slower than record making and requires patience in all concerned. On the other hand, it has many merits. It affords excellent opportunities to the [collector] for observing the musical intelligence and ability of the singer, his variability in repetition to repetition in melody, form, text, etc., as would not be noted under the rather more strenuous and rapid recordings by the phonograph. It also affords an excellent chance for conversation by the way, for questions bound to arise which would never occur to the collector in the more perfunctory process of making records, and would only too late be put by the transcriber. Moreover, in this more leisurely pursuit, an informant may appeal to a bystander for assistance in recollecting, or arguments may arise which, to the alert collector, may furnish valuable additional data. Longhand notation is the best method possible for checking on impromptu composing and frauds. Phonograph records and longhand notations of the same song may be compared with advantage.[19]

Although the limitations of the phonograph were real, some of the difficulty experienced by ethnographers such as Radin and Roberts might not have related to the workings of the machine itself but instead to their adjustment to an unfamiliar process of documentation in which the oral nature of their material was retained rather than immediately reduced to written form. The historically shaped sensorium of ethnographers of the period was still essentially a post-Enlightenment environment in which meaningful sound was automatically spatialized—and specialized—in the form of the written word. In Walter Ong's terms, their frame of reference was fully "chirographic," centered on the preeminence of visual evidence, and the authority of text.[20] The contemporary era characterized by Ong as that of "secondary orality," in which the voice becomes newly alive and significant through electronic media, was being ushered in by the invention of the very machine the early ethnographers used with such obvious reluctance. Some of their hesitation might have had less to do with the limitations of the machine itself than with adjustment to an unfamiliar process of documentation in which the oral nature of their material was retained indefinitely, instead of being immediately reduced to written form. Despite their success with the phonograph, Radin and Roberts obviously hesitated to endorse it unreservedly as a tool—an attitude typical of Boas's students, reflecting both their experience and the opinion of Papa Franz himself.

Boas's influence on the course of ethnography, and the attention this influence indirectly drew to the usefulness or mechanical means of recording, predated and extended well beyond his circle of colleagues and students at Columbia. By the turn of the century, he had already systematically developed his agenda for the professionalization of American anthropology in ways that promoted the use of the phonograph in government-sponsored fieldwork. As early as 1887, he had corresponded with John Wesley Powell, director and founder of the BAE, concerning the publication of his first ethnological research in the Baffin Islands. By the early 1890s, he was fully engaged in the Byzantine politics of the organization and was offered a position directing editorial work for the Bureau.[21] Although he turned down this offer, he benefited from the agency throughout the nineties in ways that he could not from other more archaeologically oriented museums and institutions. The BAE indirectly subsidized his work on linguistics and mythology by purchasing his manuscripts and field notes at a generous price. For his part, he did not hesitate to express his views concerning administration and policy both to Powell and to Samuel Langley, head of the Smithsonian Institution, of which the BAE was a part. In the course of Boas's prolonged "systematic self-professionalization" as an anthropologist, he had concluded that the growth of the field and the future of the BAE required that "those lines of human activity that do *not* find expression in material objects—namely language, thought, customs, and I may add, anthropometric measurements—be investigated thoroughly and carefully," a conviction he impressed upon Langley in correspondence concerning a possible successor to Powell in 1893.[22]

Correspondence with Powell and his associate, William John McGee, in 1893 reveals Boas's early commitment to the essential importance of collection of full texts of cultural materials; we have seen that it was in this same year that he first experimented with the phonograph as an ethnographic tool. As the policy shift influenced by Boas drew the BAE collecting projects and publication initiatives ever more deeply into areas concerned with such nonmaterial aspects of culture as myth, music, narrative, and linguistics, the phonograph became an essential tool for the ethnographers employed by the BAE. As it happened, Powell retained control of the Bureau until his death in 1902, and although he was replaced by W. H. Holmes, no friend to Boas, the emphasis on nonmaterial forms of expression, especially linguistic and musical, remained strong. The Bureau publication of Boas's *Handbook of American Indian Languages* in 1911 bears witness to an influence that would continue for at least two more decades in the BAE's history.[23]

At first glance, it is difficult to reconcile the connection between Franz Boas, champion of a relativistic approach to culture and enemy of imposed external schemata, and John Wesley Powell, who was so profoundly influenced by the evolutionary constructs of Lewis Morgan that a personal copy of the latter's work *Ancient Societies* was presented to each new employee of the Bureau.[24] Boas and Powell present a fascinating contrast: Boas the product of a richly textured and deeply rooted European intellectual synthesis of science and humanities, Powell the restless heir to generations of a very American type of military explorer-naturalists dating at least back to Meriwether Lewis. In a widely used text, anthropologist Marvin Harris ungraciously dismisses Powell as a "hayseed and a bumpkin," adding that in comparison with Boas, he was "a distressingly undisciplined dabbler." Curtis Hinsley characterizes the Bureau under Powell's direction as the embodiment of "a concept of scientific anthropology that became a historical reject, a road not taken in the professional development of American anthropology."[25] It is true that Powell and his staff were often less than theoretically rigorous and their embrace of evolutionist constructs with their accompanying ethnocentric and racist assumptions were incompatible with attitudes accepted in today's ethnographic disciplines—attitudes shaped in part by the efforts and influence of Boas. But Powell was the best-known ethnologist of his era, and his grip on the purse strings that controlled federally funded ethnographic efforts during his tenure at the BAE was firm and sure at a time when Boas was still making an uneasy transition from geographic determinism to a more broadly based study of culture. What Powell and Boas shared in abundance was their orientation toward the *past*—a preoccupation in their ethnological work that might have had roots in their previous training in geography and geology, studies that predisposed them to look for artifactual evidence for their historical speculations, whether in the form of a geological specimen, a pot shard, or a song text recorded in wax.[26]

Indeed, the BAE's roots lay in federal geological and geographical survey work undertaken in the 1870s. A veteran of the Union Army who had lost an arm at the battle of Shiloh, Major Powell began his civilian career as director of these expeditions. According to Powell's final report to the U.S. Department of the Interior in 1877, the work included "classification of Indian tribes, such classification being not only of scientific interest, but of great importance in the administration of Indian affairs," which suggests his awareness of the potential political and administrative applications of work he would later support as head of the Bureau.[27] As a result of his initiative, the agency was founded in 1879 as the Bureau of Ethnology, to be renamed the Bureau of American Ethnology in 1894.

The BAE's professional staff for the most part lacked formal ethnographic, musicological, and linguistic training, and they labored under impossibly restrictive time constraints in the field. They found the introduction of the phonograph as a tool to be a godsend in the collection of the full textual material that, through Boas's influence, became a standard requirement in their work in the 1890s and early decades of the next century. W. H. Holmes, Powell's successor, described the advantages and limitation of the phonograph in a 1906 letter:

> I will say that the recording of phonetics of primitive languages by means of a phonograph of any construction is impossible, for the reason that the phonograph renders only the physical characteristics of the spoken sound, while the primary object we have to investigate is the physiological method of producing the sound. This can be obtained only by closest observation of the speaker.

> On the other hand, the phonograph is of very great value in recording the characteristic rhythm and cadence of the spoken languages and it also is of greatest service in obtaining native texts, undistorted by the difficulties of recording the spoken word in writing, which always necessitates slow pronunciation and for this reason breaks up the syntactic unity of the sentences. I have applied successfully the method of having old people, well versed in the lore of the Indians, tell their stories into the phonograph. Then I had the same stories in the presence of the original informant repeated by the phonograph to an interpreter, who pronounced the sentences as they appear on the phonograph to me, and from this dictation I recorded the sentences, checking off the interpreter from the phonographic record. In these two respects the phonograph is the most useful instrument in linguistic studies.[28]

The device allowed them to record language, music, and ceremony—to "save the lore," in BAE ethnologist John Peabody Harrington's words—in a form from which they or others could later publish written phonetic and musical transcriptions, providing as well impressive quantifiable, artifactual evidence of their industry. Nearly a score of BAE consultants and staff made use of the phonograph from 1895 to the mid-1930s, creating an irreplaceable record of American Indian culture the value of which is still unfolding, as recordings of music and ceremony made during this era are recirculated among members of the communities in which they were originally recorded. This return of the recordings is not without irony, since both field-workers and often their subjects assumed that by the end of the twentieth century such communities would have long ceased to exist.[29]

The anthropological folklorists who reluctantly embraced the phonograph as an ethnographic tool viewed the texts they collected as a key to the understanding of larger issues in the groups they studied—as artifacts of evolutionary development, as evidence for migration and diffusion, or as templates revealing in microcosm the significant cultural patterns that played out in many aspects of social life. But there were also scholars who, by temperament or training, gravitated toward textual and musically expressive forms in their own right, without necessarily generalizing from them concerning broader cultural questions about the cultures from which the materials were collected.[30] Musicologists and the scholars whom Rosemary Levy Zumwalt labels "literary folklorists" both used the phonograph extensively in their work for reasons related to, but distinct from, the reasons motivating the anthropological collectors of folklore. No less an authority than Béla Bartók stated unequivocally, "The father of modern folksong studies was Thomas Edison."[31]

The earliest investigations concerning the purely musicological usefulness of the phonograph were undertaken by psychologist Benjamin Ives Gilman, to whom Mary Hemenway entrusted the analysis of the Zuni cylinders made by Fewkes in 1890. Gilman's work on these cylinders earned for him credit from pioneer ethnomusicologist Erich Moritz von Hornbostel as "the first scholar to use the phonograph in a scientific approach to the study of music."[32] Gilman was primarily interested in the technical reliability of phonograph recordings and in their usefulness in comparative musicological studies. He scrupulously described his technique in transcribing the Fewkes cylinders. Using a harmonium tuned to concert pitch, he notated the programs of ten cylinders, having refrained from listening to any other Indian music so that his ear would be "clean." Despite the problems posed by fluctuations in the speed of recordings made with Fewkes's first machine, a treadle model, Gilman was enthusiastic about the accuracy of the phonograph:

> The apparatus proves to be a means by which the actual sound itself of which a music consists may, even in many of its more delicate characteristics, be stored up by the traveler, in a form permanently accessible to observation. . . . [The recording] can be interrupted at any point, repeated indefinitely, and even within certain limits magnified, as it were, for more accurate appreciation of changes in pitch, by increasing the duration of notes. A collection by phonographic cylinders like that obtained by Dr. Fewkes forms a permanent museum of primitive music, of which the specimens are comparable in fidelity of reproduction and convenience for study, to casts or photographs of sculpture or painting.[33]

Gilman's interest in the phonograph as a fieldwork tool was of the armchair variety: he was intrigued by the accuracy of the device because it suggested the possibility of a scientific study of comparative music. The machine raised "the hope that some proportion of the resulting close determinations of pitch might prove significant," revealing subtle "habitudes of performance" of different peoples and individuals.[34] He grasped the distinction between the notation of a performance, which he believed only possible through the use of an objective mechanical device such as the phonograph, and the notation of a piece of music, the result of taking down by ear, which is "a record of the observer's idea of what the performers of certain observed sequences of tone would have performed had their execution corresponded to their intention, or (perhaps) had their intention not wandered also from a certain norm."[35] He concludes that notation made by ear from repeated hearings represents not observations but what he terms "a theory of observations"—the listener's paradigm for an ideal performance.[36]

Gilman's work indirectly demonstrated an aspect of phonograph use unremarked upon at the time but significant nonetheless. He was essentially an indirect participant in the ethnographic process: Fewkes's cylinders offered a scholar far from Zuni a body of apparently objective data to work with—a separation virtually impossible under any other circumstance. Gilman's role in the early history of the phonograph is defined by this curious quality of separation from the source. His most important legacy aside from his work with Fewkes's Pueblo recordings is his 1893 anthology of 101 cylinders containing "exotic music" that he recorded at the World's Columbian Exposition in Chicago, which included Javanese, Samoan, Turkish, and Kwakiutl performances, a collection inspired and financed by the generous Mrs. Hemenway.[37]

Not all researchers were as impressed with the capacity of the phonograph to record musical performances. Musicologist H. E. Krehbiel, intrigued by Gilman's enthusiasm, pounced on the opportunity to test a machine on display at an exhibit in Frankfurt-on-Main. In a letter to the *Tribune* later printed in the *Musical Visitor,* he dismissed Gilman's assessment of the phonographic potential with an arch charm more deadly than any full-scale systematic critique: "I confess that I part with regret from the Zuni melodies which Dr. Fewkes imprisoned on his phonograph cylinder and Mr. Gilman transcribed for us (those quarter tones opened up such a delightful field for speculation); but since I toyed with a phonograph and pitch pipe at the Frankfurt exhibition yesterday they are banished from my collection."[38]

The dispute over the machine's usefulness in recording music remained unreconciled in Great Britain as well, but there the authoritative weight of opinion held against the phonograph. Like the American specialists in Indian linguistics, the British specialists in folksong placed great value on the skill required in making scrupulously accurate transcriptions—musical, in their case. It is perhaps no wonder, then, that Percy Grainger's vigorous recommendation of the phonograph as a tool met with such a cool reception on the part of the Folk-Song Society in 1908. In a letter commenting on a draft of Grainger's article "Collecting with the Phonograph" written for the Society journal, folksong doyenne Anne Geddes Gilchrist expressed her reservations to the equally eminent Lucy Broadwood:

> In my own experience of seeing records being taken by my brother of the performances of singers, both cultured and otherwise, we have found it not absolutely reliable as a recorder (though a good instrument). It is faulty both as regards "dynamics" and timbre of the sounds recorded, and fails to reproduce sibilants –the initial "s" of a word particularly. As to pitch, I have also had some occasional doubts as to which instrument—the human or the artificial—was a little "out"! The chief weakness of the phonograph, I think (apart from the general slight or more than slight distortion of tone) is its limited range of piano to forte.[39]

For the trained musician, the fidelity of the phonograph clearly left something to be desired. The technical limitations led many collectors who used the machine to limit their performers to individuals whose vocal quality recorded well and to restrict vocal mannerisms that would cause distortion.[40]

Paradoxically, despite technical reservations such as those quoted above, both Gilchrist and Cecil Sharp also objected to the phonograph as a means of recording that was *too* precisely accurate. They believed that ultimately the subjective response of the human ear best caught and conveyed the content of a performance. Although Sharp was to make use of the cylinder phonograph from time to time, he disliked the machine, expressing his reasons at some length in a letter to Percy Grainger in 1908. After remarking that he felt that it made singers self-conscious, that it was useless for singers whose voices were too weak to register, and that he was not satisfied with the clarity with which it recorded words, Sharp makes clear his most strenuous objection: that in the documentation of folksong "it is not an exact, Scientifically accurate memorandum that is wanted, so much as a faithful artistic record of what is actually heard by the ordinary auditor."[41] He comments that just as a photograph is generally inferior to a painting in conveying a scene, a phonographic recording is inferior to an auditor's rendering of a performance in standard notation.[42] This analogy was also drawn by Gilchrist, who passionately maintained that "the trained ear or eye of an artist is surely able to reproduce with more real *truth*—because with understanding and sympathy—the sounds or the sights impressing the sensitive surface—whether human or artificial—of an 'innocent' receptive medium."[43] Ideological objections also prevented the phonograph from becoming popular among many British collectors. To British folksong enthusiasts such as Gilchrist, Sharp, and Vaughan Williams, the introduction of a phonograph into the homes of their informants must have felt something like introducing a tightly leashed but hungry cat into a dovecote. Maud Karpeles relates:

> More than once it happened that Cecil Sharp would be sitting quietly with an old couple, listening with enjoyment, when the peaceful atmosphere would be disturbed by the noisy entrance of the grandchildren, who would be shocked to find their grandparents singing their silly old songs to the gentleman, and would endeavor to reinstate the family reputation by turning on the gramophone with the latest music hall records; songs of which one old man said: "Can't make no idea to it, no more than that chair; 'tis a gabble of noise with no meaning to it."[44]

The phonograph was the Enemy, the means of disseminating debased commercial products of the music hall among the as-yet "uncontaminated" rural populace. To use it in their work while attacking it in print must have struck them as inconsistent at the very least.[45] Of the powerful clique of musicians controlling the direction of the English Folk-Song Society, only Percy Grainger valued an initial recording of collected tunes in "as *merely scientific* a form as possible."[46] Grainger's use of the adverb "merely" indicates his belief that the best transcriptions were those, technical or otherwise, that would give an objective rather than impressionistic rendering of a performance. In contrast, the interest of most members of the Society was aesthetically and, in a well-bred manner, sociologically motivated along a Romantic Herderian vein: to them, the subjectively modified response of an educated ear to a performance was intrinsic to the value of a transcription of folk music. Whereas the American collectors of American Indian material assumed that the technology represented by the phonograph would accelerate assimilation to Anglo society and thus improve the lot of the people they were recording, the British folksong collectors were for the most part musicians committed to the promulgation of folksong in an arranged and idealized form as the proper expression of the British people, to be preserved from the taint of progress.

American collectors of Anglo-American folksong were far readier to accept the advantages and make the best of the disadvantages of the phonograph than were their British counterparts. On the whole, the American folksong collectors of the cylinder era were not representatives of institutions or even participants in an organization with a fixed and clear program such as that of the English Folk-Song Society. They operated as private agents, fulfilling their own private agendas, often devoted to the folksong of a particular region. John A. Lomax, although supported by a Harvard traveling fellowship in his expeditions to collect cowboy songs in 1908 through 1910, had no clear tie to the university aside from the sponsorship of George Lyman Kittredge and Barrett Wendell. Helen Harkness Flanders devoted herself wholeheartedly to Vermont folksong, independent of any institutional agenda or program. Phillips Barry similarly devoted himself to New England in general. To these private scholars and local enthusiasts the phonograph was a boon precisely because they were *not* accomplished, professionally skilled musicians. It allowed them to collect extensively without the proficiency demanded by transcription by hand. Folksong scholars in the tradition of Francis James Child and George Lyman Kittredge, their primary interest was in the texts of the songs, but they were too thorough to neglect melody when a simple means of collecting it was available.

The machine was also valued by small regional societies, groups of amateur scholars devoted to the lore of their area, who worried that the material they sought to collect would be gone forever before they could set it down. Alice Mabel Bacon, reporting on the work and methods of the Hampton Folk-Lore Society of Virginia in 1898, lamented the delay in collecting African-American music in her region, giving as a reason the lack of any professional musician in the club to transcribe. "If we can obtain a graphophone, and thus make records not only of songs, but of sermons, prayers, etc., and so gather, as we cannot now gather, some complete records of entire religious services, we are convinced that through this means we may add much to the common fund of knowledge of the Negro music."[47]

The urgency expressed by the Hampton Folk-Lore Society is typical of the sentiments of the local enthusiasts as well as those scholars engaged in the collection of Indian cultural expression. For individuals convinced that each passing day diminished the harvest of traditional materials to be gathered, the phonograph, whatever its limitations, offered exceptional speed and efficiency in the field.

The efficiency of the phonograph as a tool in the field was reiterated by Marius Barbeau in a programmatic address to the American Folklore Society in 1918, a plea for consistent professional standards in the documentation of fieldwork. An experienced collector equipped with a phonograph, he said, could make an adequate record of data in a single day that an untrained observer will only imperfectly record in a month of work; with good informants, an expert field folklorist "finds no difficulty in collecting an average of forty or fifty songs or ballads in a day's work, the texts being taken in stenography, and a few stanzas recorded on the phonograph."[48] The collector today trembles not only at the demands such an "average" day's work would represent, even with a tape recorder, but also at the staggering richness of available materials the offhand reference to forty or fifty song texts implies!

Despite its many limitations, the phonograph represented a valued tool for many collectors in the early part of the century; it could expedite fieldwork undertaken under pressure, produce a body of data conforming to contemporary notions of scientific objectivity, and compensate for skills many collectors lacked in written transcription of music of phonetic texts. In addition, for many women collectors, it might have represented compensation of another order.

The typical role of women in the late nineteenth and early twentieth centuries located her at the protected center of the domestic nest—a role turned topsy-turvy in virtually every significant respect by the requirements of serious and extended field research. Indeed, this very inversion of gender expectations might account for the surprisingly large number of women who made substantive contributions in the area—women whose professional activities in anthropology and folklore included a social agenda, overt or covert. Whether or not they framed their involvement in fieldwork as revolutionary—and some did—the adventure of escaping the usual routine of women's lives of the period was intensely attractive to a wide range of temperaments, from indomitable Matilda Coxe Stevenson to gentle Helen Heffron Roberts.

Escape into a male-dominated professional sphere had its price. Franz Boas was exceptional in his encouragement of women as ethnographers, but his sponsorship was not an entree into the almost exclusively male precinct of institutional employment.[49] Relatively few women had had access to even the limited formal academic training available in fieldwork-related disciplines at the turn of the century, and they were further burdened with the expectation that their work would display an inappropriate level of "feminine" subjectivity. Perhaps reacting to these critical stereotypes, a striking number of women collectors used the phonograph expertly and extensively, including Alice Cunningham Fletcher, Elsie Clews Parsons, Constance Goddard DuBois, Helen Heffron Roberts, Laura Boulton, Natalie Curtis Burlin, Helen Hartness Flanders, Gladys Reichard, Theodora Kroeber, and the tireless Frances Densmore.

Not only was the phonograph a useful tool in preempting sexist assumptions concerning the nature of the data collected by women but mastery of its technology also implied a satisfyingly "masculine" proficiency in mechanical matters usually considered a male preserve. Such symbolic appropriation of "manly" skill in emergent technologies was a notable feature of gender politics of the period—Jane Gay, Alice Cunningham Fletcher's companion in the field, wrote lively popular accounts of their adventures among the Nez Perce in which she habitually referred to herself in the third person as "she" when her role was that of "the Cook," but *"he"* when acting as "the Photographer."[50] The use of up-to-date equipment provided an emblem of competence for women in the field, allowing them to demonstrate facility in areas usually marked off as male territory.[51]

In the end, both men and women accepted or rejected the phonograph for a variety of reasons. For some, it provided a convenient and practical means to document the forms of verbal and musical expression considered the essential units of a community's traditional culture; others considered it too cumbersome and intrusive to use on a regular basis. Some collectors welcomed the opportunity to make use of a dynamic new technological innovation; others saw the very novelty of the phonograph, and the social change its dissemination heralded, as a symptom of precisely that progressive force against which they were valiantly holding the line. Some regarded the device as a means to achieve a scientific objectivity in their work; others saw it as a cheap evasion of the skill in transcription essential to any well-trained ethnographer.

Then as now, every field-worker engages not only in a professional process of documentation and analysis but also in an inner enactment of a privately composed drama as suspenseful, risky, and exhilarating as the hunt—a heroic drama in which we cast ourselves as protagonist. In the end, the choice each field-worker made concerning the use of the phonograph often depended on a combination of practical and ideological factors—but depended as well on how readily he or she accepted the role of the phonograph as a dramatis persona in the fieldwork scenario. A clumsy prop? A steady supporting performer? Or even an upstaging scene-stealer? The phonograph could be any of these, in the valorous effort to save "the songs more pristine than the songs of Troy."[52]

NOTES

This chapter is reprinted by permission of the author. It was originally printed in Brady, Sarah. *In a Spiral Way: How the Phonograph Changed Ethnography* (Jackson: University Press of Mississippi, 1999).

1. John Peabody Harrington files, Federal Cylinder Project, American Folklife Center, Library of Congress.
2. Curtis M. Hinsley Jr., "Ethnographic Charisma and Scientific Routine: Cushing and Fewkes in the American Southwest, 1879–1893," in *Observers Observed: Essays on Ethnographic Fieldwork*, vol. 1 of *History of Anthropology*, ed. George Stocking Jr. (Madison: University of Wisconsin Press, 1983), 68.
3. Gladys Reichard, "Franz Boas and Folklore," in *Franz Boas, 1858–1942*, ed. Alfred L. Kroeber, *Memoirs of the American Anthropological Association* 61 (Menasha, WI: American Anthropological Association, 1943), 55.
4. Rosemary Lévy Zumwalt, *American Folklore Scholarship: A Dialogue of Dissent* (Bloomington: Indiana University Press, 1988), 31–32.
5. George W. Stocking, "Introduction: The Basic Assumptions of Boasian Anthropology," in *The Shaping of American Anthropology: A Franz Boas Reader*, ed. George W. Stocking (New York: Basic Books, 1974), 85.
6. Theodora Kroeber, *Alfred Kroeber: A Personal Configuration* (Berkeley: University of California Press, 1970), 51.
7. Rosalie H. Wax, *Doing Fieldwork: Warnings and Advice* (Chicago: University of Chicago Press, 1971), 31–32.
8. Stocking, "Introduction," 11.
9. The influence of William James on more recent folklore scholarship through the work of George Herbert Mead is discussed in Simon J. Bronner, "'Toward a Common Center': Pragmatism and Folklore Studies," *Folklore Historian* 7 (1990): 23–30. Boas's reluctance to pronounce on collected data is a persistent leitmotif in critical accounts of his influence. Marion Smith strikes a typically exasperated tone:

> The exhaustive collection of data which seems at the time to have little or no connection with any specific problem is peculiarly a feature of [Boas's] approach. . . . Masses of data may therefore be worked over with no clear knowledge of what's to be gained at the end. A new hypothesis or a new slant on an old problem will "emerge" or be "revealed" or "suggested." The data will "speak for themselves. . . . Boas was always too self-critical to rely completely on his own observations. He needed the documentation of the texts, the family history, to test his own precision.

Marion Smith, "Boas' 'Natural History' Approach to Field Method," in *The Anthropology of Franz Boas*, ed. Walter Goldschmidt, *American Anthropological Society Memoir* 89 (Menasha, WI: American Anthropological Association, 1958), 54–56.

10. Franz Boas, "The Aims of Ethnology," in *Die Ziele der Ethnologie* (New York: Hermann Bartsch, 1889). Reprinted in *The Shaping of American Anthropology: A Franz Boas Reader*, ed. George W. Stocking (New York: Basic Books, 1974), 1.
11. Desley Deacon, *Elsie Clews Parsons: Inventing Modernity* (Chicago: University of Chicago Press, 1997), 100–107.
12. Franz Boas, "On Alternating Sounds," *American Anthropologist* 2 (1889): 47–53. Reprinted in *The Shaping of American Anthropology: A Franz Boas Reader*, ed. George W. Stocking (New York: Basic Books, 1974), 75.
13. Franz Boas, "Note: Teton Sioux Music," *Journal of American Folklore* 28 (1925): 319; Dorothy Sara Lee, *Early Anthologies*, vol. 8 of *The Federal Cylinder Project: A Guide to Field Cylinder Collections in Federal Agencies*, Dorothy Sara Lee, gen. ed. *Studies in American Folklife*, 3:8 (Washington, DC: American Folklife Center, Library of Congress, 1984), viii.

14. He remarked much later with regard to Frances Densmore's work, "the study of form is not easy, because in transcriptions made from the phonograph—and I presume that most of the material in Miss Densmore's book has been so transcribed—accents are not reliable, because mechanically accents are introduced on those tones that correspond to the rate of vibration of the diaphragm." Franz Boas, "Note: Teton Sioux Music," 319.

15. The Pearson Circle was one of several memorable discussion groups established by Goldenweiser, a popular and charismatic student at Columbia, that were modeled on groups formed in Russian universities to study the emerging topics in psychology, philosophy, and history of sciences. The circle was named for Karl Pearson, author of the influential *Grammar of Sciences*. Desley Deacon, *Elsie Clews Parsons: Inventing Modernity*, 99–101.

16. Melville J. Herskovits, *Franz Boas* (Clifton, NJ: Augustus M. Kelley, 1973), 22; Robert H. Lowie, *Robert H. Lowie, Ethnologist: A Personal Record* (Berkeley: University of California Press, 1959), 3. An excellent discussion of the intellectual climate of the early years of anthropology at Columbia can be found in Deacon, *Elsie Clews Parsons*, 97–107.

17. Simon J. Bronner, *American Folklore Studies: An Intellectual History* (Lawrence: University Press of Kansas, 1986): 55.

18. Helen Heffron Roberts and Robert Lachmann, "The Re-recording of Wax Cylinders," *Zeitschrift für vergleichende Musikwissenschaft* 3 (1935): 75–83. Reprinted in *Folklore and Folk Music Archivist* 6 (1963): 4–11.

19. Helen Heffron Roberts, "Suggestions to Field Workers in Collecting Folk Music and Data About Instruments," *Journal of the Polynesian Society* 40 (1931): 57–58.

20. Walter S. J. Ong, *The Presence of the Word: Some Prolegmena for Cultural and Religious History* (New Haven: Yale University Press, 1967): 87–88; Walter S. J. Ong, *Orality and Literacy* (New York: Methuen, 1982): 136.

21. Stocking, "Introduction: The Basic Assumptions of Boasian Anthropology," 59–60; George W. Stocking, *The Ethnographer's Magic, and Other Essays in the History of Anthropology* (Madison: University of Wisconsin Press, 1992): 64–68.

22. Curtis M. Hinsley, Jr. *Savages and Scientists: The Smithsonian Institution and the Development of American Anthropology, 1846–1910* (Washington, DC: Smithsonian Institution Press, 1981), 251. The description "systematic self-professionalization" is Robert Lowie's— *Robert H. Lowie, Ethnologist: A Personal Record*, 183.

23. Stocking, *The Ethnographer's Magic*, 60–91.

24. Carl Resek, *Lewis Henry Morgan, American Scholar* (Chicago: University of Chicago Press, 1960), 150.

25. Hinsley, *Savages and Scientists*, 37–38.

26. The topic of Boas's non-evolutionary orientation toward the past, and its implications in his concern with the evidential value of texts, is explored in Stocking, "Introduction: The Basic Assumptions of Boasian Anthropology," 85–86. Stocking further explores the implications of this stance in relation to his approach to linguistics and his work with the BAE in Stocking, *The Ethnographer's Magic, and Other Essays in the History of Anthropology*, 89–91; see also Dell Hymes, "Linguistic Method in Ethnography: Its Development in the United States," in *Method and Theory in Linguistics*, ed. P. L. Garvin (The Hague: Mouton, 1970).

27. Neil Merton Judd, *The Bureau of American Ethnology: A Partial History* (Norman: University of Oklahoma Press, 1967): 5.

28. W. H. Holmes, Letter, 1906. National Anthropological Archives. Photocopy in files of Federal Cylinder Project, American Folklife Center, Library of Congress, Washington, DC

29. Erika Brady, "The Bureau of American Ethnology: Folklore, Fieldwork, and the Federal Government in the Late Nineteenth and Early Twentieth Centuries," in *The Conservation of Culture: Folklorists and the Public Sector*, ed. Burt Feintuch (Lexington: University Press of Kentucky, 1988).

30. Zumwalt, *American Folklore Scholarship*, 122.

31. Béla Bartók, Liner notes to *Hungarian Folk Songs*, Folkways FE 4000 (1950).
32. Dorothy, *Early Anthologies*, vii.
33. Benjamin Ives Gilman, "Zuni Melodies," *Journal of American Ethnology and Archaeology* 1 (1891): 63–91. 68.
34. Benjamin Ives Gilman, *Hopi Songs*, (Boston: Houghton Mifflin, 1908): 25.
35. Gilman, *Hopi Songs*, 27.
36. Gilman, *Hopi Songs*, 25.
37. Dorothy, *Early Anthologies*, viii.
38. H. E. Krehbiel, Letter, 1891, *Musical Visitor* 20, no. 10 (1891): 256–257. Reprinted in *Ethnomusicology* 2 (1958): 116–117.
39. Michael Yates, "Percy Grainger and the Impact of the Phonograph," *Folk Music Journal* 4 (1982): 265–275, 266.
40. Charles Hofmann, ed., *Frances Densmore and American Indian Music: A Memorial Volume*, Contributions from the Museum of the American Indian, vol. 23 (New York: Heye Foundation, 1968), 101–113.
41. Yates, "Percy Grainger," 269.
42. Yates, "Percy Grainger," 269.
43. Yates, "Percy Grainger," 269.
44. Maude Karpeles, *Cecil Sharp: His Life, His Work* (Chicago: University of Chicago Press, 1967), 34.
45. A discussion of Cecil Sharp's dislike of the phonograph both as collecting tool and as cultural force is offered in Karpeles, *Cecil Sharp*, 34 and 41.
46. Yates, "Percy Grainger," 266.
47. Alice Mabel Bacon, "Work and Methods of the Hampton Folk-Lore Society," *Journal of American Folk-Lore* 11 (1898): 17–21, 19–20.
48. C-Marius Barbeau, "The Field of European Folk-Lore in America," *Journal of American Folklore* 32 (1919): 184–197.
49. Deacon, *Elsie Clews Parsons*, 258–272.
50. Joan Mark, *Stranger in Her Native Land: Alice Fletcher and the American Indians* (Lincoln: University of Nebraska Press, 1988): 185.
51. It might also be argued that women ethnographers were unencumbered by what appears to have been a peculiarly male rejection of the use of technical equipment as an impediment to their self-image as an assimilated participant in the life of the community—in Freilich's terms, a "marginal native." Morris Freilich, *Marginal Natives: Anthropologists at Work* (New York: Harper and Row, 1970). Although women in the field often established warm and even intimate relationships with community members, especially other women, they seldom displayed the rather adolescent over-identification that resulted in embarrassing photographs of male anthropologists in loincloths, squatting over tinder and flint.
52. John Peabody Harrington files, Federal Cylinder Project, American Folklife Center, Library of Congress.

THREE
Ballad Collectors in the Ozarks

Norm Cohen

Who is a songcatcher? When old Fred High of High, Arkansas, collects songs from his neighbors, and then Max Hunter collects songs from Fred High, and then Vance Randolph collects songs from Max Hunter . . . which one is the songcatcher? Ballad collectors Mary Parler and Randolph made this point in the brochure to an album of Hunter's recordings: "Nearly all folksingers are collectors, in a sense. They visit other singers, write down the words of their songs, and 'ketch the tunes' by ear."[1] Our society is divided into the literate and the illiterate—the big fish and the little fish. By default, the literate get to write the rules: we get to decide who the songcatchers are. Consequently, in this chapter, I focus on the bigger fish as the prime songcatchers, knowing full well that this is not the perspective of the smaller fish. By way of compensation, some of those smaller fry will also be featured, in part because they are remarkably interesting subjects themselves.

The Ozark Plateau (or Ozark Mountains, or just Ozarks) is an upland region mainly extending across southern Missouri and northern Arkansas with spillovers into southeastern Kansas, eastern Oklahoma, and southwestern Illinois. The Ozarks were settled mainly by Americans moving west from the Appalachians. In 1860, for example, only half of all Missourians had been born in that state, while a quarter came from Kentucky, Tennessee, Virginia, Ohio, and North Carolina (in order of decreasing significance).[2] In Arkansas the westward migration was even more evident: 51 percent of all Arkansans had come from Tennessee, with an additional 14 percent each from North Carolina and Georgia.[3] The early musical lore of the Ozarks consequently mirrors that of the

Appalachians, though after the Civil War, the region increasingly developed its own musical culture.

The main focus of this chapter will be the music of the Missouri–Arkansas region, including those portions of the state not strictly part of the Ozarks, since the major collectors did not stop their efforts when the terrain became horizontal. In this survey I have benefited greatly from the bibliographic essays of Mr. Ozarks himself—Vance Randolph— who published several surveys of folk song collecting in these regions.[4] Randolph's reports of who collected what and when are essential reading for anyone seriously interested in Ozark music. Upon his death, his title surely passed quietly to the late William K. McNeil, whose meticulous and extensive scholarship, undertaken from his base at the Ozark Folk Center, constituted the most important contribution to the field in the last several decades.

If I were to adhere strictly to this volume's pre-1940 focus, the survey would be dominated by the contributions of two giants in the folksong field: Henry Marvin Belden and Vance Randolph. Between them they inaugurated and closed out the first four decades of Ozark folksong scholarship. Because so much research of significance has been done since the 1940s, I will allow myself the luxury of discussing at least briefly the major songcatchers of the next decade as well.

Harry Belden (as his close friends called him) and Vance Randolph were poles apart in their careers and song-collecting activities. Belden was an academic through and through, based at a university throughout his career, an armchair collector who did not work in the field yet still inspired numerous other collectors and was responsible for their work being made available to the larger community. Randolph was disparaged as an "amateur" throughout the early part of his career; he often lived from hand to mouth, had no regular employment, battled alcoholism, and was forced to accept writing assignments under pseudonyms to keep from starving. Yet the two of them deeply respected and appreciated each other. If they, as subjects, dominate this chapter, it is a just reflection of their importance.

HENRY MARVIN BELDEN (1865–1954) AND HIS STUDENTS

Belden's long life began in Wilton, Connecticut, in 1865. In his first thirty years he graduated from Trinity College in Hartford, taught for a few years, commenced graduate school at Johns Hopkins (1889), spent a year at the University of Nebraska (1893), completed his dissertation at the University of Strasbourg, and accepted an appointment in the English department at the University of Missouri in Columbia (1895). About eight years later, he was involved in the formation of a new campus organization called the English Club, devoted to reviving interest in creative literary work. At each meeting, members—including students and faculty—read their own stories, poems, songs, and papers. At one of these meetings, a student (probably Maude Williams) worked into her story a song that she had known from childhood. An astonished Belden recognized it as a text of a Child ballad and was told there were a lot more like it back home. Aware that Child's opinion had been that the old ballad tradition was stone cold in the New World, Belden urged his students to gather other texts, and that summer Williams sent him songs that became part of the *collectanea* of the Missouri Folk-Lore Society.

The following year, the student-written report of the English Club noted that the Club could pursue the important task of collecting Missouri ballads, inasmuch "as very little has ever been done in this direction before."[5] In January 1905, Belden read a paper at the Modern Language Association meeting in Chicago titled "Folk-Songs in Missouri," in which he announced the survival of many old British ballads in rural sections of the state and that his club had so far found eleven examples.[6] The following year, he published the first batch of Missouri songs collected by his students in the *Journal of American Folk-Lore*, "Old Country Ballads in Missouri."[7] In the last weeks of that year, the Missouri Folk-Lore Society was officially established, with Belden named as secretary. In 1907, Belden issued a six-page pamphlet, *A Partial List of Song-Ballads and Other Popular Poetry Known in Missouri* that enumerated seventy-six items.[8] A second edition in June of 1910 boasted 145 items.[9] Between 1905 and 1912, Belden published eight journal articles based on the Missouri material. He also encouraged two of his students to publish their own articles on Missouri play-party songs.

By 1916, a large number of songs had been amassed—enough for Belden to discuss with Franz Boaz the possibility of the American Folk-Lore Society publishing the collection. Belden worked for the next year on preparing a manuscript for publication. Although the manuscript was completed in 1917, a succession of delays, including the war, the influenza epidemic, other academic pursuits, and the disintegration of the Missouri Folk-Lore Society, conspired to forestall publication until 1940.[10] During the intervening years, although very little further collecting took place, Belden busied himself searching other collections and resources in order to refine his headnotes. When published, the volume included 610 variants of 284 songs and ballads, gathered by over one hundred collectors, most of whom had been students at the University of Missouri. Belden retired from the university in 1935, but his folk song activities continued up until his death, principally with the coediting (along with Arthur Palmer Hudson) of the Frank C. Brown collection of North Carolina songs and ballads.[11] Belden suffered a stroke on May 12, 1954, and died five days later. Searches for his archival materials turned up empty-handed—unaccountably, until a letter from his son was found that revealed that Belden had felt that everything of importance had been published, and so the papers were destroyed after his death.[12]

One of Belden's first student colleagues was Goldy Mitchell Hamilton (1881–1955), who took her AB and MA in English at the University of Missouri–Columbia in 1903 and 1904, respectively, and was one of the original members of the English Club and the Missouri Folk-Lore Society. Following graduation, she held a succession of teaching positions—in each of which it seems she kindled enthusiasm for ballad collecting. For example, between 1909 and 1911 Ms. Hamilton taught English at West Plains High School. There her students were so taken by the prospect of ballad collecting that they wrote an article for the school yearbook, *The Zizzer*, describing ballads and their importance and included ten texts that they had collected. Belden himself supplied comments on the ballads. These and other student *collectanea* Hamilton duly forwarded to Belden for the Missouri Folk-Lore Society collection. Altogether, she was the most prolific contributor to Belden's final publication. Hamilton used a 1911 article on the Missouri play-party by another of Belden's students—Mrs. L. D. Ames[13]—to prompt her own students, most of them from northeast Missouri, to report the play-party songs that they had known, and published a collection of them in 1914 in the *Journal of American Folk-Life*.[14] In 1913, she gave a paper at the Missouri Folk-Lore Society (among talks by folksong scholars George Lyman Kittredge and W. Roy MacKenzie) about the Meeks family murder, an 1894 tragedy that inspired several local ballads.[15]

Among Belden's other students in that period who contributed to the Missouri Folk-Lore Society ballad-collecting project were Leah Yoffie, Maude Williams, Mr. W. S. Johnson, Lois Welty, Ethel Lowry, Miss Colquitt Newell, Earl Cruickshank, Mr. C. H. Williams and his brother, George, and Mrs. J. S. Lochtenberg. Leah Rachel Clara Yoffie continued her interest in folklore and published articles in to the 1940s on children's and Jewish lore in the St. Louis area.

VANCE RANDOLPH (1892–1980)

Though he suffered much criticism from academics early in his career, Vance Randolph lived to see his reputation rescued, and, as with old wine, the passage of time has only improved it. Randolph was born in Pittsburg, Kansas, in 1892. By 1919, when he moved to Pineville, Missouri, where he lived for most of his life, he had completed college and earned an MA in psychology, taught high school biology, and served in the U.S. Army. In 1924, while pursuing graduate work at the University of Kansas, he met Margaret Larkin, cowboy song collector, and her friend, the poet Carl Sandburg, who carried out some Ozark collecting himself while visiting in Missouri. Both of them urged Randolph to pursue song collecting rather than his graduate work in psychology, and Randolph returned to Pineville without the degree. His interest in Ozark lore included not only songs but also Ozark speech, folk beliefs, and play-parties. His first books, *The Ozarks* (1931) and *Ozark Mountain Folks* (1932), which both included some his earliest efforts at song collecting, followed many months of editing weekly newspaper columns on old songs, including "The Songs Grandfather Sang" in the *Pineville Democrat* and then in *Ozark Life*, and years of sporadic collecting in Kansas, Oklahoma, and around Pineville.[16]

Initially, Randolph held no special regard for the Ozarks, but he was aware that, unlike New England, the Southwest, or the Appalachians, the region had not been heavily canvassed by collectors. (Belden's Missouri collecting was not confined to the Ozarks.) Swayed by the practice of the time, he was primarily interested in the older British ballads (Child ballads) and believed that only older residents would be valuable informants. He was soon disabused of both prejudices, and *Ozark Folk Songs* shows more than most regional collections the impact of songs composed for commercial hillbilly recordings in the 1920s and 1930s. Randolph accepted the importance of collecting tunes as well as texts but was painfully aware of his own limitations. He resorted to various devices to recover tunes, including bringing his informants to the home of a local piano teacher who could work out the tunes on piano and then write them out. In the 1920s he tried an Edison dictating machine on some trips, and later a wire recorder, but was satisfied with neither. Not until 1940–1942 did he procure from Alan Lomax at the Library of Congress's Archive of Folk Song the use of a good "portable" recording machine. Thus equipped, Randolph revisited many of his earlier informants (in most cases, neighbors) and recorded some of the same songs and ballads on acetate discs. From these recordings came more than one third of the items in the first volume of *Ozark Folk Songs*.

In spite of the fact that Randolph's *Ozark Folk Songs* provided some eight hundred tunes for 1,635 items, well ahead of most prior collections, it still received harsh criticism upon publication. Musicologist Charles Seeger, while exonerating Randolph of much of the blame, charged that "the whole process of collection, transcription, selection, and editing of the music was amateurish from start to finish."[17] Folklorist Branford Millar criticized the incomplete references to other collections and questioned the inclusion of many songs from the Civil War and later.

Suffering poor health intermittently and lack of regular financial comforts, Randolph's last years were spent bedridden in the depressing surroundings of a Fayetteville retirement home with his then nearly blind wife and academic companion, Mary Celestia Parler. At least he had the satisfaction of seeing his work vindicated, the branded red "A" for Amateur erased, and replaced by the golden "F" for Folklorist. Randolph's collection is housed in the Special Collections Department of the University of Arkansas Library. A sampling of thirty-five selections from his 1941–1942 recordings is available on CD.[18]

THE THESIS WRITERS

In the 1930s, a half-dozen or so graduate students in music or English departments returned to their native hills and vales to gather material for the master's thesis. One of these, Mr. Lynn Ellis Hummel, probably wrote his thesis while he was a music teacher in Monett, Missouri, public schools.[19] Hummel wrestled with the problematic singing customs of the native Ozarkers.

> For the most part the hillman has a nasal twang to his singing which is very much in evidence in the singing in almost any country church in the Ozarks today. Many of the younger singers pitch their songs very high amounting almost to a falsetto. This is true of both men and women. The elimination of this nasality was one of the biggest problems I had to face in teaching choral music in the high school in Mountain Grove.[20]

His thesis contains words and music of 116 songs. The collection includes (among others) twenty Child ballads, a section labeled "Temperance Songs," play-party songs, nursery and comic songs, and religious songs. Hummel's musical background was evident in his introduction, and he spent considerable space on musical characteristics of Ozark singing and of the tunes.

Maude Wright was a native of Hot Springs, Arkansas, who earned her BA at Ouachita College in Arkadelphia, Arkansas, and her MA in music at Louisiana State University, by which time she had already gained experience teaching elementary school and college. Her thesis included seventeen text/tunes collected in Garland, Clark, and Ashley counties with an introductory essay on folksong scholarship but very little about her informants.[21]

Grant McDonald's MA thesis included thirty-eight texts and thirty-seven tunes from Ozarks collected from the spring of 1937 through 1938 while he was teaching music at high school at Spokane, Missouri.[22] His thesis was entitled *A Study of Selected Folk-Songs of Southern Missouri*, granted through the University of Iowa.

Irene Jones Carlisle took her BA at Texas Christian University in 1928 and didn't return to school for two decades, by which time she was a noted poet, with publications in several periodicals and a book of poems published in 1945.[23] During World War II she worked as a welder in the Oakland, California, shipyards and wrote what is her best known poem, "Welder," which can still be viewed on the website for the Rosie the Riveter organization.[24] Carlisle collected folksongs in the 1940s[25] and then again when she was gathering material for her MA thesis.[26] Carlisle collected her material in Washington, Carroll, and Sebastian counties between February and June of 1951. She used a tape recorder and deposited her tapes at the University of Arkansas Library. In 1942, Randolph collected from her, and in 1960, at which time she was living in Fayetteville, she recorded half a dozen songs for collector Max Hunter.

A music teacher at the College of Ozarks in Clarksville, Arkansas, John Stilley was collecting Ozark songs and fiddle tunes as early as 1939. He wrote his master's thesis at Northwestern University Music School in 1942.[27] Stilley collected songs, ballads, and fiddle tunes from his family and neighbors, and also from a few classmates at the College of the Ozarks. In many cases, the informant and date of collection are not given; those that are dated were obtained in 1940–1941. In 1992, W. K. McNeil published the thesis in two successive issues of *Mid-America Folklore*, with brief remarks by Stilley (then living in Flagstaff, Arizona) and editorial annotations.[28] Stilley originally provided no background information on the eighty-four items, presenting it as a raw sample of what was still being sung in the Arkansas Ozarks. The thesis had been missing for many years from the Northwestern library; fortunately, Stilley had kept a copy.

Having lost his high school teaching position in 1940 in north Arkansas due to an insolvent school district, Theodore Garrison returned to school to earn an MA, hoping to increase his chances of finding employment. Casting about for a thesis topic, he recalled having heard about John Lomax's exploits collecting and publishing folk songs from Texas and decided the same could be done for his native Arkansas. He collected his material the next year, but other events, including a war, intervened and kept him from completing the thesis until 1944. Garrison collected his material from eleven Searcy countians, including two of his relatives. His headnotes identify each informant (name, location, and date) and provide references to other versions. Brief biographical sketches gave more background on the singers. After obtaining his MA, Garrison became an instructor at the University of Arkansas and published two articles about Arkansas folksongs.[29] In 2002, W. K. McNeil edited Garrison's thesis for publication in *Mid-America Folklore*, adding supplementary material to both headnotes and biographical notes.[30]

OUTSIDE ACADEME

The distinction between academic and nonacademic collectors is, unfortunately, not to be dismissed out of hand. While the nonacademics often preserved important materials that can reveal much regional lore, their materials are unfortunately of distinctly less use for later scholarly analysis because they generally lack any information about the informants, where and when the songs were collected, and where or when they were learned (some of these accusations can also be made about the academic collections). The prime example is perhaps Carl Sandburg's material as it appears in *The American Songbag* (1927)—an excellent singing collection (including six obtained in the Ozarks) but devoid of information about the provenance of the material presented.[31]

One of the earliest nonacademics was Col. DeWitt Clinton Allen (1835–1920), a lawyer born in Clay County, Missouri, who gave an address before the Missouri Historical Society in 1914 entitled "Old Ballad Days in Western Missouri."[32] Clinton's use of the term "ballad" does not conform to current scholarly use, but his speech included fragments of twenty-two songs and ballads recalled from his youth in the 1840s and '50s. Although he probably sang them in his 1914 presentation, the tunes have not been preserved. They included imported ballads such as "Barbara Allen," songs and ballads written by Thomas Moore and Robert Burns, and a tolerably complete "Joe Bowers."

Another early songcatcher was Charles van Ravenswaay (1911–1990), whose curriculum vitae included directorships of the Missouri Historical Society, Old Sturbridge Village in Massachusetts, and the Henry Francis duPont Winterthur Museum and Gardens in Wilmington, Delaware. Primarily interested in history and art history, van Ravenswaay earned a BA at Washington University in St. Louis in 1933 and an MA the following year. In the early 1930s, van Ravenswaay collected local folklore and folk songs from schoolchildren in the area, which he used to provide background in his historical writings. His papers, deposited at the Western Historical Manuscript Collection at University of Missouri–Columbia, include perhaps two hundred children's rhymes, poems, and game songs, ballads and songs, and spirituals.

Also in this category were the several writers who conducted old songs columns in local newspapers. Fifty or one hundred years ago many such columns in different parts of the country enjoyed a large and interactive readership, and they remain an unexplored treasure of old songs that could provide sausage for many thesis and dissertation mills. In the Ozarks, they include work by Otto Ernest Rayburn, W. H. Strong, May K. McCord, and others.

Otto Ernest Rayburn (1891–1960) was a schoolteacher, writer, and publisher of numerous works about the Ozarks, as well as a prodigious collector of folk materials. Rayburn edited three journals: *Ozark Life* (Kingston, Ark., 1925–1930), *Arcadian Magazine* (Eminence, Mo., 1931–1932), and *Arcadian Life* (Caddo Gap, Ark., 1933–1941). According to Randolph, files of the three periodicals hold at least 112 local song texts. The most extensive repository of Rayburn's *collectanea* is his *Ozark Folk Encyclopedia*, described by Randolph as 250 volumes of some 120,000 pages; according to the Special Collections Department at the University of Arkansas, where it is housed, it consists of 229 folders of clippings, notes, letters, photos, and various miscellaneous. *Forty Years in the Ozarks* is Rayburn's autobiography.[33] Rayburn also functioned as an informant for Randolph, and eight of his song texts appear in *Ozark Folk Songs*.

W. H. Strong wrote a series of articles on folk songs for Rayburn's *Ozark Life* from July 1927 through August/September 1928. The whereabouts of the manuscript originals were unknown to Randolph at the time of his survey. Miss Lucile Morris conducted "The Old Songs" weekly in the Springfield *Sunday News and Leader* (26 August 1934 to 3 March 1935). The files show 102 Ozark texts. Mr. C. V. Wheat edited "Songs and Ballads of Yester Years" in the Aurora *Weekly Advertiser* from 1934 to 1942. Altogether, some 1,650 texts were printed, but with some repetition.

Particular mention should be made of May Kennedy McCord, whose "Hillbilly Heartbeats" column appeared weekly in the Springfield *Leader-News* from 1932 to 1938, then thrice weekly in the Springfield *News* until 1942. McCord (1880–1979) grew up in Galena, Missouri, where her father operated a general store, and she early took an interest in the stories and songs that she constantly heard around her. Her mother taught her to play guitar, and by 1931, when Carl Sandburg came to Springfield to speak on the university campus, McCord was singing and playing songs and ballads. In 1942 she inaugurated a fifteen-minute daily radio program in St. Louis, where she featured folk songs; she continued radio work off and on until she was in her 80s. Though Randolph was a little suspicious of her credentials, he recorded a number of her songs.

One last candidate for this category is Ray Wood, whose *Mother Goose in the Ozarks* offers more than fifty rhymes and riddles, many of which were obviously sung rather than recited.[34] Wood gave no sources, other than to say that he collected them. Randolph noted that they were collected near Fort Smith, Arkansas, where Wood ran a column entitled "That Ain't the Way I Heard It" in the *Southwest Times Record*.

SOME COLLECTORS IN THE 1940S AND 1950S

Ruth Ann Musick (1897–1974)

Though she is best known for her folklore work in West Virginia (where she moved in 1946), Musick was born in Kirksville, Missouri, outside of which her parents worked on a farm. She received her BS in Kirksville State Teacher's College (now North Missouri State University), an MA in mathematics in 1928, and a PhD in English in 1943 and taught both English and mathematics in her early career. Meanwhile, she became interested in the folklore of her native Missouri, and her first folksong collecting was in that state. Her first two publications concerned Missouri dance calls and folksongs.[35] In 1951, she collaborated with Vance Randolph in preparing a review of Missouri folk song–collecting activity.[36] Her early Missouri *collectanea* were chosen for publication in the American Folklore Society's Memoir Series in 1947, but inadequate funding ambushed the project; her manuscript remains unpublished — presumably with her other papers at Fairmont State College in West Virginia, where she taught.[37]

Mary Celestia Parler (1904–1981)

Mary Parler taught folklore and English at the University of Arkansas from 1949 to 1975. In 1949, she started the University of Arkansas Folklore Research Project, and in 1950 she helped to found the Arkansas Folklore Society. Throughout her teaching career she encouraged her students to undertake folksong fieldwork, and their *collectanea* form a large part of the Folklore Collection at the University of Arkansas—not only the recordings but also typescripts of them (eighteen volumes). Altogether some 3,640 sound recordings were made under her direction. Her collection includes nonmusical lore as well—riddles, proverbs, superstitions and beliefs, and more. She married Vance Randolph in 1962 and they worked together until their deaths one year apart.

In 1963, she compiled and published *An Arkansas Ballet Book*, a "cross-section of the many ballads and ballad-derivatives [sic] in the University of Arkansas Archive of tape-recorded songs."[38] The book contains forty-three song texts collected between 1950 and 1961 by her, Max Hunter, and Merlin Mitchell. In 2003, the Center for Arkansas and Regional Studies at the University of Arkansas–Fayetteville issued *Anthology of Arkansas Folksongs*, a two-CD set containing fifty-seven selections, edited and annotated by Alan Spurgeon, Rachel Reynolds, and Robert Cochran.

Max Hunter (1921–1999)

Though he lived in urban Springfield, Missouri, most of his life, Hunter's parents were from rural southwest Missouri. His first jobs were as a refrigerator repairman and then salesman, and his territory was southern Missouri and northwest Arkansas. There he began to collect songs from his customers as a hobby. Using a tape recorder, if he liked what he heard he would transcribe the text and play the tape over and over until he had learned the tune. Then he erased the recording.

In 1956, he appeared at a folk festival in Eureka Springs, Arkansas, and sang and talked about several ballads he had learned from his family. There he met Randolph and Parler, who urged him to continue with his collecting but to preserve his recordings. In the next two decades he built up a collection of more than two thousand songs, which he eventually donated to the Springfield–Greene County Library in Springfield. The collection now has a website, and 1,594 text transcriptions are available online.[39] His singing can be heard on two recordings: *Ozark Folksongs and Ballads*, recorded by Sandy Paton (1963), and *The Balladere: Max*

Hunter Sings Original Folksongs, Vols. 1 / 2, a double-CD set edited from very informal recordings Hunter had made of himself singing traditional songs he had collected, with running spoken commentary.[40]

Loman D. Cansler (1924–1992)

Cansler was born in Dallas County, Missouri, and in 1950, armed with a BA and MA in education from the University of Missouri, began his career as a high school teacher and counselor, first in Fayette, Missouri, and later in North Kansas City High School. Cansler was at work on his master's degree when, prowling the library stacks, he came across folk song collections by Belden and Sandburg and others, and noticed that among the songs in those collections were some he had grown up with— and were still being sung. His interest awakened, he started talking to his parents about the songs, and in 1953 he bought a tape recorder and began collecting from his grandfather and other family members. His grandfather's songs (seven texts included) were the basis for his article, "Boyhood Songs of My Grandfather."[41] Eventually he recorded two LP albums for Folkways: *Missouri Folk Songs* and *Folk Songs of the Midwest*.[42]

John Quincy Wolf, Jr. (1901–1972)

Born in Batesville, Arkansas, Wolf attended Arkansas College (now Lyon College), then Vanderbilt (MA, 1923), and finally Johns Hopkins University, where he earned a PhD in English. Most of his professional career was spent teaching English poetry at Southwestern College (now Rhodes College) in Memphis. He began collecting Ozark folksongs in 1941 after attending the Old Settlers' Picnic and folk festival at Blanchard Springs. Later, he collected blues (in the Memphis area) and Sacred Harp material. Arthritis forced him to give up his Ozark collecting in 1963 and to retire in 1970. In 1999, his widow donated his recordings and other papers to Lyon College, where it forms the Wolf Collection. Among his best-known "discoveries" was Ozark ballad singer Almeda Riddle, from whom he recorded over one hundred songs.[43]

Fred High (1878–1962)

Though he published only a single folksong publication, and that after 1940, Frederick Green High's work is so idiosyncratic that I cannot resist detailing him for this volume. High was born in High (named for his ancestors), Arkansas, where his family had settled in 1845, and lived within "twelve foot of where I was born" all his life. His schooling was limited to a total of 207 days because he couldn't afford to purchase the required books. "He has operated a molasses mill, a canning factory, and several other enterprises, and for thirty-five years, until the post office was discontinued, he was postmaster of High. Now [in 1952] he supplements the income from his farm by manufacturing molasses for a few customers." When Irene Carlisle compiled her MA thesis she noted that High was one of her most outstanding contributors: "He has an astonishing store of songs, most of which came to him through his own family."[44] High contributed songs to Vance Randolph, Mary Parler, John Quincy Wolf, and Max Hunter, as well as to Carlisle.

In about 1952, High compiled and published his own song collection, *Old, Old Folk Songs*—one of three books he wrote.[45] His brief introduction stated, "I, Fred High . . . have compiled 73 Old, Old Time Songs of several kinds to suit young and old. Some long, some short and I hope it pleases you all. I am 73 years of age past, and this book contains one song for each of my years here on earth."[46] Most of the songs have a by-line, but it isn't clear whether High means that the named individual was the person who wrote the song or rather (more reasonably) the one who sang it for him. Thus, "Mary Martha & Laserth" was "Writen by my sister on my birthday jan the 15–51" and "Poor Oma" is by "Mother."[47] High's collection is as important as some with much greater pretensions, and serves as a reminder that everyone who sings folk songs is a songcatcher in his or her own right.

SINCE THEN

Like the announcement of Mark Twain's demise that he was fond of quoting, reports of the death of traditional songs in the Ozarks have been premature. For decades, virtually every collector was confident that he or she was gathering in the last leaves of traditional folksong, only to be handily survived by the tradition itself. Collecting in the Ozarks continued into the last years of the twentieth century—not only songs and ballads, but also fiddle music, a subject neglected in this account for want of space. While the nature of the songs and ballads might change slowly, the tradition itself thrives.

NOTES

1. Mary Parler and Vance Randolph, pamphlet accompanying *Max Hunter of Springfield, Ozark Songs and Ballads* (Folk-Legacy FSA-11, 1963).

2. Norm Cohen, *Folk Music: A Regional Exploration* (Westport, CT: Greenwood Press, 2005), 110.

3. Cohen, *Folk Music*, 110.

4. Vance Randolph, "Ballad Hunters in Northern Arkansas," *Arkansas Historical Quarterly* 7 (Spring 1948): 1–10; Randolph and Ruth Ann Musick, "Folksong Hunters," *Midwest Folklore* 1 (April 1951): 23–31.

5. Quoted by Susan L. Pentlin and Rebecca B. Schroeder, "H. M. Belden, the English Club, and the Missouri Folk-Lore Society," *Missouri Folklore Society Journal* 8–9 (1986–1987).

6. H. M. Belden, "The Study of Folk-Song in America," *Modern Philology* 2 (1905): 573–579.

7. H. M. Belden, "Old-Country Ballads in Missouri," *Journal of American Folk-Lore* 19 (1906): vol. 1, 231–240, and vol. 2, 281–299.

8. H. M. Belden, *A Partial List of Song-Ballads and Other Popular Poetry Known in Missouri with Some Hints for the Collector* (Columbia: Missouri Folk-Lore Society, 1907).

9. H. M. Belden, *A Partial List of Song-Ballads and Other Popular Poetry Known in Missouri with Some Hints for the Collector*, 2nd ed. (Columbia: Missouri Folk-Lore Society, 1910).

10. Henry M. Belden, ed., *Ballads and Songs Collected by the Missouri Folk-Lore Society* (Columbia: University of Missouri, 1940).

11. Henry M. Belden and Arthur Palmer Hudson, eds., *The Frank C. Brown Collection of North Carolina Folklore* (Durham: Duke University Press, 1952).

12. Pentlin and Schroeder, "H. M. Belden."

13. L. D. Ames, "The Missouri Play-Party," *Journal of American Folklore* 24 (July–September 1911): 295–318.

14. L. D. Ames, "The Play-Party in Northeast Missouri," *Journal of American Folklore* 27 (1914): 289–303.

15. See: http://missourifolkloresociety.truman.edu/hamilton.html

16. Vance Randolph, *The Ozarks* (New York: Vanguard Press, 1931); Vance Randolph, *Ozark Mountain Folks* (New York: Vanguard Press, 1931). In his first books, Randolph provided very picturesque accounts of the collecting process in the Ozark backwoods, describing in rich detail the Ozarkers who gave him texts. When I visited Randolph in 1979 and asked him if the texts in the early books were included in his larger *Ozark Folk Songs*, he said he could not recall. It is interesting, though, that while the characters named in the 1931 and 1932 accounts are absent from *Ozark Folk Songs*, several of the texts in those earlier works are—except for greater use of non-standard pronunciations—word-for-word identical with texts in *Ozark Folk Songs*. Perhaps back then Randolph was more concerned with painting an accurate though impressionistic picture of the Ozarks rather than providing an ethnographic account. It would not be difficult to believe of a man who wrote pamphlets under the pseudonym of "Belden Kittredge"—in homage to two of his favorite ballad scholars.

17. Charles Seeger, "Review of Randolph, *Ozark Folksongs*," *Modern Language Association: Notes*, 2nd series, 4 (June 1947): 469–470.

18. *Ozark Folksongs*, edited by Norm Cohen (Rounder CD 1108, 2001).

19. Lynn Ellis Hummel, "Ozark Folk-Songs" (master's thesis, University of Missouri, 1936).

20. Hummel, "Ozark Folk-Songs," 2.

21. Maude Wright, "Folk Music of Arkansas" (master's thesis, Louisiana State University, 1937).

22. Grant McDonald, "A Study of Selected Folk-Songs of Southern Missouri" (master's thesis, University of Iowa, 1939).

23. Irene Carlisle, *Music by Lamplight* (La Porte, IN: Dierkes Press, 1945).

24. See www.rosietheriveter.org

25. See two articles by Irene Carlisle ("And Doors of Ivoree," *Arkansas Gazette*, Little Rock, 3 May 1942 and 10 May 1942) about ballad hunting near Fayetteville, including partial texts of eighteen songs.

26. Irene Carlisle, "Fifty Ballads and Songs from Northwest Arkansas" (master's thesis, University of Arkansas, 1952).

27. John W. Stilley, "Ozark Mountain Folk Songs" (master's thesis, Northwestern University, 1942).

28. "The Stilley Collection of Ozark Folk Songs," *Mid-America Folklore* 20:1 (Spring 1992), 1–64; and 20:2 (Fall 1992), 77–109.

29. Theodore Garrison, "Some Survivals of British Balladry among Ozark Folk Songs," *Arkansas Historical Quarterly* 5 (Autumn 1946): 246–262; "The Native American

Influence in Folk Songs of North Arkansas," *Arkansas Historical Quarterly* 6 (Summer 1947): 165–179.

30. "Forty-Five Folk Songs Collected from Searcy County," *Mid-America Folklore* 30:1/2 (Fall 2002): 7–215.

31. Carl Sandburg, *The American Songbag* (New York: Harcourt Brace, 1927).

32. Col. DeWitt Clinton Allen, *Glimpses of the Past* (Missouri Historical Society, 1935), 133–150.

33. Otto Ernest Rayburn, *Forty Years in the Ozarks* (Eureka Springs: Ozark Guide Press, 1957).

34. Ray Wood, *Mother Goose in the Ozarks* (Baywood, TX: self-published, 1939). The book includes a foreword by J. Frank Dobie.

35. Ruth Ann Musick, "A Missouri Dance Call," *Journal of American Folklore* 59 (1946): 323–334; Ruth Ann Musick, "Three Folksongs from Missouri," *Hoosier Folklore* 5 (September 1946): 29–34.

36. Vance Randolph and Ruth Ann Musick, "Folksong Hunters in Missouri," *Midwest Folklore* 1 (1951): 23–31.

37. See Judy Prozzillo Byers, "Ruth Ann Musick—The Show-Me Mountaineer: A Missourian Adopted by West Virginia," *Missouri Folklore Society Journal* 8–9 (1986–1987).

38. Mary Celestia Parler, *An Arkansas Ballet Book* (Fayetteville: University of Arkansas, 1963; reprint, Norwood Editions, 1976).

39. See http://lcweb2.loc.gov/diglib/legacies/MO/200003214.html

40. *Ozark Folksongs and Ballads* (Folk Legacy LP FSA-11, 1963), recorded by Sandy Paton; *The Balladere: Max Hunter Sings Original Folksongs, Vols. 1 / 2*.

41. Loman D. Cansler, "Boyhood Songs of My Grandfather," *Southern Folklore Quarterly* 18 (September 1954): 177–189.

42. Loman D. Cansler, *Missouri Folk Songs* (Folkways 5324, 1959); Loman D. Cansler, *Folk Songs of the Midwest* (Folkways 5330, 1973).

43. See www.lyon.edu/wolfcollection

44. Carlisle, *Fifty Ballads*.

45. Fred High, *Old, Old Folk Songs* (self-published, 1949).

46. High, *Old Songs*, no page number.

47. High, *Old Songs*, no page number.

FOUR

Songcatchers in the West: Cowboy Songs

Guy Logsdon

When western songs are mentioned, many folks automatically think of traditional cowboy songs or songs sung by Hollywood cowboys, but there are far more traditional songs from the West than those found in the cowboy genre. There are songs of the Mormons and songs from miners, railroaders, buffalo hunters, loggers, depression and dust bowl migrants, hobos, labor unions and many additional song subjects along with old-time fiddle tunes. However, there were and are many folksong scholars and songcatchers who have devoted much of their time to songs of the cowboy, for the romanticized cowboy is the "mythical folk hero" of the United States.

The work, the values, and the songs of the trail-driving cowboys of the late 1800s and working cowboys through the years were and are much different from those of the romanticized "hero" cowboy of Hollywood and television. The real working cowboy was and is a "hired man on horseback," who seldom had a good singing voice. As is the case with society in general, many cowboys could not even carry a tune, much less sing a song.

The "singing cowboy" narratives started in 1874 when Joseph G. McCoy, the man responsible for starting the trail driving days from Texas to Kansas, recorded his experiences in *Historic Sketches of the Cattle Trade of the West and Southwest*.[1] He wrote that when Texas cattle were corralled and restless when waiting to be shipped, he and others sitting on a fence would sing to them, and the human voice would settle them down. He wrote, "Singing hymns to Texan steers is the peculiar forte of a genuine cow-boy, but the spirit of pure piety does not abound in the sentiment," and continued, describing that a young cowboy "loves tobacco, liquor and women better than any other trinity."[2] In later years songcatchers often wrote that due to content, many songs could not be printed; also, very few versions of hymns sung by cowboys were collected.

He and other early day participants often used the word "singing" instead of "yelling"; the "whoopin' an' hollerin'" at livestock was and is far more common than singing to them, but at night some of the young cowboys did sing, hum, whistle, and use other sounds to prevent sudden noises from stampeding the herds and to cover their own fear of the darkness.

As the "trail driving" cattle days slowly died, the romanticized singing cowboy narratives became more common, and songs depicting actual cowboy life and death slowly emerged. As dime novelists, historians, journalists, folklorists, and others slowly transformed the working cowboy into a singing cowboy, the visions of singing to prevent or stop stampedes, singing to the rhythm of the horse's gait, and other lore became standard stories, but any cowboy who could sing—astride his galloping horse, bent over in his saddle, sucking dust down his throat—had rare vocal and physical talents. Nevertheless, the singing cowboy slowly evolved into Hollywood's "horse opera."

In the early 1930s, Ken Maynard, though lacking vocal skills, became the first "reel" cowboy to sing in a motion picture, but Gene Autry was the singer for whom the genre was created.[3] In the years that followed, some of the commercial and Hollywood songs entered tradition, and belief in the singing cowboy image became deeply embedded in the national culture of the United States. The early cowboy songcatchers would not be surprised, for some of the trail-days songs were adaptations of popular songs of the time.

In the late 1800s, cowboy poems appeared in print before songs, but it was the 1980s before much attention was paid to cowboy poetry. The "real" cowboy image was always masculine, and the "reel" cowboy portrayed even more masculinity. During the early decades of the twentieth century, poetry was often thought to be a female or "sissy" endeavor, yet many of the popular cowboy songs were poems before anonymous individuals set them to music. The well-known song "The Strawberry Roan" was written by the cowboy Curley Fletcher at an Arizona rodeo in 1914. It was printed as a poem, but by the 1920s it was being sung.[4] The identity of the individual who started singing it is still unknown; it may have been a cowgirl, not a cowboy. The romanticized reel cowboy hero could be seen and heard singing, but not quoting poetry. What would John Wayne's image have become if he had been a poetry-reciting cowboy?

NATHAN HOWARD "JACK" THORP

The first documented songcatcher who traveled collecting cowboy songs was Nathan Howard "Jack" Thorp, born in 1867—the year the trail drives started northward out of Texas. New York City was his birthplace, and as a son of a wealthy New York lawyer he was educated at Saint Paul's School in Concord, New Hampshire. Little biographical information is known about Thorp other than he spent his summers on a brother's ranch near Stanton, Nebraska, and as his father had fallen on hard financial times, he did not attend college.

At the age of nineteen he moved to New Mexico with his Nebraska cowboy skills. He had been a polo player in New York, so he started his cowboy life as a buyer of horses to be shipped to New York to become polo ponies. He was an educated, cultured young man who wanted to become a cowboy, and he succeeded. As he matured he became a cattleman and horseman as well as a poet and storyteller; not only was he a western songcatcher, but he also contributed songs to the cowboy genre as he played his mandolin-banjo traveling over many trails.

During his second year in New Mexico, while hunting stray horses north of Roswell, by accident he rode into a cowboy night camp and heard a cowboy singing "Dodgin' Joe," a song about "the fastest cutting-horse in Texas"—a song that had not appeared in any collection. He asked to hear more songs, and when he heard them became inspired to hunt for songs, not horses. The next morning on horseback he started the first known western songcatching trek. It was March of 1889, and he rode and collected songs over a trail that covered approximately 1,500 miles. His travels in the saddle took him into Indian Territory (now Oklahoma) and down to Dallas and San Antonio before returning to his home range in New Mexico. Years later he told about his inspiration to collect and his experiences as a songcatcher in "Banjo in the Cow Camps," published in the *Atlantic Monthly* in August of 1940 and reprinted in his autobiography *Pardner of the Wind* (1941).[5] His *Atlantic Monthly* essay is still one of the best—possibly the best—article written about the singing of the hired man on horseback.

He wrote that he carried a notebook in which he "jotted the words to any cowboy song," and "in the nineties, with the exception of about a dozen, cowboy songs were not generally known . . . only ones I could find I gathered, a verse here and a verse there, on horseback trips . . . most of the time spent in cow camps, at chuck wagons and line camps."[6]

He collected the song "Sam Bass" verse by verse until he had eight in a coherent sequence; years later others expanded the song into eleven verses. As many other songcatchers did, Thorp expurgated and bowdlerized the songs when necessary. He wrote:

> Take into account that many of the songs had to be dry-cleaned for unprintable words before they went to press . . . it wasn't always parlor talk . . . the entire range version of The Top Hand . . . the words would have burned the reader's eyeballs . . . I expurgated and had to change even the title, and the song has appeared exactly as I rendered it in all cowboy song books published since.[7]

In 1908, Thorp took a small manuscript of songs he had collected and written to the News Print Shop in Estancia, New Mexico, and printed it for the cost of six cents a copy for two thousand copies. The title was *Songs of the Cowboys*, a small fifty-one-page red paperback book containing twenty-three songs.[8] It was the first book of cowboy songs to be published and has become extremely rare. The first song in the book, "Little Joe, the Wrangler," was written by Thorp and is now well known among western singers and fans; a few lesser-known songs in it were also written by him.[9] In subsequent years, not knowing the original source, other cowboy songbooks often included songs from Thorp's small publication without giving credit, much to his chagrin.

In 1921, *Songs of the Cowboys* was expanded and published by the Houghton Mifflin Company; it continued 101 songs either collected or written by Thorp.[10] His dedication was to thirty-one "COW-GIRLS AND PUNCHERS," and is one of the most sincere and appreciative statements written by a songcatcher:

> Many of you I have worked with in the past, on the range, the trail, and in the branding pens. All of you I have known well . . . . Those who are alive I hartily [sic] thank for having given me their assistance in collecting these songs. May this little book tend to recall the times, good and tough, we had together.[11]

In the following years his poems appeared in regional journals as well as *Poetry*, and as a storyteller he wrote *Tales of the Chuckwagon* (1926) which was printed privately.[12] His autobiography, *Pardner of the Wind*, was written in collaboration with Neil M. Clark; J. Frank Dobie wrote Clark with great praise for Thorp, saying, "All Jack needed was a good listener. He never seemed to run out and yet his stories always had pertinence and were based on character more than anything else."[13]

A few songs and statements about cowboy singing had been printed in books and journals prior to Thorp's publication. In her book of recollections and experiences, *Texan Ranch Life* (1894), Mary J. Jaques included "The Jolly Cowboy" and a lengthy version of "The Dying Cowboy" to supplement her statements about cowboys singing for diversion or recreation, not while working cattle.[14] Grace B. Ward wrote the article "Cowboy Songs and Dance," published in *Pearson's Magazine* (1903); among the songs were "Sam Bass" and "The Dying Cowboy," and she emphasized that the singing was around campfires at night.[15] Sharlot M. Hall was an Arizona ranch woman who was also a poet; she wrote a story "Songs of the Old Cattle Trail" for *Out West* (1908).[16] She used four songs to illustrate her story that had a cowboy singing cattle to sleep with "Lorena," a song popular during the Civil War and equally popular for many years among trail hand cowboys; the songs she used were sad songs.

JOHN A. LOMAX

John A. Lomax, the best-known American songcatcher, was born in 1867—the same year as Jack Thorp, and the year the trail drives started. Two years later his family decided to leave his Mississippi birthplace and move to Texas where they settled into farm life near Meridian, near the Chisholm Trail. As a farm boy he heard many cowboy songs and other folk songs. In his late teens, he started putting them on paper; his family stressed education, at least getting one year of college. Motivated by a desire to learn, John Avery Lomax graduated from the University of Texas in 1897. He stayed at the university working different positions and, in 1903, became an English teacher at the A&M College of Texas, which later became Texas A&M University. He and Bess B. Brown were married in 1904 and had two sons and two daughters.

In 1906, he accepted a scholarship to attend Harvard and took with him his ballads and a keen interest in folksongs. He was encouraged by George L. Kittredge and Barrett Wendell to continue capturing western ballads. At Harvard he received a grant of five hundred dollars as a Sheldon Fellow, which funded travel expenses and a cylinder recorder. He started collecting in 1908 and became the first western songcatcher to use a recording device in his collecting travels; however, many cowboy informants would not sing into the horn without encouragement from alcohol. Lomax later wrote, "Not one song did I ever get from them except through the influence of generous amounts of whiskey, rye and straight from the bottle or jug."[17]

Not all of his songs were field-collected, as newspapers and magazines carried information about his project, which resulted in many songs being sent to him. He also found some that were already in print. Lomax, too, had to expurgate, bowdlerize, rewrite, and edit many of his field-collected songs and some that were sent to him. Years later he wrote an old cowboy's statement about singing:

> In the singing about camp, a cowboy would often cut loose with a song too vile to repeat; great cheers and hurrays would usually follow and there would be calls for more. After the climax in this class of songs had been reached, some puncher would strike up an old-time religious hymn, and that also would be cheered to the echo.[18]

Lomax did not always credit his sources when his *Cowboy Songs and Other Frontier Ballads* was published in 1910, and, as in the Thorp book, no melody lines were printed.[19] Thorp became angry at the "learned professor" for not crediting him for songs taken from his publication. It is not known if Lomax had a copy of Thorp's book or if individuals copied songs or tore out pages and sent them to him. In 1916, an expanded edition was published again with no credit given to Thorp.[20] Humorously, but spurred by anger, Thorp took his copy of the Lomax 1916 edition and went through marking each of his songs with comments such as "expunged by me." Thorp also took songs from that 1916 edition and used them in his 1921 edition of *Songs of the Cowboys*, but the texts were not always identical. As a result there is difficulty in identifying some of the songs as collected by Lomax or collected by Thorp.[21]

D. K. Wilgus, in his *Anglo-American Folk Song Scholarship Since 1898* (1959), presented the problems Lomax had in expurgating and bowdlerizing his songs, along with his methods of collecting and presenting his material.[22] Wilgus also discussed both Thorp and Lomax and the controversy of sources and credits. In 1967, John O. West wrote an article titled "Jack Thorp and John A. Lomax: Oral or Written Transmissions?" in the journal *Western Folklore*, in which he provides additional information about Lomax using Thorp's texts.[23] The controversy had no negative effect on the popularity of Lomax and *Cowboy Songs and Other Frontier Ballads*, for the 1910 and 1916 editions went through numerous printings and had a major influence among cowboy singers and others interested in folk songs. In 1919, his collection of cowboy poetry was published by Macmillan and contained poems that became songs such as "A Border Affair" by Charles Badger Clark, Jr.; this collection has seldom been quoted by western scholars.[24]

John A. Lomax and family continued to live in Texas, except for two years in Chicago. He was a founding member of the Texas Folklore Society and served as president of the American Folklore Society.[25] His son Alan joined him in the early 1930s in his collecting ventures and became another well-known songcatcher. Together they compiled and edited many major collections, including a 1938 revised and enlarged edition of *Cowboy Songs and Other Frontier Ballads* in which a melody line was printed for many of the songs.[26] This edition was reprinted at least five times during the early 1940s. In 1986 it was reprinted in a paperback edition with a long and informative introduction by Alan Lomax and Joshua Berrett.

In 1933, Lomax was appointed Honorary Curator of the Archive of Folksong at the Library of Congress. Alan went with him and continued the family legend. It has been estimated that John A. Lomax traveled over two hundred thousand miles in his years as a songcatcher before he died in 1948. A few years before his death he was asked to write a chapter for a proposed anthology of regional folklore, but the book was never published and his chapter was returned and lay dormant for many years. However, it was published in 1967 as *Cow Camps and Cattle Herds* with the introduction written by John A. Lomax, Jr.[27] It is a belated but extremely important contribution to cowboy lore and the Lomax legacy.

Another Lomax article had a major influence on how cowboy songs are characterized. It was published with the byline Mrs. John A. Lomax and was a story she had written entitled "Trail Songs of the Cowpuncher" for the *Overland Monthly* (1912).[28] She used information from his collections and included the statement that the rhythm of a cowboy song was set to the gait of the horse. Since then, many scholars, journalists, and others involved in collecting and studying cowboy songs and lore have stated or written the same belief. However, in her husband's cowboy songbook many of the songs are in 3/4 (waltz) time. Horses did not and do not waltz, and a slow-paced, stiff-legged horse did not and does not inspire one to sing.

J. FRANK DOBIE

J. Frank Dobie was another scholar who wrote many books about the West, particularly Texas, and he wore many different shoes in his life. He was a teacher, historian, folklorist, and author, and became known to many people as "Mr. Texas." Born in 1888 on a Texas ranch, his parents made sure that he and his siblings were educated; he was sent to Alice, Texas, to live with grandparents and graduate from high school. Dobie attended Southwestern University in Georgetown and there met his future wife and lifetime partner, Bertha McKee. After graduating in 1910, he became a high school teacher; the following year he returned to Southwestern University and taught there for two years. He then went to Columbia University to earn a master's degree.

In 1914, Dobie went to the University of Texas as an English teacher and became a member of the Texas Folk-Lore Society, which had been organized five years previously. In 1917, he left the University to serve two years in the field artillery during World War I. He was back at the University in 1919 but resigned in 1920 to run his uncle's ranch. He returned to Austin the next year. It was in 1920 when his first article about cowboy songs, "The Cowboy and His Songs," was published in *Texas Review*.[29] In 1922, Dobie's interest in cultural traditions led him back into the Texas Folk-Lore Society, and he became the secretary-editor of the Society and expanded the publication series that has retained its quality and continues to contribute valuable material to those interested in western cultural heritage.

Dobie is seldom considered to be a songcatcher; however, in volume six of the publications of the Texas Folk-Lore Society, *Texas and Southwestern Lore*, he contributed a lengthy article "Ballads and Songs of the Frontier Folk" (1927).[30] His attitude about folksongs and singing was set forth in his opening statement:

> The songs in the collection that follows are generally commonplace and devoid of literary merit. Yet because of their merit to social history, their reflection of a people's experiences and attitudes towards life, they are worth preserving. Moreover, if considered in their proper setting, they do have a kind of literary merit. . . . [I]n short, under proper conditions thousands of people have derived from just these songs the true effect of literature.[31]

The songs and commentary that followed indicate that Dobie was a song-catcher, for he gave sources and events during which he gathered them. When known, he told where and why his informant learned them, and he gave his evaluation of vocal quality. The song genres are numerous: the first song, "The Song of the Happy Hunters," is about hunting javelinas (wild hogs). The variation is indicated by "The Honest Tramp," "The Drunkard's Dream," "Not Long Since a Young Girl and I Fell in Love," "The Haunted Wood," "Away Here in Texas," "Texas Rangers After the Mob," "Cowboy's Hymn," and many others. In volume seven, *Follow de Drinkin' Gou'd* (1928), he continued with "More Ballads and Songs of the Frontier Folk."[32] The songs varied from "The Maid of Monterrey" to "The Wyoming Nester" to "The Cowboy's Stroll."

In the book *Backwoods to Border* (1943), Dobie included an article, "A Buffalo Hunter and His Song," in which he used three songs to illustrate the diversity sung by buffalo hunters—"The Buffalo-Skinners," "The White Captive," and "Sherfield."[33] In each of his essays, a melody line was provided for some songs. He took songs from existing songbooks and gave proper credit, but indeed, he collected many of them. His "Buffalo Hunter" essay was an expanded version of one of his weekly newspaper columns for the *Dallas News*—a series he started writing in 1939 and continued until his death in 1964; his Sunday column was titled "My Texas."

Since Dobie did not have a doctorate, the University of Texas administration would not give him professorial advancement. So, in 1923, he accepted the chairmanship of the English department at Oklahoma A&M College (now Oklahoma State University) in Stillwater. He continued to edit the Texas Folklore Society publications and became the president of the Oklahoma State Folklore Society, originally organized in 1915. While at Oklahoma A&M, he published his article "Cowboy Songs" in *Country Gentleman* (1925).[34] In this article, he quoted one cowboy saying "there never was a stampede while the fiddle was going," and continued with, "a peculiar form of cowboy song for quieting cattle is the yodel. The most famous of the yodels is called The Texas Yodel."[35]

After two years in Oklahoma he returned to the University of Texas, where he spurred his research, collecting, and writing to a hard human gallop. In 1947, he was engaged in controversy in Texas: he was an avowed liberal, which did not make him popular with the governor or the president of the University, so he resigned that year.

J. Frank Dobie wrote twenty books of history, folklore, and culture; numerous entries in books written by others; 502 articles and stories for magazines; and many other items. He was a songcatcher, but his interests went beyond songs. He died in 1964.

DANE COOLIDGE

Dane Coolidge was a songcatcher who has been overlooked by many. He was born in Massachusetts in 1873, but the family moved to the Los Angeles area in 1877, where his father became the owner of an orange farm at Riverside, California. He earned a degree from Stanford University and studied at Harvard University from 1898 to 1899. Coolidge was a naturalist who worked as a field collector of animals for federal agencies as well as for the British Museum, and he became a photographer of wildlife and cowboys in the west, eventually taking over 3,700 photographs—many of which were taken during the days of glass plate negative photography. He would exchange a photograph of a cowboy if the cowboy would write out the words of the song or songs he knew and sang.

Coolidge became well versed in American Indian and cowboy lore, and, in 1912, wrote an article, illustrated with his photographs, "Cow Boy Songs" for *Sunset* and later "Cowboy Songs and Ballads," published in *Poetry* (1917).[36] In a well-written literary narrative, he stated,

> It may teach us not to scorn the beautiful music which often goes with ribald songs. A ballad changes a hundred and a thousand times; no two men sing it alike and it changes from pathos to parody and back again . . . cow-boy songs, like most true ballads, are apt to deal with old, unhappy, far-off things. . . . Most of the real funny ones, according to cow-boy standards, will probably remain in the *Index Expurgatorius* of the scholar for some time to come.[37]

He also wrote at least forty books, of which many were western novels. He authored three books with the term "Cowboys" in the title—each published in the late 1930s after his itinerant collecting days were slowed down. Each of these books included photographs he had taken. The first was *Texas Cowboys* (1937) and had two chapters, "Cowboy Songs and Stories" and "Herd Songs and Ballads," in which songs were printed, including "Barbara Allen."[38] His second book was titled *Arizona Cowboys* (1938), and the third *Old California Cowboys* (1939).[39] *Arizona Cowboys* contains photos taken during 1903–1904, and *Old California Cowboys* had three chapters: "Cowboys in California," "Cowboys in Arizona," and "Cowboys in Old Mexico." Coolidge died in 1940.

MARGARET LARKIN

Margaret Larkin was born in New Mexico in 1899 with (as she later claimed) a guitar in her lap. She grew up among cowboy singers and tellers of tales and absorbed cowboy and Hispanic lore. She became a lady with many talents and interests—poet, collector and singer of cowboy songs, trade union activist, journalist, writer of nonfiction, and other activities, and became friends with Jack Thorp, Carl Sandburg, and many writers and poets in the Santa Fe and Taos artist colonies. She attended the University of Kansas where her poetic skills won awards. Her poetry was published in many forms, and she wrote award-winning plays.

Larkin was attracted to the east in the late 1920s where she worked as a journalist, publicist, and press agent and became interested in the social problems intensified by the Great Depression. She was one of the first to realize the value of folk songs as a tool for expressing social protest. Her interest went beyond cowboy songs when in 1929 she met Ella May Wiggins, who was a mill worker in North Carolina and had a natural talent for writing ballets about working conditions and life. Wiggins was murdered shortly after Larkin met her—most probably by mill owners. Larkin returned to New York City and gave concerts using Wiggins's songs and became one of the earliest singers of social protest songs in a concert mode in New York City. She also became known as a singer of cowboy songs. She compiled forty songs and two variants considered to be singable into *Singing Cowboy: A Book of Western Songs* (1931), with piano arrangements by Helen Beck.[40] Her texts were as she had learned them, and when possible she gave sources as well as locations. Larkin also wrote extensive notes that were not romanticized. She stated that not all cowboys sang and stressed that the importance and function of singing was an individual cowboy decision. Her belief was that the songs were not work songs and that it was a happy accident if one fit the gait of a horse.

The Oklahoma playwright Lynn Riggs became friends with Larkin while in Santa Fe. In 1931, when his play *Green Grow the Lilacs* was produced on Broadway, he used songs that he had learned in Oklahoma, but when they added "Singing Interludes," Riggs turned to Larkin for advice and the use of some of her songs. When the play became a road show, Larkin was in the troupe as a folksinger and guitarist, and a small booklet, *Cowboy Songs, Folk Songs and Ballads from* Green Grow the Lilacs (1932), was published to be used with the script by local productions of the play.[41]

By the late 1930s, Margaret Larkin had become deeply involved in left-wing activities. Her husband was a member of the Communist Party, but that marriage ended in divorce. She met playwright-novelist Albert Maltz, and they shared similar views about a writer's social responsibilities. They moved to Hollywood, where he earned awards from the Academy of Motion Picture Arts and Sciences. However, in 1947 he was subpoenaed to appear before the House Committee on Un-American Activities and became one of the Hollywood Ten who refused to answer questions. He served a prison term, and when he was released, they and their two children moved to Mexico. She and Maltz divorced in 1964; she remained in Mexico where she died in 1967.

INA SIRES

Little information has been found about the songcatcher Ina Sires, but her *Songs of the Open Range* (1928), which included full piano accompaniments for all twenty-nine songs, made her a genuine songcatcher.[42] Sires was born in the Texas Panhandle near Lamesa and grew up on a ranch; after graduating from Baylor University, she taught school in Arizona, Kansas City, and Montana, and when her collection was published, she was teaching in the Dallas Public Schools. In 1927, she wrote that she had used the books of both Thorp and Lomax, but she did not indicate which ones, nor did she give any sources. She did write that she obtained tunes from cowboys and that she field collected some songs as she worked, lived, and traveled in western states:

> I have several ballads that so far as I know have not appeared in print, but my chief work has been to preserve the melodies. I have secured these directly from the cowboys, by visiting ranches, attending dances, and riding on round-ups in the western states where people still dance all night to the tune of the fiddle.[43]

She continued the romance of cowboy singing by writing that cowboys sing their herd to sleep at night, that they sing to the gait of their horse, and other misinformation. She also indicated that she started collecting five years earlier, and her notes about each song were mixed with accuracy about cowboys as well as pure romanticism. In an advertisement leaflet, it was written that she was available for "Lecture and Songs, Given in Costume . . . The Cowboy as The Builder of The West is a humorous, interesting, instructive lecture, full of laughs, full of real history . . . songs that kept the herds quiet, that expressed the faith, love and joy of the real cowboy in his big out-of-doors."[44] How long she gave the lectures, when she died, or where her papers were deposited have not been documented.

JULES VERNE ALLEN, "THE SINGING COWBOY"

Jules Verne Allen, known as "The Singing Cowboy," was born at Waxahachie, Texas, in 1883. It has been written that he started working cattle at the age of ten and became a horse wrangler in the late 1890s, which was the job of taking care of the horses, keeping them together, and preparing them for work. It was the lowest level of work in a cow camp and usually given to boys or young men. He worked cattle from the Mexican border to Montana, and played the guitar and sang cowboy songs. He also became a rodeo cowboy, and he eventually worked in law enforcement and volunteered for service during World War I.

When the radio became popular in the 1920s, Allen became a popular cowboy personality singing over stations in Dallas, San Antonio, and Los Angeles as "Longhorn Luke and His Cowboys" and "Shiftless," and recorded ten songs as "The Original Singing Cowboy" for Victor in April 1928. A small songbook, *Cowboy Songs Sung by Longhorn Luke and His Cowboys*, was published in San Antonio by his radio sponsor.[45] He also performed at various events in New Mexico, and in 1929 the governor appointed him as the "official singer of New Mexico's cowboy folk songs." In his book *Cowboy Lore* (1933), he had chapters about cowboy life, cattle brands, and terms and sayings.[46] His unit "Songs of the Range" was one hundred pages long in the book of 163 pages, and each song had full piano accompaniments. As an introduction to the songs he wrote:

> Out of many Cowboy songs I have selected those I thought contributed most to Cowboy lore. . . . [M]ost of them are presented here just as I learned them on the range; in a ranch house or near the corral years ago. . . . The songs in the following pages were taken down from my voice just as I sing them.[47]

He may have been a songcatcher, but many of Allen's songs were from the Lomax book. His romanticized explanation about cowboy life and singing make it necessary to question all of his claims about his cowboy life. His recording career did not extend into the 1930s, but he remained a popular radio and solo performer through the 1930s. He died in 1945 and apparently left no documents in any archives.

CHARLES ANGELO SIRINGO

Charles Angelo Siringo was born in 1855 in Dutch Settlement, Texas. His Italian father died a year after his birth, and his Irish mother had to care for him and his sister. As a young boy—twelve years old—he was hired to be a cowboy and worked for and with some cattlemen and cowboys who became legendary western figures, such as Shanghai Pierce. By 1876 he had worked his way up to be a trail driver and with cowhands drove a herd of 2,500 cattle up the Chisholm Trail to Kansas. He also helped to establish the LX Ranch in the Texas Panhandle. He married in 1884 and settled in Caldwell, Kansas. He started writing his autobiography *A Texas Cow Boy: or, Fifteen Years on the Hurricane Deck of a Spanish Pony* (1886).[48] It has been documented as being the first autobiography written by a working cowboy. The title page continued with "By Chas. A. Siringo, An Old Stove-Up 'Cow Puncher,' Who Has Spent Nearly Twenty Years on the Great Western Cattle Range." The following year they moved to Chicago where he signed on with the Pinkerton's National Detective Agency. As a cowboy detective, he traveled the West in pursuit of outlaws and was involved in early labor union disputes.

His wife died, and he had at least one failed marriage before retiring to his ranch in Santa Fe, New Mexico, in 1907. There he wrote a second book *A Cowboy Detective: A True Story of Twenty Two Years with a World Famous Detective Agency* (1912).[49] In 1916, he became a New Mexico Ranger chasing rustlers for two years, and in 1919 he wrote and self-published another book about himself, *A Lone Star Cowboy* (1919), and compiled a small paperback booklet, *Song Companion of a Lone Star Cowboy: Old Favorite Cow-Camp Songs* (1919).[50] There were fourteen songs in the forty-eight pages that sold for twenty-five cents, and he wrote that they were songs that put many longhorn herds to sleep on a dark and stormy night, adding his touch to the romanticization of cowboy songs. How much influence the Lomax book had on his choices is not known. In any case, the *Song Companion* remains an extremely rare and valuable little songbook.

Siringo wrote other books—the last of which was *Riata and Spurs: The Story of a Lifetime Spent in the Saddle as Cowboy and Detective* (1927), a combination of two earlier titles.[51] He was a popular figure in his day, meeting many historical western and national figures. Siringo moved to the Hollywood cowboy movie world, but appeared in no movies. He died in California in 1928.

NOTES

1. Joseph G. McCoy, *Historic Sketches of the Cattle Trade of the West and Southwest* (Kansas City, MO: Ramsey, Millett, and Hudson, 1874).

2. Guy W. Logsdon, *"The Whorehouse Bells Were Ringing" and Other Songs Cowboys Sing* (Urbana: University of Illinois Press, 1989). Pages 283–287 encompass a summary of McCoy's statements about cowboy singing.

3. *Sons of the Saddle*, 16 mm, 76 min. Ken Maynard Productions, Inc., 1930.

4. Curley Fletcher, "The Outlaw Bronco," *Globe Arizona Record*, 16 December 1915.

5. N. Howard (Jack) Thorp and Neil M. Clark, *Pardner of the Wind* (Privately printed, Caldwell, Ohio, 1945; reprinted Lincoln: University of Nebraska Press, 1977), 41–42. This book was copyrighted in 1941 but not published until 1945, and unfortunately Jack Thorp did not live to see it published. In December 1979 I located Neil Clark in Santa Fe, New Mexico, and obtained the manuscript, photos, correspondence, and Clark's *Pardner of the Wind*.

6. Thorp and Clark, *Pardner of the Wind*, 41–42.
7. Thorp and Clark, *Pardner of the Wind*, 41–42.
8. N. Howard Thorp, *Songs of the Cowboy* (privately printed, 1908; reprinted Lincoln: University of Nebraska Press, 1984).
9. Thorp, *Songs of the Cowboy*. Before meeting Clark, I had obtained Thorp's personal copy that he had given to Clark; it has many holograph notes by Thorp about the source or authorship of some songs. Clark loaned it to Austin E. and Alta S. Fife when they edited *Songs of the Cowboys* (New York: Clarkson N. Potter, 1966), including song variations, annotations, notes, and other information; this edition is a major contribution to cowboy songcatching and the study of Thorp.
10. N. Howard Thorp, *Songs of the Cowboys* with an Introduction by Alice Corbin Henderson (Boston: Houghton Mifflin, 1921).
11. Thorp, *Songs of the Cowboys*.
12. N. Howard Thorp, *Tales of the Chuckwagon* (privately printed, 1926).
13. Dobie to Clark, 11 February 1941, letter in the Thorp-Clark Collection in the Guy Logsdon Collection.
14. Mary J. Jaques, *Texan Ranch Life* (London: Horace Cox, 1894).
15. Grace B. Ward, "Cowboy Songs and Dance," *Pearson's Magazine* (January 1903).
16. Sharlot M. Hall, "Songs of the Old Cattle Trail," *Out West* (March 1908), 216–221.
17. John A. Lomax, *Adventures of a Ballad Hunter* (New York: Macmillan, 1947), 41.
18. John A. Lomax and Alan Lomax, *Cowboy Songs and Other Frontier Ballads*, rev. and enlarged (New York: Macmillan, 1938), xvi–xvii.
19. John A. Lomax, *Cowboy Songs and Other Frontier Ballads* (New York: Sturgis and Walton Co., 1910).
20. John A. Lomax, *Cowboy Songs and Other Frontier Ballads* (New York: MacMillan, 1916).
21. Lomax, *Cowboy Songs*. I obtained Thorp's copy when I purchased his *Songs of the Cowboys*. For more of Lomax and Thorp, see Logsdon, *The Whorehouse Bells*, 299–302.
22. D. K. Wilgus, *Anglo-American Folk Song Scholarship Since 1898* (New Brunswick: Rutgers University Press, 1959).
23. John O. West, "Jack Thorp and John Lomax: Oral or Written Transmission?" *Western Folklore* 26 (1967): 113–118.
24. John A. Lomax, *Songs of the Cattle Trail and Cow Camp* (New York: Macmillan, 1919).
25. For the Lomax biography and contributions, see Nolan Porterfield, *Last Cavalier: The Life and Times of John A. Lomax* (Urbana: University of Illinois Press, 1996)—this is an outstanding biography. For his personal accounts, see Lomax, *Adventures of a Ballad Hunter*.
26. John A. Lomax, *Cowboy Songs and Other Frontier Ballads* (New York: Collier, 1938).
27. John A. Lomax and John A. Lomax, Jr. *Cow Camps and Cattle Herds* (Austin: Enrico Press, 1967).
28. Mrs. John A. Lomax, "Trail Songs of the Cowpuncher," *Overland Monthly* (January 1912): 24–30.
29. J. Frank Dobie, "The Cowboy and his Songs," *Texas Review* 5:2 (January 1920): 163–169.
30. J. Frank Dobie, "Ballads and Songs of the Frontier Folk," Publications of the Texas Folk-Lore Society VI, *Texas and Southwestern Lore* (Austin: University of Texas Press, 1927): 121–183.
31. Dobie, "Ballads and Songs," 121.
32. J. Frank Dobie, *Follow de Drinkin' Gou'd*, Texas Folk Lore Society (1928).
33. J. Frank Dobie, "A Buffalo Hunter and His Song," *Texas and Southwestern Lore* (Texas Folk Lore Society) 18 (1943): 1–6.
34. J. Frank Dobie, "Cowboy Songs," *Country Gentleman* (January 10, 1925), 9.
35. Dobie, "Cowboy Songs," 9.

36. Dane Coolidge, "Cow Boy Songs," *Sunset: The Pacific Monthly* 29:5 (November 1912): 503–510; and "Cowboy Songs and Ballads," *Poetry* 10 (August 1917): 255.
37. Coolidge, "Cowboy Songs and Ballads," 255.
38. Dane Coolidge, *Texas Cowboys* (New York: E.P. Dutton, 1937).
39. Dane Coolidge, *Arizona Cowboys* (New York: E.P. Dutton, 1938); Dane Coolidge, *Old California Cowboys* (New York: E.P. Dutton, 1939).
40. Margaret Larkin, *Singing Cowboy: A Book of Western Songs* (New York: Knopf, 1931).
41. Lynn Riggs, *Cowboy Songs, Folk Songs and Ballads from Green Grow the Lilacs* (New York: Samuel French, 1932).
42. Ina Sires, *Songs of the Open Range* (New York: C. C. Birchard and Co., 1928).
43. Ina Sires, "Songs of the Open Range," *Texas and Southwestern Lore* (Austin: Texas Folk-Lore Society, 1927); Sires, *Songs of the Open Range*; piano arrangements were by Charles Repper.
44. This leaflet, with her photograph in costume, is in the Guy Logsdon Collection.
45. Jules Verne Allen, *Cowboy Songs Sung by Longhorn Luke and His Cowboys* (San Antonio: Clegg Company, 193-).
46. Jules Verne Allen, *Cowboy Lore* (San Antonio: Naylor Printing Co., 1933).
47. Allen, *Cowboy Lore*, 63.
48. Charles Angelo Siringo, *A Texas Cow Boy: or, Fifteen Years on the Hurricane Deck of a Spanish Pony* (Chicago: Siringo and Dobson, 1886).
49. Charles A. Siringo, *A Cowboy Detective: A True Story of Twenty Two Years with a World Famous Detective Agency* (Chicago: W. B. Conkey Company, 1912).
50. Charles A. Siringo, *A Lone Star Cowboy* (self-published, 1919); Charles A. Siringo, *The Song Companion of a Lone Star Cowboy: Old Favorite Cow-Camp Songs* (self-published, 1919).
51. Charles A. Siringo, *Riata and Spurs: The Story of a Lifetime Spent in the Saddle as Cowboy and Detective* (Boston: Houghton Mifflin, 1927). For more information about Siringo, see the "Handbook of Texas Online" at http://www.tshaonline.org/handbook/online; see also Ben E. Pingenot, "Charlie Siringo: New Mexico's Lone Star Cowboy," *Cattleman*, November 1976.

FIVE

Songcatchers in the West: Other Traditions

Guy Logsdon

The geographic region of the West covers a vast area and many state boundaries, massive elevation variations, numerous ethnic groups, and different migration movements and routes. During the 1930s, there was a massive migration into the West Coast region with most migrants going to California looking for work. There have been many misconceptions about the reasons for the massive migration, with the Dust Bowl being identified in our history as the primary cause and the Great Depression as the secondary reason. While the dust storms may have driven a few away from their homes, it was the collapse of the cotton industry and subsequent displacement of tenant and sharecropper cotton farming families, especially in Oklahoma, that drove migrants westward. The area in western Oklahoma designated as a portion of the Dust Bowl had a very small population of cattlemen and wheat farmers, and very few left their ranches and farms. There were approximately seventy-one thousand migrants—mostly from the cotton farming regions of eastern and southern Oklahoma. In the southern states, the tenant and sharecropper families were often African-Americans, most of whom migrated northward to Cleveland, Chicago, Detroit, and other northern cities, but their migration did not attract the attention that the western migrants did.

Woody Guthrie has been popularly identified with the Dust Bowl since the late 1930s, and his was an authentic experience in Pampa, Texas, that he shared in his songs and stories. He was a songcatcher as well as a songwriter, for he heard many traditional songs and melodies as he traveled from Okemah, Oklahoma, to Pampa and on to California. He used some of the melodies as tunes for his lyrics. Woody wrote that he heard *Otto Gray and His Oklahoma Cowboys* sing "Midnight Special" at the Crystal Theater in Okemah in 1925.[1] This was long before Lead Belly made the song popular. How many traditional songs and tunes he gathered in his memory is not known, but he seemed to have the unusual ability to catch songs and keep them in his memory reserve.

ECONOMIC MIGRANTS

In the mid 1930s, the Farm Security Administration established migrant camps for the estimated 250,000 migrants—both domestic and foreign—in California. They were usually one-room temporary structures where families could stay. In some camps the fee was one dollar a week, and some of the camps had a library, a post office, and a community building. John Steinbeck became interested in the way migrants were treated in California, and in 1936 he followed migrants as they traveled seeking work. In October 1938, he wrote a series about their conditions and treatment for the San Francisco News. In his opening article Steinbeck wrote, "The migrants are needed, and they are hated."[2]

The seven articles were published in pamphlet format as *Their Blood Is Strong* (1938) in order to raise money to rally widespread support for the abolition of this waste of human lives. It sold for twenty-five cents, and the cover was composed of two photographs by Dorothea Lange—a baby nursing on its mother's breast sitting on bedding under a tree, and a migrant tent with bed and bedding outside.

Along with Lange's famous 1936 photograph, "Migrant Mother," taken in Nipomo, California, greater national attention was directed to the migrant problems, and in 1939 Steinbeck's *Grapes of Wrath* increased concerns.[3] However, it was *Their Blood Is Strong* that inspired two young men to become songcatchers.

CHARLES L. TODD AND ROBERT SONKIN

Charles L. Todd was a graduate student at City College of New York (now the City College of the City University of New York) and had an interest in folk music. At City College he met Robert Sonkin, who was a speech student and a linguistics specialist interested in American dialects. The combination of interests and abilities developed into an outstanding songcatching team whose efforts have not received the attention they deserve. Todd's parents lived in California, and in the summer of 1938 he planned a visit home and obtained a contract to write a magazine article on the California problems.

Todd contacted Alan Lomax at the Archive of American Folk Song, Library of Congress, requesting support to record individuals in the camps, as during his visits he learned that the migrants had carried their traditional folk life with them. Lomax made the Archive's recording equipment available—"a Presto disc recording machine, recordable discs, needles, and batteries . . . at a weight of approximately eighty pounds."[4] They received information on how to collect cultural heritage along with documentation methodology and other forms of assistance. Todd and Sonkin started their trek in late summer 1940 and visited seven camps before returning to their classes, continuing the trip in September of 1941.

The recording conditions were usually difficult but reflected life in a migrant setting. They recorded in "sewing rooms; ironing rooms; arts and crafts sheds; nurseries; camp libraries."[5] Their notes were excellent; copies of them are in the Archive of Folk Culture along with the recordings that survived. The first song on their typescript, "Catalog of Recordings . . . Summer of 1940," was "The Old Apple Tree in the Garden" sung by Ruth Elliot at the Arvin camp. This was followed by three conversations with three different men; "Dust Storm," "Sleet Storm," and "Tall Stories." They recorded songs, poems, and instrumental music such as "Firebrands for Jesus," "Cotton Fever," "Pistol Pete," "Talkin' Blues," "Billy in the Low Ground," and other musical genres. Their notes tell their experiences in each camp along with explanatory information about each item recorded, with typed lyrics of each song filed alphabetically.

In 1964, they wrote an article entitled "Ballads of the Okies" for the *American Folk Music Occasional* in which they expressed their opinion of why there is such a diversity of folk songs.

> There are hollers, shanties, break-downs, sinful songs and Christian songs: there are songs addressed to mules, ponies, rattlesnakes, jackrabbits, boll weevils, geese, chickens, pigs, and crawdads. There are ditties about rye whisky and cocaine. There are ballits which tell of the death of Dewey Lee, the fate of Edward Heckman, the hanging of John Hardy, the shooting of Jesse James, and the betrayal of Bold Jack Donahue. In short, name your favorite American institution, be it a bucking bronco, a groundhog, or a public enemy, with a little traveling, you'll probably find a song about it somewhere.[6]

As songcatchers, these two men created an amazing archive that tells the story of a tragic period of life for many people who were affected by the dust storm, the collapse of the cotton industry, and the Great Depression. Todd and Sonkin were concerned about the survival of heritage in migrant settings, and the complete story of their sincere dedicated songcatching ventures and the cultural heritage they saved is yet to be comprehensively told.

BENJAMIN ALBERT BOTKIN

Boston was the birthplace in 1901 of B. A. Botkin, who through his "Treasury" books, such as *A Treasury of American Folklore: Stories, Ballads, and Traditions of the People* (1944), *A Treasury of Western Folklore* (1951), and other titles and journal articles, made cultural traditions and folklore of America available in millions of homes around the world.[7] Through hard scholastic effort Botkin earned scholarships to Harvard University, where he earned his BA, and in 1921 he completed his MA in English at Columbia University. In the fall of 1921 he started his teaching career in the English department at the University of Oklahoma. In 1923, he returned to New York City to work and study, and in 1925 he went back to the University of Oklahoma and started gathering traditions from students and other Oklahomans and eventually became president of the Oklahoma Folk-Lore Society and the Oklahoma Writers.

His Oklahoma fieldwork became his doctoral dissertation at the University of Nebraska (PhD awarded in 1931) and remains a major resource for the study of the American play-party. It was published as *The American Play-Party Song* (1937).[8] However, he first wrote about his song-catching efforts in the article "The Play Party in Oklahoma," published in *Publications of the Texas Folk-Lore Society 7, Follow de Drinkin' Gou'd* (1927).[9]

He edited the first book published by the University of Oklahoma Press in 1929, *Folk-Say: A Regional Miscellany*; it was also the first publication of the Oklahoma Folk-Lore Society.[10] He remained affiliated with the University of Oklahoma until 1940; however, in 1937 he received a scholarship to study at the Library of Congress, where he became the national folklore editor of the WPA Federal Writers Project and in 1942 the head of the Archive of Folk Song, Library of Congress. His contributions to collecting, disseminating, and popularizing the folk life, including folk songs, of America are legend. Botkin died in 1975, and his papers are in the University of Nebraska–Lincoln Libraries, and there is a web site for the archival collection.

SIDNEY ROBERTSON COWELL

There were other songcatchers in California, especially when that state was still identified as a western frontier. The *Works Progress Administration California Folk Music Project* was launched in 1938 by Sidney Robertson, who in 1941 became Sidney Robertson Cowell. She was born in San Francisco, California, as Sidney William Hawkins in 1903. She became Sidney Robertson in 1924, when she not only graduated from Stanford but also married Kenneth G. Robertson.

Her degree was in romance languages and philology, and when her husband studied psychiatry at the University of Paris, she accompanied him as an interpreter and also studied piano while there. Back in the San Francisco area, she taught music, continued to study music, and in 1934 divorced her husband. She went to New York City where for two years she was director of the Social Music Program at the Henry Street Settlement in the Lower East Side. In 1936 she became music assistant to Charles Seeger who was chief of the music unit at the Special Skills Division of the Resettlement Administration, Washington, D.C. The following year she became the regional representative of the Special Skills Division of the Resettlement Administration; when the Fourth National Folk Festival was held in Chicago, she recorded music from four European countries and also recorded in the field in Wisconsin and Minnesota.

By 1937 she was back in Washington making plans and seeking funds to collect folk music in California. The music division of the Library of Congress supported the project providing that the field recordings would be deposited in the Archive of American Folk Song. The University of California, Berkeley, as a cosponsor, gave her office space in the music division. Both the Library of Congress and the University of California sponsored her application for Works Progress Administration approval for the California Folk Music Project, and the project started October 28, 1938.

In 1940, funds were not renewed and the doors of the California Folk Music Project were closed, but Sidney Robertson remained busy. She coedited, with Eleanora Black, *The Gold Rush Song Book* (1940)—a small collection containing only fifty-five pages of texts and tunes.[11] She also compiled the *Check List of California Songs* (1940).[12] The original recordings of the California Folk Music Collection, approximately thirty-eight hours in twelve languages and eighteen ethnic groups and performed by 185 musicians, remain available in the Library of Congress along with field work documents, photographs, and numerous other ethnographic material.

In 1941, she and Henry Cowell were married. He was a composer, who as a teenager had studied with Charles Seeger at the University of California and became a world music scholar and a musician influential in musical experimentation and teaching. Under the name Sidney Robertson Cowell, she and Alan Lomax compiled *American Folk Song and Folk Lore: A Regional Bibliography* (1942).[13] Later, she and her husband coauthored *Charles Ives and His Music* (1955).[14] Sidney Robertson Cowell died in 1995.

LEONIDOS WARREN PAYNE, JR.

Dr. Leonidos Warren Payne, Jr., was born in 1873 in Alabama and earned his PhD from the University of Pennsylvania in 1904. He became a member of the University of Texas faculty in 1906 as a professor of English with an interest in folk linguistics and became a songcatcher. In 1909, he was a cofounder with John A. Lomax of the Texas Folklore Society and became the first president of the Society. He also was a primary contributor to the Society's early publishing ventures, *Publications of the Texas Folklore Society*. The first issue was published in 1916 with the lead statement a short history of the Society. The first article in the first issue was "Texas Play-Party Songs and Games," written L. W. Payne, Jr., and R. E. Dudley (1916), and the second article, "Finding List for Texas Play-Party Songs" (1916), was written by Payne.[15]

In this second publication, Payne wrote about the ballad "One Evening As I Sat Courting," which he had collected from a student from Fort Worth; in a later volume he wrote a short statement about a lost treasure legend. Subsequent articles were "Some Texas Versions of The Frog's Courting" (1926), "Songs and Ballads, Grave and Gay" (1927), and "Recent Research in Balladry and Folk Songs" (1930).[16] He died in 1945; his biography, written by Hansen Alexander, *Rare Integrity: A Portrait of L. W. Payne, Jr.*, was published in 1986.[17]

WILLIAM A. OWENS

A prominent Texan devoted to songcatching and the lore of the West was Dr. William A. Owens, born in Pin Hook, Texas, in 1905. His father died shortly after his birth, so he grew up in small town agriculture poverty. Owens wanted an education, and in order to earn degrees he worked many odd jobs in East Texas, eventually earning a teaching certificate and becoming a country school teacher for two years. Owens attended Southern Methodist University and earned his BA in 1932 and MA in 1933.

He became an academician and worked his way upward to teaching at Texas A&M University before earning his PhD at the University of Iowa in 1941. His dissertation was "Texas Folk Songs," which was subsequently published with its original title as volume 23 in the *Publications of the Texas Folklore Society* (1950).[18] The first edition had piano arrangements by Willa Mae Kelly Koehn, the second edition melody transcriptions were by his daughter, Jessie Ann Owens, and both editions contained his commentaries about the songs.

His first book was a "Special Edition for the Texas Folk-Lore Society," but not a numbered publication. It was distributed in 1936 to members as *Swing and Turn: Texas Play-Party Games*.[19] Throughout his career he wrote short stories, numerous articles, and reviews along with twelve books—including novels—and he won many awards for his writing. He was in the army during World War II, earning a Legion of Merit award while serving in the Philippines, and resumed teaching at Texas A&M when he returned to Texas. In 1946 he joined the faculty at the University of Texas and the following year started teaching at Columbia University, retiring in 1974.

During those Columbia years he maintained a relationship with the University of Texas, serving as director of the Oral History of Texas Oil Pioneers from 1952 to 1958, interviewing many of the Texas oil trailblazers. With years of interviews, he coauthored with Mody Boatright *Tales from the Derrick Floor: A People's History of the Oil Industry*, published in 1970.[20] William A. Owens died in 1979, and his massive archival collection was acquired by the Cushing Memorial Library at Texas A&M University. A full inventory of his papers is found on the website, Texas Archival Resources Online.[21]

ROBERT WINSLOW GORDON

Born in 1888, Robert Winslow Gordon was the man who organized the Archive of Folk Song in the Library of Congress. As a Maine native he attended Harvard and fell under the influence of George Lyman Kittredge, developing a strong interest in ballads, and in 1912, while earning his doctorate, taught freshman composition and was an assistant under Kittredge. In 1918 he was offered a job at the University of California, Berkeley, and accepted it.

As an academician dedicated to collecting and researching folk songs, he soon experienced contempt and criticism from his English department colleagues. They were particularly irritated by his monthly column in *Adventure Magazine*, "Old Songs That Men Sing." He edited the column from 1923 to 1929 and from around the nation received 3,858 letters containing songs and queries.[22] He was dismissed by the University of California in 1924.

While unemployed, Gordon continued to collect and research folk songs using his own funds, occasionally receiving grants and getting a few writing contracts. One of those contracts was with the *New York Times*. His series "The Folk Songs of America," started on 2 January 1927, and the last of his fifteen essays was in the 22 January 1928 issue. In December 1938, the National Service Bureau—a division of the Works Progress Administration—with the sponsorship of the Joint Committee on Folk Arts issued his typescript articles with the title *Folk-Songs of America*. Each song had his extensive research as part of his essay, and the 110-page publication covers songs and research across the nation—mountain songs, all types of African-American songs, outlaw songs, lumberjack songs, nursery songs, songs of the pioneers, cowboy songs, and others. It is an important collection that is difficult to find.

In 1928 the Library of Congress funded the establishment of the Archive of American Folk Song, now the Archive of Folk Culture. Gordon was appointed as the archivist and placed his collection on deposit. It should be noted that it was Robert W. Gordon who started the archive that often has been attributed to John A. Lomax.

The Library of Congress administration became unhappy with him and he was dismissed in 1933 but continued to work at different jobs in Washington. Unfortunately, he could not continue with his pursuit of folk songs and stories of their origin; depression took control of him. Gordon died in 1961.[23]

AUSTIN E. AND ALTA S. FIFE

Austin E. and Alta S. Fife were the ultimate songcatcher team. Austin was born in 1909 and Alta in 1912. They met at Utah State University and started their collecting treks in the late 1930s while Austin was a graduate student at Stanford University, where he was also a research assistant to a specialist in Hispanic folklore. His major field was French language and literature, and later he studied at Harvard. With his introduction to folklore, the Fifes decided to apply the research methods to their Mormon heritage and western life. When time allowed, they traveled across the west collecting Mormon lore and western and cowboy songs and poems, along with other forms of western lore.

The first essay by Austin Fife was published in 1940, but World War II suspended his folkloristic efforts.[24] After serving in the air force, he enjoyed a variety of grants and fellowships. The Fife's first joint book was about Mormon lore—*Saints of Sage and Saddle: Folklore among the Mormons* (1956).[25] Their next book project was Jack Thorp's *Songs of the Cowboys* (1966).[26] In each work, they did extensive research about each song, such as comparing texts others collected and seeking authorship identities, and melody lines were provided for some of the songs. They accomplished this by listening to field-recorded singers, commercial recordings, and other reproduced sound. They also included a facsimile of Thorp's original 1908 book.

Austin's teaching career took them to different communities until 1960 when they decided to return to Utah State University—where in 1966 the Fife Folklore Archives was established—and they continued to travel and collect using recording equipment, cameras, and writing supplies. Their songcatching and research efforts were compiled into important books such as *Cowboy and Western Songs: A Comprehensive Anthology* (1969; reprinted 1999) with music editor Mary Jo Schwab.[27] The work remains a major collection of western songs with fourteen categories as diverse as "The West before the Cowboy," "Frontier Realism," "Red Men and White," "Love across Cultures," "Westerners at Work," and "Swing Your Partner." In *Ballads of the Great West* (1970) they presented 113 western poems and songs in four sections, "The Physical and Human Environment," "The Cowboy and Other Western Types," "Dramatic Situations and Events," and "Code of the Cowboy."[28] The ballads were presented as poems, and sources were identified along with commentary about each poem. In the introduction, the Fifes presented an excellent analysis of western poems and songs:

> These poems are presented under the rubric of "folk" or "primitive," we note notwithstanding at least three different kinds of poems having some common stylistic features. . . . These are bona fide folk and popular poems written by unpretentious and typically unknown poets who have something to say and who say it in the most direct and natural way they can. The story counts for everything . . . there are poems by articulate and sophisticated poets who achieve a folk or primitive effect by sheer artistry . . . there are poems with a burlesque flavor which capture and portray westernism by willful exaggeration of unpolished or uneven quality.[29]

Also published in 1970, *Heaven on Horseback: Revivalist Songs and Verse in the Cowboy Idiom* was a study of the religious side or Christian Ethic of the cowboy; the forty-nine songs and poems are in categories that deal with nature, death, hymns, and prayers, and there are melody lines for the songs.[30] The Fifes identify their sources and provide their explanation of each entry.

The Fife Folklore Archives is one of the major research facilities in the nation. It is a library and an archives organized into collections: the Fife Mormon Collection (folk songs and narratives), the Fife American Collection (a large body of cowboy and western folk songs and ballads, including collections from N. Howard Thorp, Charles Siringo, and others), Fife Slide Collection of Western U.S. Vernacular Architecture (hay derricks, gravestones, mail box supports, fences, and other slides), and their fieldwork tapes are in the appropriate collection. The Fieldwork Collection contains 125 reel-to-reel tapes, 184 acetate discs, 48 bound volumes of field transcriptions and research extracts, and over 3,000 annotated slides. Some of their early recordings and research materials were deposited in the Archive of Folk Culture, Library of Congress.

LESTER A. HUBBARD AND THOMAS E. CHENEY

Two other Mormon songcatchers add depth to the folk songs of the Latter-day Saints. Lester A. Hubbard caught and saved hundreds of songs from family members and friends, and Thomas E. Cheney gathered songs and lore in Utah and Idaho. L. A. Hubbard was born in Utah in 1892, but very little information about his life as a songcatcher is available, other than that he grew to maturity in a singing family environment and became a professor at the University of Utah–Salt Lake City. In 1961, a collection of 250 songs selected from over 1,000 gathered by him was published under the title *Ballads and Songs from Utah* with musical transcriptions by Kenly W. Whitelock.[31] In his introduction, Hubbard wrote:

> The songs and ballads in this collection, with few exceptions, were acquired in Utah from Latter-day Saints. . . . Most of the singers, whose parents had been Mormon pioneers, knew stories of the migration to Utah, the economic problems involved, and the authority of the Church leaders in directing and controlling the religious, social and economic lives of the group. . . . The songs recorded on discs and the texts acquired from diaries and notebooks containing a diversity of materials also supplement our knowledge of Utah and her people during the second half of the Nineteenth Century.[32]

Since the songs could not cover all of the problems, issues, and progress that the Mormons confronted and accomplished during that period, he continued with a concise outline of nineteenth-century events. He wrote about the function of songs, singing, and music in the lives of the early day Mormons, as well as about some of the sources of the songs:

> On Sunday evenings young people frequently sang in the home where an organ or other musical instrument was available. . . . Some families reserved one evening each week for singing and storytelling. . . . Singing provided entertainment at the public herding grounds. . . . Mrs. Salley A. Hubbard [his mother] contributed 134 songs and ballads and twenty-nine fragments, most of which she had learned when she was a girl in Willard [Utah]. . . . From her father, who played the violin, and her mother and sisters, who frequently sang when they worked, Mrs. Hubbard learned many of the songs which she still remembered when she was eighty-three years old. . . . All of the songs memorized did not receive the approval of the orthodox and serious-minded elders. Some of the young people, she said, strove to be independent of parental and Church mandates.[33]

The songs and ballads were categorized into ten general subjects including "Versions of Child Ballads," for many of the Francis James Child ballads were widely known in folk song circles across the nation. There were sixty-two "Love and Courtship" songs, of which most ended in tragedy; there were "Crimes and Criminals," "Songs of the West," "Nursery Songs," "Utah and the Mormons," and other subject areas. The collection shows that the diversity of songs was the same among Latter-day Saints as it was nationwide, for the Mormon immigrants came from foreign countries as well as the United States. The identity of the singer, the dates and places of his songcatching, and pertinent comments by the singers accompany each song as well as historical information about the song or ballad. In 1978, Lester A. Hubbard died in Salt Lake City.

Born in Idaho in 1901, Thomas E. Cheney grew up with a desire for an education. After high school and a short normal school education, he became an elementary school teacher and continued his education at Utah State Agriculture College (now Utah State University), majoring in English. In the tradition of the LDS Church he served his two-year mission work in Southern California before returning to his hometown as a teacher and administrator. During the summer sessions he attended the University of Idaho for graduate studies and became interested in traditional folk culture through the study of balladry.

His master's thesis, "Folk Ballad Characteristics in a Modern Collection of Songs," involved approximately seventy-five ballads gathered from Mormons in Utah and Idaho, comparing the ballads with those in the Francis James Child publications. He completed his master's in 1936 and became an English faculty member at Brigham Young University. Cheney continued his songcatching ventures during his summer breaks and put together 250 songs and ballads for the American Folklore Society to publish. Over time, the number was decreased to one hundred titles and published as volume 53 of the Publications of the American Folklore Society Memoir Series as *Mormon Songs from the Rocky Mountains: A Compilation of Mormon Folksong* (1968).[34]

The one hundred songs were grouped in "Songs Dealing with Mormon History," "Songs of Mormon Country Locale," "Mormon Customs and Teachings Satire and Sin," and chapter 1 was an excellent "Introduction to Mormon Folksong." He acknowledged in his "Preface" that not all of the songs were collected by him and not all were composed by or about Mormons, and that he had twenty hours of tape recordings from the contributors to his master's thesis. As with Hubbard, through the years he put together a collection of over one thousand items, and while gathering songs he held rigidly to the rule of accepting songs only from oral tradition or from manuscript journals preserved by the families of the early folksingers. He also gave credit to the Fifes for allowing him to use songs from their collections and cited the source of each song. His historical background for each song is thorough and at times lengthy. Not all songs were printed with a melody line. Thomas E. Cheney participated in many activities that involved Mormon songs and lore and was president of the Folklore Society of Utah in 1963–1964; he died in 1993.

CHARLES J. FINGER

Western songcatchers sometimes emerge from unexpected places and backgrounds. Charles J. Finger was born in England in 1867 and attended college in London and Germany, staying on in England when his parents moved to the United States. He became a sailor in 1890 on a ship headed to Chile, where he then worked as a sheepherder, tour guide, and at various odd jobs before going to New York City. From there he went to San Angelo, Texas, where once again he became a sheepherder.

He started writing newspaper articles and taught music lessons before becoming a United States citizen, and he married the daughter of a sheep rancher. They moved to Alamogordo, New Mexico, where he worked for a railroad company, and in 1905 they had moved to Ohio with another railroad company. During that time he continued to write. His stories attracted attention, and three were published in the magazine *Mirror* in 1919. His jobs seemed to disappear from company closures and death of owners, so in 1920 they moved to Fayetteville, Arkansas. There he continued to write and also published a literary journal, *All's Well, or The Mirror Repolished*.

His songcatching interests were first published in 1923 as *Sailor Chanties and Cowboy Songs* in the Haldeman-Julius *Little Blue Book* series.[35] A few years later, *Frontier Ballads Heard and Gathered* (1927) was published by Doubleday Page and Company.[36] Following the title page, his collection was described (all in capital letters) as:

> SONGS FROM LAWLESS LANDS with some of their tunes as heard and set down by Charles J. Finger many here printed for the first time together with a true account of the manner of their singing by gold hunters in the Andes, men on shipboard, hard-cases who were beach combers, fellows in the calaboose, south sea smugglers, sealers, bartenders, and some who have gained fame.[37]

Finger was trained in music and enjoyed hearing the vocalizing of traditional singers. He wrote, "When I first heard an old-timer sing an old-time song, I had a real thrill. It was an exciting event. Not so much the song as the manner of singing astonished and delighted me."[38]

His songs covered many individuals, occupations, and events, with most supported by melody lines. He wrote about his experiences when gathering a song as well as with the story behind the song and the singer. Finger was a unique songcatcher who wrote many books and included songs and verse when pertinent. He died in 1941, and his papers and collections are at the University of Arkansas.

D. K. WILGUS

Dr. D. K. Wilgus was not only an outstanding scholar and popular professor of English and Anglo-American folksong, he was a dedicated songcatcher and field collector of legends. He was born Donald Knight Wilgus in Ohio in 1918 and earned his three degrees at Ohio State University. He served in the U.S. Army during World War II and in 1950 went to Western Kentucky State College (now University), accepting an appointment as associate professor of English. In 1961 he was promoted to professor of English, and while there he established the Kentucky Folklore Record and did extensive fieldwork in the region.

In 1963 he started a long and prolific academic career at UCLA, where he and Wayland Hand, who had been teaching folklore for many years, initiated a folklore department. In 1965 it became the Department of Folklore and Mythology, and as professor of English and Anglo-American folksong he served as head of the department. His contributions to the study of hillbilly music, blues, commercial country-western music, and other genres were numerous, and he conducted song collecting in Ireland as well as the United States. D. K. Wilgus gathered and researched all varieties of traditional music including American Indian ballads.

He edited the *Kentucky Folklore Record*, for five years edited *Western Folklore*, and served in many folk society offices including the presidency of the American Folklore Society. While his books, articles, reviews, and other publications are numerous, his scholarly study *Anglo-American Folksong Scholarship Since 1898* (1959) is the definitive study of twentieth century folksong in this country.[39]

At the time of his death on Christmas Day 1989, his research and collections were massive. There were eleven thousand commercial recordings, over fifty thousand manuscript items, and one thousand field recorded tapes, song folios, photographs, folk and country music periodicals, and many other related items. His widow, Dr. Eleanor Long-Wilgus, donated a large portion to the Southern Folklife Collection at the University of North Carolina Wilson Library; his Kentucky collection to the Southern Appalachian Archives, Hutchins Library, Berea College; and the D. K. Wilgus Folksong Collection remained at UCLA. D. K. Wilgus is another great songcatcher to whom this nation's students, scholars, and collectors will always be indebted.[40]

MINING AND HOBO SONGS

As stated earlier, not all western songs were and are about cowboys, pioneers, Indians, outlaws, conflicts, and other themes usually associated with the West. For many people, mining is not a western image; however, Montana, as with many other western states, has mining as an occupation, and the World Museum of Mining is a Butte, Montana, attraction. Oklahoma had lead and coal mines, and since the American Indians, who owned the land before statehood, would not work underground, many European immigrants traveled to Indian Territory to work in the mines, no doubt carrying ethnic traditional songs. When General George Custer said that gold had been found in the Black Hills of the Dakotas, people rushed there hoping to get rich, only to discover that there was no gold — instead they found Indian resistance against intrusion on their land. The song "The Dreary Black Hills" reflected some of their problems.

Nevertheless, traditional mining songs are not easily found in the West other than gold mining songs in California, where both commercial and traditional songs about the forty-niners became plentiful—for music and gambling were the primary ways for miners to kill time. John A. Stone, using the name "Old Put," wrote songs in the 1850s about California gold hunters and published them in his *Original California Songster* (1855), giving in a few words what would occupy volumes detailing the hopes, trials, and joys of a miner.[41] His *Golden Songster* (1858) contained the largest and most popular collection of California songs ever published.[42] He also was an entertainer and sold thousands of copies of his books. A few of his songs became traditional folksongs such as "Sweet Betsy from Pike," in which his lyrics were set to an adaptation of the melody of "Villikins and His Dinah."

Mart Taylor was another song writer and entertainer who wrote *The Gold Digger Book* (1856), containing the most popular humorous and sentimental songs; one or two of his songs also may have entered oral tradition.[43] There are collections and studies of western and gold mining songs by compilers and editors who were not songcatchers—they selected their songs from books written by songcatchers and other compilers. The history of the songs in some of the collections justifies the editors' efforts, and the songbook by Robertson and Black, *The Gold Rush Song Book* (1940), must not be overlooked.

GEORGE MILBURN

George Milburn was born in Coweta, Indian Territory (Oklahoma), in 1906 and attended the University of Tulsa as well as two state universities. He was an educated, literate individual who chose to ride the rails with hobos, and, while at the University of Oklahoma, he assembled eighty-six songs and poems into *The Hobo's Hornbook Collected and Annotated by George Milburn* (1930).[44] In his opening essay "Poesy in the Jungles," he wrote,

> Not many investigators in the field have attained to enough familiarity with the road to differentiate between genuine hobo ballads and the pseudo ballads offered by co-ed ukulele virtuosos and catarrhal phonograph yodelers . . . the term is used to define the songs and poems originated by American vagrants and current among them. . . . Hobos are migratory workers, while tramps have sources of livelihood other than toil.[45]

Milburn's annotations express his strong opinion that hobos seek seasonal work, while tramps do not. He provides much information about the hobo and his world, and wrote about the ballad "The Boomer Shack," "many such pseudo-pathetic ballads . . . are current in the jungles."[46] Some of the songs have melody lines.

NOTES

1. Woody Guthrie, *Woody and Lefty Lou's Favorite Collection Old Time Hill Country Songs* (Gardena, CA: Spanish American Institute Press, 1937); two earlier editions were mimeographed and mailed to their fans. For additional information see Ed Cray, *Ramblin Man: The Life and Times of Woody Guthrie* (New York: Norton, 2004).
2. John Steinbeck, *Their Blood Is Strong* (San Francisco: Simon J. Lubin Society, 1938), 1.
3. John Steinbeck, *The Grapes of Wrath* (New York: Viking, 1939).
4. From the American Folklife Center, Library of Congress web page "Voices of the Dust Bowl." Recordings and additional information by and about Todd and Sonkin are also available online at http://memory.loc.gov/ammem/afctshtml/tshome.html
5. Charles Todd and Robert Sonkin, "Ballads of the Okies," *American Folk Music Occasional* 1 (1964): 87.
6. Todd and Sonkin, "Ballads," 87.
7. B. A. Botkin, *A Treasury of American Folklore: Stories, Ballads, and Traditions of the People* (New York: Crown Publishers, 1944); B. A. Botkin, *A Treasury of Western Folklore* (New York: Crown Publishers, 1951).
8. B. A. Botkin, *The American Play-Party Song* (Lincoln: University of Nebraska Press, 1937).
9. B. A. Botkin, "The Play Party in Oklahoma," *Publications of the Texas Folk-Lore Society* 7 (Austin: University of Texas Press, 1928): 7–24.
10. Benjamin Albert Botkin, *Folk-Say, a Regional Miscellany* (Norman: University of Oklahoma Press, 1930).
11. Sidney Robertson and Eleanora Black, *The Gold Rush Song Book* (San Francisco: Colt Press, 1940).
12. Sidney Robertson, *Check List of California Songs* (Berkeley: mimeographed, 1940).
13. Sidney Robertson Cowell and Alan Lomax, *American Folk Song and Folk Lore: A Regional Bibliography* (New York: Progressive Education Association, 1942).
14. Sidney Robertson Cowell and Henry Cowell, *Charles Ives and His Music* (New York: Oxford University Press, 1955).
15. L. W. Payne, Jr., and R. E. Dudley, "Texas Play-Party Songs and Games," *Publications of the Texas Folklore Society* 1 (1916): 28–29; L. W. Payne, Jr., "Finding List for Texas Play-Party Songs," *Publications of the Texas Folklore Society* 1 (1916).
16. L. W. Payne, Jr., "Some Texas Versions of the Frog's Courting," *Publications of the Texas Folklore Society* 5 (1926); L. W. Payne, Jr., "Songs and Ballads, Grave and Gay," *Publications of the Texas Folklore Society* 6 (1927); L. W. Payne, Jr., "Recent Research in Balladry and Folk Songs," *Publications of the Texas Folklore Society* 8 (1930).
17. Hansen Alexander, *Rare Integrity: A Portrait of L. W. Payne, Jr.* (Austin: Wind River Press, 1986).
18. William A. Owens, "Texas Folk Songs," *Publications of the Texas Folklore Society* 23 (1950).
19. William A. Owens, *Swing and Turn: Texas Play-Party Games* (Dallas: Tardy, 1936).
20. Mody C. Boatright and William A. Owens, *Tales from the Derrick Floor: A People's History of the Oil Industry* (Garden City, NY: Doubleday, 1970).
21. Texas Archival Resources Online, http://www.lib.utexas.edu/taro/
22. *The Gordon Collections: Manuscript and Recorded Collections Acquired and/or Indexed by Robert Winslow Gordon in the Archive of Folk Culture*, Library of Congress Folk Archive Finding Aid, LCFAFA no. 9, 1991. This four-page guide was compiled by Joseph C. Hickerson and Gregory Jenkins and is available from the Archive of Folk Culture, Library of Congress.
23. Debora Kodish, *Good Friends and Bad Enemies* (Urbana: University of Illinois Press, 1986).
24. Austin E. Fife, "The Legend of the Three Nephites among the Mormons," *Journal of American Folklore* 53 (January–March 1940): 1–49.

25. Austin E. and Alta S. Fife, *Saints of Sage and Saddle: Folklore among the Mormons* (Bloomington: Indiana University Press, 1956).

26. Jack Thorp, *Songs of the Cowboys* (New York: Clarkson N. Potter, 1966). The Fifes version included song variations, annotations, notes, and other information added to Thorp's original 1908 publication.

27. Austin E. and Alta S. Fife, *Cowboy and Western Songs: A Comprehensive Anthology* (New York: Clarkson N. Potter, 1969).

28. Austin E. and Alta S. Fife, *Ballads of the Great West* (Palo Alto: America West Publishing, 1970).

29. Fife, *Ballads*, 24–25. A complete bibliography of the Fife's writings is impossible in this chapter; the Fife Folklore Archives website will provide much more information (http://library.usu.edu/folklo/).

30. Austin E. and Alta S. Fife, *Heaven on Horseback: Revivalist Songs and Verse in the Cowboy Idiom* (Logan: Utah State University Press, 1970).

31. L. A. Hubbard, *Ballads and Songs from Utah* (Salt Lake City: University of Utah Press, 1961).

32. Hubbard, *Ballads*, xxi.

33. Hubbard, *Ballads*, xix.

34. Thomas E. Cheney, *Mormon Songs from the Rocky Mountains: A Compilation of Mormon Folksong* (Austin: University of Texas Press, 1968).

35. Charles J. Finger, *Sailor Chanties and Cowboy Songs* (Gerard, KN: Haldeman-Julius Co., 1923).

36. Charles J. Finger, *Frontier Ballads Heard and Gathered* (Garden City: Doubleday, 1927).

37. Finger, *Frontier Ballads*, title page.

38. Finger, *Frontier Ballads*, 1; see also: Finger, *Sailor Chanties*. For additional information and a description of the Finger Collection see the University of Arkansas Libraries, Charles J. Finger Papers web page (http://libinfo.uark.edu/specialcollections/findingaids/finger.html).

39. D. K. Wilgus, *Anglo-American Folk Song Scholarship Since 1898* (New Brunswick: Rutgers University Press, 1959).

40. William Lynwood Montell, a former student, friend and fellow folklore scholar, wrote an excellent obituary in the *Journal of American Folklore* 109 (Winter 1991): 72–73.

41. John A. Stone [Put], *Put's Original California Songster* (San Francisco: D.E. Appleton, 1868, c1855).

42. John A. Stone [Put], *Put's Golden West Songster* (San Francisco: D.E. Appleton, 1858).

43. Mart Taylor, *The Gold Digger Book* (Marysville, CA: 1856).

44. George Milburn, *The Hobo's Hornbook: A Repertory for a Gutter Jongleur* (New York: Ives Washburn, 1930).

45. Milburn, *Hobo's Hornbook*, xi.

46. Milburn, *Hobo's Hornbook*, 63–64.

SIX

Folk Song Collectors in the Midwest

James P. Leary

In 1940, the eminent folklorist Stith Thompson briefly prefaced Paul G. Brewster's *Ballads and Songs of Indiana* with an astute, still-pertinent observation, "To those who have been accustomed to think that American folksong survives only in mountain recesses of the South, the increasing number of fine collections recently issued from less isolated regions comes as evidence of a surprising vitality."[1]

Then as now, if inclined at all to think of folk songs and singers from way back before the mid-twentieth century's folk revival, most Americans might imagine an overall-clad, jug-toting Anglo-American banjo-picker atop old Smokey, or a gang of African-American laborers singing in steamy flood-enriched fields as they pick cotton or cut cane. These familiar images—vigorously cultivated at the nineteenth century's turn by journalists, local color writers and painters, commercial recording companies, and more than a few folklorists—associated the South over all other regions with what was homemade, agrarian, archaic, simple, and authentic in an America that was increasingly mechanized, urban, up-to-date, complicated, and artificial. Yet Thompson, a scrupulous scholar who founded what would become the nation's leading folklore department at Indiana University, favored hard evidence over nostalgia-tinged antimodernism, no matter how alluring it might be.

Surely Mary O. Eddy's similarly titled *Ballads and Songs of Ohio* (1939) was one of the "fine collections" Thompson invoked.[2] Less prominent but no less savvy than the Hoosier academic, Eddy also challenged the notion that folk song resided most prominently in such places as the southern Appalachians where people were relatively homogeneous and set apart from the larger world. Sketching 150 years of Ohio settlement by

Christianized Indians, Pennsylvania Germans, Germans from Europe, Virginians, New Englanders, former Anglo-American denizens of the Middle Atlantic states and, most recently, "an immigration of all sorts of people attracted by the industries of the larger cities," Eddy argued that the continuous immigration and cultural diversity characterizing Ohio were just as conducive to fostering folksong as were prolonged settlement and isolation.[3] Indeed, patterns of sustained patchwork settlement prevailed throughout the Midwest, including communities established by French and Irish via Canada, by Mediterranean, Nordic, and Slavic peoples, and by African-Americans from the Deep South. Amidst the cultural mosaic characterizing Midwestern places, Eddy continued, "it is possible to find, side by side, songs of many types and from many sources."[4] In the decades prior to America's entry into World War II, other Midwestern songcatchers made much the same point, either explicitly or implicitly through the songs and tunes they set down. Their considerable yet largely neglected discoveries offer important insights into the nature of American folk song and American life.

Paradoxically, H. M. Belden, the Midwest's first regionally oriented folksong scholar of note, was among the last to publish his findings. Belden's *Ballads and Songs Collected by the Missouri Folk-Lore Society*, begun in 1903, previewed by 1907 in *A Partial List of Song-Ballads and Other Popular Poetry Known in Missouri*, and completed in 1917, was to have been published the next year by the American Folklore Society in cooperation with the Missouri Folk-Lore Society, but World War I and the subsequent demise of the Missouri society in 1920 delayed the wide-ranging, meticulously annotated anthology's appearance until 1940.[5] Had it been published as planned, about the time Cecil Sharp inspired so many with his southern Appalachian folk song discoveries, perhaps the genre's vitality in the Midwest would have been more a surety than a surprise.

HENRY MARVIN BELDEN

Henry Marvin Belden (1865–1954), like many ballad and folksong scholars of his generation, was an English professor. Born a New Englander in Wilton, Connecticut, Belden graduated from Trinity College in Hartford, then entered Johns Hopkins in 1889, eventually earning his doctoral degree in 1894 after a stint abroad at the University of Strasbourg. In 1893, however, Belden had ventured to Lincoln, teaching for a year at the University of Nebraska, and in 1895 he joined the English faculty at the University of Missouri where he would remain until retirement in 1937. Thoroughly familiar with Francis James Child's five-volume *The English and Scottish Popular Ballads* (1882–1898), including Child's notion that such songs were no longer sung, Belden was delighted to learn otherwise.[6]

> In the spring of 1903, at a meeting of the English Club which I was privileged to attend, a local-color story was read in which one of the characters sang a song that I recognized as one of the old English ballads recorded by Child. Upon inquiry, I was told that many such songs were known and sung by country folk in Missouri.[7]

From that moment, he began collecting folk songs in earnest. Reflecting on his preliminary findings in a 1905 essay for *Modern Philology*, "The Study of Folk-Song in America," Belden stated that such songs had not vanished in the new nation; rather, new examples had been and were being composed.[8] And as was the case with ancient ballads, their existence was sustained through a combination of print and oral tradition. Consequently, "inclusion rather than exclusion should be the rule in the work of collection."[9] Additionally, at a time when the texts of songs were chiefly sought, while the lives of singers and the contexts of performance were an afterthought at best, Belden advised collectors to record the circumstances of song-gathering, the family and cultural background of singers, information on the source of their particular version, and anything they might know about the song's history and significance. He soon put his guidelines into practice, organizing the Missouri Folklore Society in 1906, and enlisting the aid of schoolteachers especially.

The resulting collection of 287 songs with variants from all over Missouri was, for its time, resplendently inclusive, although not without shortcomings. As an English professor of Anglo-Protestant origins—a heritage shared overwhelmingly by his school-teaching assistants at a time when pupils were regularly punished for speaking another tongue—Belden emphasized the English language and decidedly Anglo-American materials, despite the immense presence of German speakers throughout Missouri, and of Slavs and Italians especially in St. Louis. As a white person in an era of segregation, and also as someone who seldom ventured from the library into the field, Belden gleaned no songs from Missouri's longstanding black citizenry. Sadly, only blackface ditties like "Zip Coon" masked a rich tradition that ranged from spirituals to ballads chronicling the celebrated St. Louis bad man "Stagolee." Finally, as a male relying almost entirely on female assistants, and as a genteel scholar with a respectable position, Belden uncovered none of the enormous repertoire of bawdy songs encountered easily in the Ozarks by the racier, unaffiliated songcatcher Vance Randolph.

Still, the range of Belden and cohorts was impressive—particularly for 1917: Child ballads; both romantic and comic ballads of British origin; Irish songs, including a bilingual text for "Shule Aroon" and a few like "Kelley's Irish Brigade" concerning Irish Americans; ballads composed in America regarding love, crime, disasters, migrations, work experiences, and war, including several, like "Give the Dutch Room," in Germanized English; religious and homiletic songs; comic and melancholy lyric songs, including some from minstrelsy; play-party rhymes and related children's nonsense songs; carols; and four songs in French from Ste. Genevieve County, where Francophone communities were established in the eighteenth century. Each song was preceded by notes about its historical origin, dissemination, and relationship to particular singers in specific places. And Belden drew upon this data to temper romantic associations of folk songs with foggy mountaintops: "the collection covers . . . all sections of the state. And it does not show the hill country—the Ozarks—to be more given to ballad singing than the richer northern and middle regions."[10]

Belden's affiliation with an English department, enlisting of students and correspondents, slight tilt toward the repertoire of women, reliance on the transcription of texts and tunes instead of audio recording, high standards for annotation, contention that folk songs flourished in many places, and Anglo-American emphasis (albeit mitigated by an awareness and partial inclusion of other groups and tongues) were exemplary of the academic training, collecting and editorial methods, and cultural orientation of fellow songcatchers toiling throughout the Lower Midwest in the years preceding World War II. A somewhat different pattern, as we shall see, prevailed in the Upper Midwest. Among Lower Midwestern songcatchers, a few, like Emelyn Gardner, who worked throughout southern Michigan, grew up elsewhere, but most were natives of the region, including Gardner's collaborator Geraldine Chickering, Mary O. Eddy from Ohio, Paul Brewster and Leah Jackson Wolford from Indiana, Charles Neely from Illinois, Earl J. Stout from Iowa, and Louise Pound from Nebraska.

LOUISE POUND

The remarkable Louise Pound (1872–1958) was born in Lincoln shortly after her parents settled there in 1869. She earned BA and MA degrees from the University of Nebraska, with emphases on English and music, before receiving a PhD from the University of Heidelberg in 1900. The first (and for decades the only) woman in the University of Nebraska Sports Hall of Fame, Pound excelled at tennis, golf, cycling, skiing, figure skating, and basketball—winning the University of Nebraska tennis title against male competitors in 1891 and 1892. Her accomplishments as a scholar were no less extraordinary in the fields of dialect and folksong study. She founded and edited the journal *American Speech*, served as president of both the American Dialect Society and the American Folklore Society, and in 1955 was the first woman elected president of the Modern Language Association of America. Fortuitously, Pound commenced a lifelong friendship with H. M. Belden during his brief tenure at the University of Nebraska in 1893 and, soon after becoming an English professor there in 1900, she initiated a systematic study of the state's folksongs.[11]

The resulting *Folk-Song of Nebraska and the Central West* (1914) prominently acknowledged Belden's encouragement, as well as the contributions of her students and of teachers throughout the state who captured nearly 350 songs in many variations.[12] Organized in thirty-two categories, with cross-references, the entirely English-language and mostly Anglo-American examples closely mirrored the content and arrangement of Belden's findings, and were linked in turn with the settlement of the Cornhusker state by two strands of "American born" settlers: those hailing from New England, New York, and Pennsylvania, and those who arrived from Southern states.

Beyond conveying mastery of current folksong scholarship, Pound's commentary demonstrated what, at the time, was a new and refreshing awareness of the relationship between community-based folk singing and the performances of traveling professionals: "colored 'minstrels'" with their "pseudo-plantation melodies," "[Dwight] Moody and [Ira] Sankey and other [religious] revivalists," crusading leaders of "temperance gatherings," "itinerant vendors of patent medicines," "circuses and wandering bands of entertainers."[13] Pound likewise showed keen awareness of the ways in which local song makers drew on verse structures, themes, rhetoric, and tunes from prior traditional songs to create new compositions. The richest section of her compilation, "Pioneer and Western Songs," illustrated this very process through the experiences of cattle ranchers and dry land farmers. "The Kinkaider's Song," to the tune of "My Maryland," invoked Congressman Moses Kinkaid's 640-acre Homestead Act, while lauding the cheerful grit of sod house dwellers in the arid, windswept sand hills of western Nebraska:

> You ask what place I like the best,
> The sand hills, oh the old sand hills;
> The place Kinkaiders make their homes
> And prairie chickens freely roam.[14]

As a native Nebraskan and a friend of novelist Willa Cather—whose *O Pioneers!* (1913) and *My Ántonia* (1918) concerned Swedes and Czechs on Nebraska's prairies—Pound was well aware of her state's non-Anglo-American folk song–singing peoples. Accordingly, she included sections on "Irish or Pseudo-Irish Ballads and Songs," "Negro or Pseudo-Negro Songs," "Songs Dealing with Indian Material," and a singing game with German-English elements, "Dutchman, Dutchman, Won't You Marry Me." More significantly, her collection was framed by a prophetic declaration from Addison E. Sheldon, secretary of the Nebraska Academy of Sciences.

> Besides the folk-song of Nebraska in the English tongue there is another Nebraska folk-song, more varied in its origins. Included in it are

the songs of the Nebraska Indians, especially those of the Pawnee tribe; songs of the Canadian voyageurs who were the first white explorers, and folk-lore of the many European peoples who have found homes here for themselves and their children. This is a rich field for the lovers of folk-lore, and progress in its study and organization is just beginning.[15]

In 1922, appropriately for a scholar from the nation's geographic crossroads, Louise Pound published *American Ballads and Songs*, the first volume to attempt an overview of the entire country's Anglo-American folksong traditions.[16] The texts and tunes included, although linked through notes to British and to Eastern and Southern American versions, drew heavily from Nebraska and its neighboring states: Colorado, Kansas, South Dakota, and especially Iowa, Missouri, and Wyoming.

ALBERT H. TOLMAN

Just as H. M. Belden sparked Louise Pound's innovative, expansive scholarship, other English professors in the Midwest inspired students to produce important folk song collections. In 1916, Albert H. Tolman (1856–1928) published "Some Songs Traditional in the United States" in the *Journal of American Folklore*, assessing and extending—chiefly with examples from Illinois and Indiana—the folk song surveys of Phillips Barry in New England, Hubert G. Shearin in Kentucky, Pound in Nebraska, and Belden in Missouri.[17] The recipient—like Belden—of a PhD from the University of Strasbourg, Tolman was primarily a Shakespearean who attracted budding folksong scholars, among them Leah Jackson Wolford and Mary O. Eddy, through his course in "Ballad and Epic Poetry" at the University of Chicago.[18]

LEAH JACKSON WOLFORD

Leah Jackson Wolford was born in Versailles, Indiana, in 1892, received a BA from Franklin College, where she met her husband, Leo T. Wolford, and earned an MA in English from the University of Chicago. She died tragically of peritonitis in 1918, less than a week after giving birth to her first child. Wolford was raised in a staunch Baptist family where young people were admonished against dancing to the fiddle, yet encouraged to frolic through the unaccompanied songs, steps, and patterns of such play-party favorites as "Captain Jinks," "Wait for the Wagon," and "Pop Goes the Weasel." Her 1915 thesis, published three years later as *The Play-Party in Indiana* (1918), focused on fifty-eight examples from Ripley County as experienced by her parents' and her own generations.[19] Combining texts, tunes, performance directions, variations, and comparative notes, Wolford's collection was preceded by concise observations on settlement history. Ripley countians were Scottish, Irish, German, and mostly English by way of Pennsylvania, Ohio, Virginia, and Kentucky, "but for the history of these play-party games, religion was almost as important as nationality. These people were Quakers, Disciples, Baptists, or Presbyterians as to creed, but they were one in opposing the dance as a wicked sport."[20] Indeed, among the Jacksons, even the genteel parlor organ, relied upon elsewhere for hymns, was spurned. As Wolford's grandfather put it, "a music-box would spile the gals, and a stuck-up sissy wud make no man a good hep-mate."[21]

The homemade play-party, however, was encouraged, and under the watchful eye of parents provided a significant pastime for youngsters of courting age that was also integrated with seasonal patterns of agrarian communal labor.

> The importance of these social gatherings can scarcely be overrated, because the occasions for the coming together of the people were so few. There was "meeting" at the country church, and here a girl might very properly go, every second Sunday night, with a neighbor boy, provided that her brother rode on horseback behind them. There were, of course, the husking-bees, the apple-cuttings, the carpet-tackings, in their seasons, and the county fair for two days every August; but the play-party was one rural merry-making which did not have a financial side to recommend it.[22]

Wolford's subsequent account of a typical play-party event, circa 1915, extended over seven pages and was exceptionally detailed for the era, commencing with a vivid description of the participants' arrival.

> The old-time play-party began at sundown. From ten miles around the people would come—whole families bumping along in the big jolt wagon, young men on horseback, several of them having their fair partners for the game seated securely behind them; and finally came the near neighbors picking their ways through the cornfields.[23]

Throughout her study, Wolford made deft observations concerning continuity and change. In her parents' day, for example, invitations were delivered on horseback, but "today one only gives the general ring on the farmer's line telephone, and at once the neighbors are listening."[24]

MARY O. EDDY

Mary O. Eddy (1877–1967) overlapped slightly with Wolford at the University of Chicago, while studying with Albert O. Tolman from 1915 to 1917. In "Traditional Texts and Tunes," coauthored by Tolman and Eddy for the *Journal of American Folklore* (1922), the former confessed "I have no knowledge of music" and attributed "all of the airs" therein to "Miss

Eddy" who "is trying to collect all the folk-songs surviving in tradition in the State of Ohio, both the words and the airs."[25] In actuality, Eddy's eventual collection *Ballads and Songs from Ohio* (1939) included 160 songs and 98 variants gathered from singers in Steubenville on the West Virginia line, in such northern Ohio industrial cities as Akron, Ashland, Canton, and Cleveland, and especially in her hometown of Perrysville, a rural Ashland County hamlet just southeast of Mansfield.[26] Eddy's singers were almost entirely women of romantic and religious temperament. Dark, sentimental, and moralistic ballads prevailed, enlivened by insights into key sources like Miss Jane Goon, a farm woman from south of Perrysville.

> Miss Goon was of a distinctly religious turn of mind, and so she favored such homiletic songs as "Wicked Polly," "A Voice from the Tomb," "The Drunkard's Doom," "A Warning to the Young," and the like. Among her songs, however, were two of my chief treasures, neither of them religious. On a sheet of foolscap in the large family Bible was copied, in the handwriting of a sister long dead, an excellent version of "The Bramble Briar," with a story which was already legendary in medieval Italy of Boccaccio's time . . . . It was Miss Goon, too, who gave me one of the best American versions of "False Lamkin." The motivation for the crime of the bloody mason is perfect in the first stanza.
>
> > False Lamkin was a mason
> > As good as ever laid stone;
> > He built Lord Arnold's castle,
> > And the lord paid him none.[27]

Born in 1858, Miss Goon appropriately confronted readers sternly in one of eight photographs of singers adorning the collection. Mary O. Eddy would go on to publish accomplished essays on folk hymnody in *Midwestern Folklore* and *Southern Folklore Quarterly*.[28]

EARL J. STOUT AND CHARLES NEELY

Like Wolford and Eddy, Earl J. Stout and Charles Neely each came from Midwestern singing communities, and they too were inspired by an English professor, John W. Ashton of the University of Iowa. Born in 1900 in Lewiston, Maine, Ashton drew upon his own experiences and those of his students to publish widely on folk speech, tales, games, and songs.[29] As a graduate student in 1931, Stout, who hailed from Cedar Falls in northeastern Iowa, was moved by Ashton to undertake fieldwork with "relatives and personal friends," while relying as well on surveys conducted "through the kindness of high school English teachers."[30] *Folklore from Iowa* (1936) combined 1,351 instances of "Current Beliefs from Iowa" with 112 ballads and songs, many in several versions. They included a mostly familiar repertoire—a few Child ballads, British and American ballads, religious and temperance songs, play-party ditties—as well as a handful of "school songs" consisting of mnemonics and rhymed student roll calls:

> Painter's Jake and Lawyer's Joe,
> Pat and Jack and Ervino.
> Here's the girls and here they go,
> Allie, Laura, Froneo.[31]

Stout also mentioned but did not print songs sung in French and German, while publishing four Irish American songs ("The Irish Jubilee," "Down Went McGinty," "Where Did You Get That Hat," "The Irish Barber") and three in "Dutch" dialect ("I'm Going to Fight Mit Siegel," "Corporal Schnapps," "Dunderbeck").

Charles Neely (1902–1937), Ashton's other songcatching student, was on the English faculty at Southern Illinois Teacher's College, Carbondale, when he died prematurely just before his *Tales and Songs of Southern Illinois* was published.[32] Neely was a native of this hilly region, flanked by the Ohio and Mississippi Rivers and dubbed "Egypt."[33] His introduction considers the area's settlement by French, Southerners of Scotch-Irish and English extraction, Germans, African-Americans and, more recently, Italian and Slavic miners. Regarding the Germans, Neely observed, "they hand their folk heritage down from generation to generation. They tell German folk tales and sing German ballads."[34] His collection, however, offered eighty-two mostly Anglo-American, mostly supernatural narratives, along with a like number of Anglo-American ballads and songs, augmented by a few of probable "Negro origin." Besides familiar pieces, Neely presented four local ballads concerning a fire, a flood, a black prostitute from "gay and wicked" Cairo, and the execution in 1928 of a bootlegging gangster, Charlie Burger. Neely's collection is particularly enlivened by brief sketches of folks like his mother, "Mrs. Charles Neely, Sr., of Carbondale" who "still loves to sing ballads and folk-songs," as well as of the Stringtown Clodhoppers, comprised of Caterville's James and Watson families, with siblings Ivan and Inez Watson singing "with a nasal twang, while they play their guitars."[35]

OTHER PIONEERING FOLKLORISTS OF THE LOWER MIDWEST

Of the Lower Midwest's remaining pioneering songcatchers, Paul G. Brewster was born in Stendal, Indiana, in 1898. A founding member in 1937 of the Hoosier Folklore Society, he published widely on folk songs and folk games as a faculty member at Tennessee Tech. The one hundred examples in his *Ballads and Songs of Indiana* (1940) were gleaned entirely from a questionnaire administered through high school English teachers, supplemented by songs sent in as a result of solicitations in Evansville and Indianapolis newspapers.[36] Although generally lacking much information about singers and the circumstances of performance, the notes are distinguished by extraordinarily complete comparative references, especially in the case of twenty-seven Child ballads for which Brewster went beyond the American and British source limitations of fellow editors to cite an array of European variations. For the author of a supposed statewide collection, Brewster was also refreshingly frank about his anthology's restriction to Anglo-American singers from southern Indiana, admitting that "no Negro songs have been collected as yet" and also that "the Indiana collection contains no songs of any foreign groups, such as Italians, Polish, Swedish, or French."[37]

Ballads and Songs of Southern Michigan (1939) by Emelyn Elizabeth Gardner and Geraldine Chickering focused similarly on songs sampled in seven Lower Peninsula counties from people of English, Scottish, and Irish stock who "came to Michigan by way of Canada or New England— maybe a few from Virginia."[38] As a professor at Wayne State University, however, Gardner was especially active in encouraging students of the bilingual second generation to record traditions of immigrants from Armenia, Finland, Italy, Poland, and elsewhere. From 1940 to 1941, for example, Harriet Pawlowska conducted fieldwork in Detroit that resulted in the finest extant study of a European immigrant group's repertoire: *Merrily We Sing: 105 Polish Folksongs* (1983).[39]

For her part, Gardner (1872–1988) was raised on a farm in central New York state's hilly Schoharie County where she heard many traditional tales and songs, and also taught high school for five years. Gardner went on to earn degrees in English from the University of Chicago and from Michigan, then taught at Ypsilanti State College before joining the faculty at Wayne State. She collected ballads assiduously from 1890 to 1940, often relying on help from students like Geraldine Chickering, "who by reason of her enthusiasm, her democratic spirit, her sympathetic understanding, and her sense of humor is an unusually successful fieldworker."[40] Chickering alone acquired roughly four hundred "old songs in English" to accompany Gardner's equally substantial efforts.[41] Their distillation of 201 representative songs in many variants, plus a summary appendix of eighty-five that were not included, is outfitted with excellent comparative notes, unusually informative biographies of fifty-three singers who "contributed three or more items," and an impressive introduction assessing the state's songs within the context of American society and folksong scholarship.[42] Gardner's remarks on the occasional role of radio in sustaining folksong traditions, and on religious objections to secular ballads, are particularly astute.

The "Occupations" section of Gardner's anthology appropriately included sixteen songs from the lumber camps that flourished in northern reaches of Michigan's Lower Peninsula. In 1938, Gardner joined with fellow English professors Earl Clifton Beck of Central Michigan and Ivan Walton of the University of Michigan to form a folklore interest group. Walton specialized in Great Lakes songs, while Beck concentrated on those of woods workers, including toilers in the Upper Peninsula and northern Wisconsin. Beck's and Walton's emphases on the repertoires of male seasonal workers from the Upper Midwest had been initiated by another English professor, Franz Rickaby. Schooled at Harvard, Rickaby (1889–1925) taught at the University of North Dakota from 1917 to 1923, gathering several hundred ballads and songs amidst summer trips to Michigan, Wisconsin, and Minnesota. Michael Cassius Dean of Virginia, Minnesota—one of Rickaby's principal singers—was also compiler of *The Flying Cloud* (1922), a collection of more than 150 "Old Time Songs and Ballads" from kindred Upper Midwestern working class males: "Outdoor Men, Sailors, Lumber Jacks, Soldiers, Men of the Great Lakes, Railroadmen, Miners, etc."[43] In 1959, folksong scholar D. K. Wilgus declared Dean's "wretchedly printed" songster to be "a slice of the repertoire of the Northern folksinger."[44]

Significantly, more than half of Dean's texts were Irish or Irish American. Although Rickaby found Anglo-American, French Canadian, and Scandinavian woods performers, he noted that Irish tunes, song forms, performance style, singers, and poets—like Wausau's Billy Allen, composer of "Shanty Boy on the Big Eau Claire"—were sufficiently dominant for him to proclaim: "The hegemony of song belonged to the Irish." Rickaby's posthumously published *Ballads and Songs of the Shanty-Boy* (1926) was the first instance of folksong scholarship concerning the Upper Midwest.[45]

E. C. Beck (1891–1977) extended Rickaby's findings in a series of books beginning with *Songs of the Michigan Lumberjacks* (1941).[46] Raised on a tenant farm in eastern Nebraska, Beck also cowboyed and hoboed some, hearing songs aplenty, before studying at the University of Nebraska where he learned folksong scholarship from Louise Pound. His love of balladry and the outdoors brought him in touch with such Michigan woods singers as the Irish American Bill McBride in the early 1930s.

> Bill McBride had one of those remarkable memories found now and then among folk-singers . . . Bill had been a chopper, swamper, teamster, top-loader, and riverhog for some of the biggest outfits of the Great Lakes pinewoods. On a log he was as agile as a cat . . . Bill learned many songs in the shanties, on decking grounds and along the rivers, and he seems to have remembered all of them. I rode with him once for twenty-four waking hours, during twenty of which he sang and recited with almost no repetitions. There were lumberjack songs, Civil War songs, Irish ballads, English ballads, slavery songs, barroom songs.[47]

Besides publishing annotated songs of McBride and his ilk, Beck was a performer and impresario who not only entertained students and civic groups with renderings of woods songs but also formed "The Michigan Lumberjacks," a troupe of singing, jigging, tale-telling retirees, including McBride, that participated in several National Folk Festivals beginning in 1934.

Woods singers like McBride, and Minnesota's M. C. Dean, often knew Great Lakes songs too, as Ivan Walton confirmed in his field journal of 1932 after visiting an elusive singer on Beaver Island in northern Lake Michigan.

> In evening I drove out about 4 miles to home of J. W. ["Johnie"] Green a farmer about 70+, native, who has spent his life except last few years on Lakes boats in the sailing season and in lumber woods winters. This was my 4th attempt to see him, sitting on his porch smoking and not in a very friendly state of mind, and could get nothing out of him for some time until I intentionally misread the opening stanza of "The Gallagher Boys" which I had been told he knew well. He corrected me on it and then I had him check the rest of it and couple of others and after that he was quite agreeable. . . . Said a large number of Lakes sailors worked in "Woods" in winter and sang sailor songs there and woodsmen were on boats in summer and sang lumber camp songs aboard the schooners. . . . He used to be able to sing over a hundred different songs.[48]

Raised on a farm more than forty miles from the fabled Lakes, Walton (1893–1968) was nonetheless charmed by tales from a sailing cousin and by a hired man, an erstwhile deck hand, who sang a ballad celebrating the E. C. Roberts's haul from Escanaba to Cleveland laden with "The Red Iron Ore." After three years of college at Central Michigan, a stint as a journalist, and World War I service with the Army Signal Corps, Walton received a BA in English from and then became an instructor at the University of Michigan. He taught from 1919 until retiring in 1963, earning an MA in 1921, and also studying folklore briefly at the University of Chicago. The lore of the Great Lakes was Walton's lifelong passion and, from 1932 through 1960, he devoted nearly every summer to fieldwork. Yet Walton never published his rich findings, excepting a few brief essays. Fortunately, however, the posthumous *Windjammers: Songs of the Great Lakes Sailors* (2002) compiles his texts, tunes, and notes for more than one hundred songs, while his equally comprehensive field journals from the 1930s have been gathered into *Songquest: The Journals of Great Lakes Folklorist Ivan H. Walton* (2005).[49]

The best singers encountered by both Ivan Walton and E. C. Beck were also captured on sound recordings, thanks to collaborations with Alan Lomax in 1938. In the early 1890s, just as H. M. Belden and Louise Pound were meeting at the University of Nebraska, Alice C. Fletcher was making cylinder recordings not far to the north among the Omaha Indians.[50] And by 1901, Frances Densmore had begun a succession of field recordings that would document the region's Chippewa (Ojibwe), Mandan, Menominee, and Winnebago (Ho-Chunk) traditional singers.[51] Sound recording of Midwestern Anglo-American and European ethnic singers, however, did not commence in earnest until the latter 1930s when a succession of public servants, trained more often in music than in English, ventured throughout the Upper Midwest especially. Sidney Robertson was first among them.

SIDNEY ROBERTSON

Sidney Robertson (1903–1995) was a native San Franciscan who studied music at Stanford and in Paris. In 1935, her professional expertise, liberal politics, and activist inclination led to a position as music program director for the Henry Street Settlement School in New York City. In that metropolis, she encountered several folksong scholars, including Charles Seeger, who hired her the following year when he took charge of a music program within the New Deal's Farm Security Administration. Sent to the Midwest, Robertson made it her business to learn about, meet, and in some cases make recordings with many of the region's songcatchers, including Louise Pound, H. M. Belden, Mary O. Eddy, David McIntosh (Charles Neely's folksong successor at Carbondale), and E. C. Beck. Robertson, however, did most of her work in Minnesota and Wisconsin.

The appearance of performers from those states at the National Folk Festival in Chicago in May 1937 inspired her to wrangle the loan of disk-cutting equipment from the Archive of American Folk Song at the Library of Congress.[52] By that summer's end, Robertson had recorded Finnish *kantele* players and Croatian *tamburitzans* from the Mesabi Iron Range, a Scots Gaelic singer from Duluth, a French fiddler from Rhinelander, numerous "Kentucks" who had migrated to northern Wisconsin in the 1890s, and the Antigo area's Ford-Walker family whose English, Irish, and lumber camp songs she issued eventually on a Folkways LP, *Wolf River Songs*.[53] She also identified several fellow researchers, including the Minnesota Historical Society's Theodore Blegen, who had published *Norwegian Immigrant Ballads and Songs* (1936), and Marjorie Edgar, an independent scholar from Minneapolis who was the first to document Finnish American songs.[54]

Robertson's 1937 recordings and accompanying correspondence, undertaken for the Archive, prompted Alan Lomax (1915–2002), the newly appointed assistant curator, to seek her advice in spring 1938 for an Upper Midwestern survey to occur that summer. In 1936, as the Archive's curator and the first folklore editor for the Federal Writer's Project, Alan's father, John Lomax, had written both E. C. Beck and Ivan Walton in hopes of recording woods and Great Lakes singers. The findings of Robertson, who by 1938 was making field recordings in California, were an added incentive. On 14 June, she wrote encouraging Alan Lomax to "go to Michigan, Wis. and Minn. with my blessing," and followed with detailed advice. Alan in turn began to research the region and send out letters in advance to Blegen, Edgar, Beck, Walton, and others.[55] As he wrote, only half-facetiously, to his sister Bess on 2 July:

> I expect after this summer to be much more cosmopolitan than you, despite your European tour. The reason: Dear Sir: The Archive of American Folk Song plans a rapid recording survey of Michigan, Wisconsin and Minnesota during the summer. If you know of the location of any Jugoslavian baroto blowers or any Swiss chantey singers, I would greatly appreciate your calling me by long distance before morning. By the middle of September, I hope to be speaking an interesting dialect composed of Norwegian, Swedish, Icelandic, German, Canuck, Hungarian, Finnic, Polish, Russian and Oshkosh. You may expect to receive an autographed photo of me holding up my first muskie by at least the end of this month. The work is going to be very interesting. I'm going to Detroit armed with letters of introduction to all the factions of the United Automobile Workers and to the Massaba [sic] Iron Ore Range of Minnesota and the I.W.W. of Duluth for union material, that assuming a galaxy of all sorts of exotic songs and instruments plus all their Americanizations.[56]

Lomax's Michigan field recording was so absorbing the he never reached Minnesota and only managed a day's work in Wisconsin.[57] Wending his way over two months from Detroit to the northern reaches of the Lower Peninsula, then across the Straits of Mackinac to the Upper Peninsula, Lomax recorded, as he reported to the Librarian of Congress, "about a thousand songs, lumberjack, lake sailor, Irish, Southern Negro, Finnish, Serbian, Polish, Canadian French, German, Hungarian, and Croatian."[58] He might have added Lithuanian, Slovenian, Swedish, and Ojibwe. Several Michigan lumberjack and lake sailor songs were published in *Our Singing Country* (1941), while others appeared, with notes by E. C. Beck, on the Library of Congress LP *Songs of the Michigan Lumberjacks*.[59]

Wisconsin continued to intrigue Lomax, however, and he worked out a joint venture between the Archive and the University of Wisconsin's school of music. The former would supply recording equipment, blank disks, some preliminary contacts, and very basic training. The latter would do the actual fieldwork. Helene Stratman-Thomas (1896–1973), a faculty member and manager of the women's chorus, warmed to the task. Although not trained in folklore, she had heard Cornish, German, and Welsh folk songs from family and neighbors while growing up in southwestern Wisconsin. Accompanied by a sound engineer, Stratman-Thomas roamed Wisconsin in the summers of 1940 and 1941, then made a final sweep in 1946 after the lifting of wartime gasoline restrictions. She photographed many performers and chronicled her experiences in vivid field notes, as evident in this excerpt from 24 August 1940:

> We had been directed to Al Van der Tie, a young man with a very fine voice. His songs included love songs in the Walloon dialect. A little song, *I Went to Market*, was a typical mixture of the language from the old world with that of the new. The lines were composed of a smattering of both English and the French dialect. Mr. Van der Tie had learned the song from Gust Mathey, an old resident of Brussels [Wisconsin]. The celebration of the old Netherlands *kermesse* is still held among the Belgian people of Wisconsin in the early fall. At that time Belgians gather for two or three days of dancing and singing in the village streets. The famous Belgian fruit pies and good coffee are part of the celebration. Mr. Van der Tie sang a song which invites everyone to come to the *kermesse*. His young son was particularly interested and proud of the fact that the recordings of his father's songs would be sent to Washington, DC[60]

Altogether Stratman-Thomas recorded more than seven hundred songs and tunes from more than 150 individual and group performers representing over thirty American Indian, African-American, and European American cultures and nearly as many languages.[61] She even succeeded, with prodding from Alan Lomax, in recording bawdy lumberjack songs by discretely waiting in the car while her assistant, Robert Draves, ran the equipment.

The bulk of English-language folk songs gathered by Stratman-Thomas have been published. The Library of Congress LP, *Folk Music from Wisconsin*, featured performances of nine ballads concerning tarrying nobles—"Lord Lovel"; Irish robbers—"Brennan on the Moor"; suffering sweethearts—"Charming Beauty Bright" and "The Drowsy Sleeper"; faithful lovers—"The Lake of Ponchartrain"; valiant cowboys—"Billy Vanero"; snakebit farmhands—"Springfield Mountain"; disaster victims—"Milwaukee Fire"; and contesting lumberjacks—"Little Brown Bulls." Additional lyric folksongs included a children's singing game—"Pompey is Dead"; a fox hunter's ditty—"How Happy is the Sportsman"; the Irish "Shule Aroon"; two celebrations of lumber camps and woods workers—"Shantyman's Life" and "The Bold McIntyres"; a harvesters' anthem—"The Cranberry Song"; and a cante fable spread by traveling shills for Hamlin's Wizard Oil—"Reuben Wright and Phoebe Brown." Meanwhile, in *Folk Songs out of Wisconsin* (1977), Harry Peters presented Stratman-Thomas's field notes and photographs, along with texts, tunes, and brief notes for 155 of the American, English, Irish, and occupational songs she recorded.[62] The full range of Stratman-Thomas's collection was made available online by the University of Wisconsin's Mills Music Library in 2005. Her immense, culturally and linguistically inclusive collection—captured through words, sounds, and images—not only offered our richest, most representative folksong portrait of any Midwestern state, but also heralded a wave of multiculturally oriented songcatchers in the post-World War II era.

From our twenty-first–century vantage, more than sixty years after the last of the Midwest's pioneering folklorists did their catching, we should no longer be surprised by the vitality of the region's folk songs and singers. Perhaps we should even be startled that, in 1940, Stith Thompson had to urge recognition for the neglected range and depth of Midwestern folk songs. Like New York, New Orleans, and Los Angeles—teeming, polyglot, singing cities of the East, the South, and the West—the entire Midwest has been a cultural middle ground, a cosmopolitan crossroads, a musical marketplace, wherein Native and Métis peoples, Anglo-American Yankees, Yorkers, and Upland Southerners, French, Irish, Pennsylvania Germans, African-Americans, and immigrants from all parts of Europe settled and jostled, sustaining, exchanging, altering, and inventing songs that variously expressed their quintessentially American experiences and aspirations.

NOTES

1. Stith Thompson, preface to Paul G. Brewster, *Ballads and Songs of Indiana* (Bloomington: Indiana University Publications, 1940), 6.
2. Mary O. Eddy, *Ballads and Songs of Ohio* (New York: J. J. Augustin, 1939).
3. Eddy, *Ballads*, 3.
4. Eddy, *Ballads*, 3.
5. H. M. Belden, *Ballads and Songs Collected by the Missouri Folk-Lore Society* (Columbia: University of Missouri Press, 1940); H. M. Belden, *A Partial List of Song-Ballads and Other Popular Poetry Known in Missouri* (Columbia: Missouri Folklore Society, 1907).
6. Francis James Child, *The English and Scottish Popular Ballads* (Boston: Houghton Mifflin, 1882–1898).
7. H. M. Belden's 1903 experience and the dispersion of Missouri folksongs are detailed in the preface of Belden, *Ballads and Songs*, xi–xii. See also H. M. Belden, "The Study of Folk-Song in America," *Modern Philology* 2:4 (1905), 573–579; Belden, *Partial List*; and Susan Pentling and Rebecca B. Schroeder, "H. M. Belden, The English Club, and the Missouri Folklore Society," *Missouri Folklore Society Journal* 8–9:1 (1986–1987), 1–42.
8. Belden, "Study of Folk-Song."
9. Belden, *Ballads and Songs*, xii.
10. Belden, *Ballads and Songs*, xii.
11. The 1972 edition of the 1922 publication Louise Pound, *American Ballads and Songs* (New York: Charles Scribner's Sons, 1972 [1922]), includes Kenneth S. Goldstein's biographical sketch and critical assessment of Pound and her folksong scholarship, vii–xii; see also Elizabeth D. Schafer, "Louise Pound," in *American Folklore: An Encyclopedia*, Jan Harold Brunvand, ed. (New York: Garland Publishing, 1996), 585–586; and Robert Cochran, *Louise Pound: Scholar, Athlete, Feminist Pioneer* (Lincoln: University of Nebraska Press, 2009).
12. Louise Pound, *Folk-Song of Nebraska and the Central West, A Syllabus* (Lincoln: Nebraska Academy of Sciences, 1914).
13. Pound, *Folk-Song of Nebraska*, 7.
14. Pound, *Folk-Song of Nebraska*, 31.
15. Addison E. Sheldon, "Editor's Preface," in Pound, *Folk-Song of Nebraska*, 1–2.

16. Louise Pound, *American Ballads*.

17. Albert H. Tolman, "Some Songs Traditional in the United States," *Journal of American Folklore* 29:112 (1916), 155–197.

18. Both Wolford and Eddy acknowledged Tolman as a mentor in their folksong publications, and he collaborated with the latter in the second of a two-part song-by-song assessment of American balladry: Tolman, "Some Songs," 1916; and Albert H. Tolman and Mary O. Eddy, "Traditional Tunes and Texts," *Journal of American Folklore* 35:138 (1922), 335–432.

19. Leah Jackson Wolford, *The Play-Party in Indiana* (Indianapolis: Indiana Historical Society, 1959 [1918]).

20. Wolford, *Play-Party*, 114.

21. Wolford, *Play-Party*, 115.

22. Wolford, *Play-Party*, 118.

23. Wolford, *Play-Party*, 118.

24. Wolford, *Play-Party*, 118.

25. Mary O. Eddy and Albert O. Tolman, "Traditional Texts and Tunes," *Journal of American Folklore* 35:38 (October–December, 1922), 335.

26. Eddy, *Ballads*.

27. Eddy, *Ballads*, xxi–xxii.

28. Eddy's essays on religious folk songs include "Some Early American Hymns," *Southern Folklore Quarterly* 10 (1943), 119–129; and "Twenty Folk Hymns," *Midwest Folklore* 3 (1953), 35–45. See also Rebecca B. Schroeder, "Mary O. Eddy," in *American Folklore: An Encyclopedia*, 219.

29. J. W. Ashton invokes his Maine childhood in "Notes on Children's Taunts, Teases, etc.," *Western Folklore* 12:2 (1955), 126–129. Regarding his Midwestern work, see "Some Jump Rope Rhymes from Iowa," *Journal of American Folklore* 52:203 (1939), 119–123.

30. Earl J. Stout cites Ashton as his "inspirer" and reveals his collecting methods in the introduction to *Folklore from Iowa* (New York: American Folklore Society, 1936), Memoirs of the American Folklore Society, volume 29, ix.

31. Stout, *Folklore from Iowa*, 1936, 129.

32. Charles Neely, *Tales and Songs of Southern Illinois* (Menasha, WI: George Banta, 1938).

33. John Webster Spargo offered a brief biography of Charles Neely in his foreword to Neely, *Tales and Songs*.

34. Neely, *Tales and Songs*, 5.

35. Neely, *Tales and Songs*, 132.

36. Paul G. Brewster, *Ballads and Songs of Indiana*, preface by Stith Thompson (Bloomington: Indiana University, 1940), Folklore Series, no. 1.

37. Brewster, *Ballads and Songs*, 13. D. K. Wilgus singles out Brewster for his attention to European versions of ballad types in languages other than English in D. K. Wilgus, *Anglo-American Folksong Scholarship Since 1898* (New Brunswick, NJ: Rutgers University Press, 1959), 243. See also Janet M. Cliff, "Paul G. Brewster," in *American Folklore: An Encyclopedia*, 103.

38. Emelyn Elizabeth Gardner and Geraldine Jencks Chickering, *Ballads and Songs of Southern Michigan* (Hatboro, PA: Folklore Associates, 1967 [1939]), vii. Albert B. Friedman provides a biography, critical appraisal, and Gardner's remarks on Harriet Pawlowska in his foreword.

39. Gardner's student, Harriet M. Pawlowska, recorded Polish songs in Trempealeau County, Wisconsin, in the late 1940s for the Library of Congress, in addition to the earlier Detroit fieldwork she published as Harriet M. Pawlowska, *Merrily We Sing: 105 Polish Folksongs* (Detroit: Wayne State University Press, 1983).

40. Gardner and Chickering, *Ballads and Songs*, 1967 [1939], 3–4.

41. Gardner's New York state folksong scholarship appeared in *Folklore from the Schoharie Hills, New York* (Ann Arbor: University of Michigan Press, 1937).

42. Gardner and Chickering, *Ballads and Songs*, 485.

43. Michael Cassius Dean, *The Flying Cloud and One Hundred and Fifty Other Old Time Songs and Ballads* (Virginia, MN: The Quickprint, 1922).
44. Dean's *The Flying Cloud* is evaluated by D. K. Wilgus in Wilgus, *Anglo-American*, 209–210.
45. Franz Rickaby included texts, tunes, variations, annotations, and some contextual information for fifty-one lumber camp songs in *Ballads and Songs of the Shanty-boy* (Cambridge, MA: Harvard University Press, 1926). Harry Peters published excerpts from Rickaby's 1919 field journals, as well as thirty-six additional ballads gathered by Rickaby in Harry Peters, *Folksongs Out of Wisconsin* (Madison: State Historical Society of Wisconsin, 1977). Rickaby's preface acknowledges Michael Cassius Dean as a major source.
46. Earl C. Beck, *Songs of the Michigan Lumberjacks* (Ann Arbor: University of Michigan Press, 1941).
47. Beck, *Songs*, 6–7. Earl C. Beck profiles Bill McBride in Beck, *Songs*, 6–7. Beck's notes accompanied recordings of Bill McBride and other Michigan woods singers, all but one of them made in 1938 by Alan Lomax for *Songs of the Michigan Lumberjacks* (Washington, DC: Library of Congress LP AFS L56, 1959). See also LuAnne Gaykowski Kozma, "Earl Clifton Beck," in *American Folklore: An Encyclopedia*, 78.
48. Ivan Walton's 1932 field journal, Ivan Walton Collection of Great Lakes Songs, Bentley Historical Library, University of Michigan, entry on Johnny Green, Beaver Island, northern Lake Michigan.
49. Ivan Walton published an overview of Michigan Great Lakes folklore, "Marine Lore," in the Works Progress Administration's American Guide Series volume, *A Guide to the Wolverine State* (New York: Oxford University Press, 1941), 113–134. Laurie Kay Sommers offers a succinct biography of Walton, along with his field notes on John W. Green, in her study of Walton's major research site: *Beaver Island House Party* (East Lansing: Michigan State University Press, 1996), 35–38, 48. Posthumous publications, the former with an accompanying compact disk of field recordings, include: Ivan Walton and Joe Grimm, *Windjammers: Songs of the Great Lakes Sailors* (Detroit: Wayne State University Press, 2002); Ivan Walton and Joe Grimm, *Songquest: The Journals of Great Lakes Folklorist Ivan H. Walton* (Detroit: Wayne State University Press, 2005). See also Yvonne R. Lockwood, "Ivan Walton," in *American Folklore: An Encyclopedia*, 739.
50. Alice C. Fletcher, *A Study of Omaha Indian Music* (Cambridge, MA: Peabody Museum for American Archaeology and Ethnology, 1893).
51. Frances Densmore's *Chippewa Music*, originally published in two installments, 1910 and 1913, of the *Bureau of American Ethnology Bulletin* has been reprinted with an introduction by Thomas Vennum, Jr. (Minneapolis: Ross and Haines, 1973).
52. Sidney Robertson's summer 1937 recordings of the National Folk Festival in Chicago, and of traditional performers in Wisconsin and Minnesota, were made for the Archive of American Folk Song (now known as the Archive of Folk Culture) at the Library of Congress. Copies of her correspondence, also in the Archive of Folk Culture, include a letter she wrote from Duluth, Minnesota, on 25 July 1937, to Harold Spivacke, chief of the Library of Congress Music Division, in which she mentions H. M. Belden, Louise Pound, Mary O. Eddy, David McIntosh, and E. C. Beck. She also requests the use of field recording equipment in connection with discussions of lumberjack performers in Wisconsin and of Marjorie Edgar and her Minnesota Finnish and Gaelic contacts.
53. Sidney Robertson, *Wolf River Songs* (Folkways LP FE 4001, 1956). Comprehensive notes and selected recordings from the repertoire of Wisconsin's Ford-Walker extended family comprised Sidney Robertson's *Wolf River Songs*. Her complete Wisconsin recordings are accessible online as part of a site created by Nicole Saylor for the Mills Music Library at the University of Wisconsin: *Wisconsin Folksong Collection, 1937–1946*, http://digicoll.library.wisc.edu/WiscFolkSong/. Asher E. Treat of Antigo, Wisconsin, also documented the repertoire of "Kentucks" in northern Wisconsin, with particular attention to the Jacobs extended family: "Kentucky Folksong in Northern Wisconsin," *Journal of American Folklore* 52:203 (1939), 1–51. For a broader treatment of

Robertson's folksong field research, see Deirdre Ní Chonghaile, "ag teacht le cuan": Irish traditional music and the Aran Islands (Unpublished PhD dissertation, University College Cork, 2010), 182–193.

54. Blegen and Martin Ruud coauthored *Norwegian Immigrant Ballads and Songs* (Minneapolis: University of Minnesota Press, 1936). Edgar's Finnish American collection, *Songs from Metsola*, was unpublished until 2007 when Joyce Hakala included it, with new annotations, as part of her larger work, *The Rowan Tree: Lifework of Marjorie Edgar, Girl Scout Pioneer and Folklorist* (St. Paul: Pikebone Music).

55. Regarding relations between Robertson (as well as, eventually, Alan Lomax) and Minnesotans Marjorie Edgar and Theodore Blegen, see James P. Leary, "The Discovery of Finnish American Folk Music," *Scandinavian Studies* 73:3 (2001), 475–492.

56. Letters from Sidney Robertson to Alan Lomax, and from Alan Lomax to Bess Lomax, are in the Alan Lomax papers at the Archive of Folk Culture. Ron Cohen kindly brought the latter to my attention. The "Dear Sir . . . rapid recording survey" sentence is exactly the wording Alan Lomax used in contacting various knowledgeable people in Michigan, Wisconsin, and Minnesota. "Alan Lomax to Bess Lomax," 2 July 1938, in Ronald D. Cohen, ed., *Alan Lomax, Assistant in Charge: The Library of Congress Letters, 1935–1945* (Jackson: University Press of Mississippi, 2011), 88–89.

57. Lomax inventories his 1938 Upper Midwestern recordings in "Archive of American Folksong: Report of the Assistant in Charge," *Annual Report of the Librarian of Congress* (Washington, DC: United States Government Printing Office, 1939), 218–225.

58. Lomax, *Annual Report*, 218.

59. Lumberjack and Lakes songs from the region appear in Alan Lomax and John A. Lomax, *Our Singing Country* (New York: Macmillan, 1941). Alan Lomax and John A. Lomax, *Songs of the Michigan Lumberjacks* (Library of Congress LP AFS L56, 1941).

60. Helene Stratman-Thomas's field notes and a selection of her photographs appear in Harry B. Peters, *Folk Songs out of Wisconsin* (Madison: State Historical Society of Wisconsin, 1977), 23–41. Peters also includes texts, tunes, and brief information on singers for all but the bawdy English-language songs recorded by Stratman-Thomas. A selection of songs in English was included, with thorough comparative notes, in Stratman-Thomas, *Folk Music from Wisconsin* (Washington, D.C.: Library of Congress LP L55, 1960).

61. In 1985, Judy Woodward produced a series of thirteen half-hour documentary programs for Wisconsin Public that sampled the full cultural and linguistic range of Stratman-Thomas's recordings. The programs were subsequently published as a cassette/book package: James P. Leary, *The Wisconsin Patchwork: Recordings from the Helene Stratman-Thomas Collection of Wisconsin Folk Music, With Commentary* (Madison: University of Wisconsin Department of Continuing Education in the Arts, 1987). The University of Wisconsin's Mills Music Library has made all of the Stratman-Thomas recordings available online: *Wisconsin Folksong Collection, 1937–1946*, http://digicoll.library.wisc.edu/WiscFolkSong/.

62. Peters, *Folk Songs*.

SEVEN

Ballad Collectors in the Northeast

Nancy-Jean Ballard Seigel

It took a homemaker from suburban Boston, two scholars from Maine, and the wife of a U.S. senator to save New England's folk songs. Each of these women made recordings of people who were proud of singing the ballads and lyrics learned from their forebearers. However, due their advancing age and changes taking place in country life, this tradition would not continue. Eloise Hubbard Linscott, Fanny Hardy Eckstorm, Mary Winslow Smyth, and Helen Hartness Flanders traveled the highways and back roads of the Northeast, preserving the songs of yesterday for tomorrow's New Englanders. But with electricity coming into these rural homes, their culture was about to change forever. New music composed by professionals and broadcast by radio would soon drown out the traditional songs and fiddle tunes that had been popular since the early settlements. But, thanks to these four women, recordings of the old ballads and folk songs may still be heard today—sung the way they used to be sung.

FANNIE HARDY ECKSTORM (1865–1946)

Fannie Hardy Eckstorm heard her first folk songs in the wilderness of the Pine Tree State. Her father, one of the most successful fur traders in Maine, brought her along with him to places in the Northeast where no white woman had ever been. Besides learning the language and customs of the Indians, observing the habits of animals and identifying tracks, she had the opportunity to meet river-drivers, explorers, trappers, guides, and landowners. These men liked to sing and tell stories, and she enjoyed listening to them. Her journals from those wilderness expeditions became the basis for future publications not only on balladry but also natural history and Indian studies.

Eckstorm graduated from Smith College in 1888—the same year the American Folklore Society was founded. From 1889 to 1891 she was superintendent of schools in Brewer, Maine. In 1893, she married Reverend Jacob Eckstorm from Chicago and they had two children. Then tragedy struck—not once, but twice. In 1899, her husband died and then two years later she lost her daughter. She relocated to Brewer with her son and parents. Over the next forty-seven years she devoted her time to researching and writing about daily life in the woods, and about flora and fauna, Native American folklore, folk songs, and the past one hundred years of the maritime and lumber industry. Her other interests included Republican politics and the suffragette movement. *The Penobscot Man* (1901) was based on her early memories of people and events.[1] In it she captured the essential characteristics of woodsmen and river-drivers. The book established her as a writer and folklorist.

Eckstorm had collected songs for years, but she did so for sheer interest with no specific goal in mind. Then, in the early 1920s, when she was in her mid-fifties, she was shocked and angered to learn that another collector had published songs she had given him.[2] Shortly afterwards, Eckstorm met Dr. Mary Winslow Smyth, who would become a close friend and literary collaborator. A Maine native, and a professor who had published a book on Middle English literature, Smyth had been collecting in the Mount Desert Island area where she summered. The two women combined their efforts to build a collection portraying the people of Maine through the medium of traditional song.

Eckstorm was well aware that such a project would not be easy—after all, collecting was something heretofore done only by men. But since no man appeared willing, she and Smyth took up the banner themselves. Sometimes they went out together, but most often they worked alone—Eckstorm in the central and eastern areas, Smyth along the seashore. When they discussed writing a book, Eckstorm envisioned something "that would interest the summer visitor, especially if musical, in picking up songs, and which would open the eyes of the native to the wealth of them that exists on all sides. Both need instruction."[3]

The Minstrelsy of Maine (1927), a book of song texts, was a major contribution to the field of regional folksongs.[4] Its introduction, "Every Man His Own Poet," explains how important singing was to the settlers. The pioneers learned the practical skills of constructing homes, farming, and hunting, and they took great pride in expressing personal experiences through poetry—either by reciting verse or making up songs.[5] Some songs, like "The Burning of Henry K. Robinson's Camp"—which recalls the destruction of an unattended lumber camp and all its contents at a time when people relied heavily on the few possessions they owned—documented historical events and their effect on common people.[6]

The Minstrelsy of Maine was divided into two parts—songs from the woods and songs of the sea and shore. The authors included background—the who, when, and where—and more subtle details. The description of "The Gay Wedding" included a note that "it had a chorus in Irish which wouldn't be safe to sing in some parts of Bangor."[7] When lumbermen cleared a range, they moved on, and many of their songs traveled with them. "The Lumberman's Alphabet"—which listed tools men used in the woods and words like "foreman," "lice," "river," "sled," and "pine"—is a song on life in the lumber camp. It became so popular that as men went west seeking their fortunes, the song migrated with them.

Songs found along the coastline described a different kind of life. Many, like "Loss of the Albion," were tales of ancient grief allowing the listener to get to know people through their tragedies and their closeness to the sea. Smyth felt these represented the people more than deepwater maritime songs such as "Little Mohea" or "Flying Cloud," working chanteys like "Whiskey Johnny" or "Drunken Sailor," or spirited pirate songs such as "Captain Kidd."[8]

Eckstorm and Smyth recognized the influence of migrations on folk music. With many of the men off at war, especially in the years after the 1880s, the labor force at home was diminishing. When the Irish and people from the Canadian provinces came into Maine to find work, they brought with them their own singing styles and melodies. Some of their songs—like the river driving tragedy in "Jam on Gerry's Rock"—could be more ballad-like, with stories strung out over many verses. Later, by the turn of the century, when there were fewer and fewer active lumber camps, the song text was emphasized far more than the tune, as in the songs composed by woodsman Larry Gorman.[9]

With a friend—Miss Mary Cabot Wheelwright—contributing towards the expenses of their field trips, Eckstorm and Smyth went to work on a second book. Their research, eventually published as *British Ballads of Maine* (1929), would include both texts and tunes of fifty-six Child ballads.[10] By 1927, they had completed the fieldwork, and Yale University Press was interested in the manuscript. At that point they met Phillips Barry; Harvard educated and an authority on English ballads, he was not only a song collector but an expert on Irish culture and folklore as well. The three became friends and did some joint collecting in Maine.[11] Eckstorm and Smyth were so appreciative of Barry's interest in their work that they invited him to collaborate on their book. He was delighted to do this, but his contribution of scholarly notes, occasional tune transcriptions, and songs from his own collection by no means equaled the volume of material Eckstorm and Smyth provided. Barry was an important man to know, and, when it came time to submit the final manuscript to

Yale, Eckstorm felt that the publishers would be more inclined to take the book if Barry's name was listed as one of the authors. (Barry had made no such request.) When *British Ballads of Maine* was finally published in 1929, the authors appeared alphabetically—with Phillips Barry's name first. In earlier days, women sometimes didn't ask for, or get, full credit for their work.[12]

Up until this time, the southern states were assumed to be the richest source of traditional music in the United States. Eckstorm and Smyth proved otherwise because, through their work, every ballad then current in the South had also been collected in Maine. The seaports of New England provided easy connection points for folk songs migrating into New England. Many were brought by sailors traveling along the coast from points as far away as Atlantic Canada and the Gulf of Mexico. Some were sung in taverns and other points of hospitality. Women came in contact with mariners through their own families or the families of neighbors, and they too became song carriers. The song "Sally and Her True-love Billy" was traced back in this way by an eighty-two-year-old man from Mount Desert.[13]

In 1930, Barry, Eckstorm, and Smyth founded the Folk Song Society of the Northeast. Its purpose was "to collect and preserve the traditional songs, ballads, cante-fables . . . still sung in regions from which the early settlers migrated."[14] Over the next few years, the Society held meetings and published a bulletin of scholarly articles

Eckstorm and Barry corresponded actively. Because she was the elder of the two and assumed she would die first, Eckstorm gave Barry her entire collection, which he stored in a box under his dining room table in Cambridge. This box contained not only letters and notebooks related to their joint work but also material acquired before the two had ever met. But Barry died first, and his wife refused to return Eckstorm's research materials.[15] Despite several attempts, some made with the assistance of Helen Hartness Flanders, Eckstorm was unsuccessful in retrieving her collection. As a result, the whereabouts of Eckstorm's precious cylinder recordings capturing the performances of early twentieth-century Maine singers has never been found.[16] Deeply grieved over this loss, she simply discontinued work on folk songs and moved on to other areas of interest, including research and writing about her Native American materials. Both Eckstorm and Mary Winslow Smyth were scholars of high intellect, considerable energy, and broad scope. Although the preservation of balladry was a major pursuit in their lives, they also published on a variety of other interests. The Fannie Hardy Eckstorm Papers are located in the Special Collections Department at the Folger Library at the University of Maine, Orono, Maine.

HELEN HARTNESS FLANDERS (1890–1972)

Helen Hartness Flanders received her life's calling at a meeting of the Committee on Traditions and Ideals of the Vermont Commission on Country Life. In 1930, at the request of Vermont Governor John E. Weeks, a group of prominent artists and writers was convened to suggest ways of preserving the Green Mountain State's cultural heritage.[17] A proposal was made that someone should collect the songs Vermonters had learned orally—passed down from generation to generation. This music could be published in a book. The obvious candidate for this project was Flanders, as everyone knew she loved music. But, to their astonishment, she declined, stating that she didn't feel she qualified because she only knew about classical music. A friend of hers, the writer Dorothy Canfield Fisher, then offered her opinion that such a project would be a waste of time because, after all, Vermonters didn't sing. Flanders, knowing many musical Vermonters, vigorously disagreed with her. What happened next changed the course of history. As they were talking, Fisher suddenly remembered a tune—a regimental marching song—that she could trace back three generations in her family.[18] It was through this spontaneous memory jog that the Vermont collection took form. That night at supper Flanders announced to her family that she was going to collect folk songs; and furthermore, she had already heard one that very day.

Driving long hours over bumpy dirt roads to search for traditional singers was quite a departure from Flanders's accustomed lifestyle. Her father was the first millionaire in the state. She was raised in elegant surroundings and attended boarding school where (aside from the usual classes) she studied voice, piano, banjo, and mandolin. By the time she was sixteen, she spoke fluent French, had toured Europe with her family, wrote poetry, and was an accomplished pianist.

Flanders was the only folk music collector active in New England who didn't have college education. From her early years, Flanders was a voracious reader and intellectually curious and would become a scholar of literature, history, and music. She was also personally charming, outgoing, and spontaneous and was just as at ease talking with a farmer baling hay in the field as with an ambassador at a White House reception. During her collecting visits, she showed interest in the things that mattered to people—whether it was concern for a dying mother, the best recipe for canned plums, or memories of the good old days. She kept in touch with many of her singers, and they with her. One of her treasured possessions, a gift from an old woodsman in Maine, was a small rug she kept beside her bed—made from the skin of a bear he had trapped.

Helen Hartness Flanders had a phenomenal memory for words and tunes and could quickly draw comparisons between folk songs and parallel examples she recognized from literature—the story of "The Prioress's Tale" from Chaucer's *Canterbury Tales* (in "Little Harry Huston," Child 155)[19] or an ancient Greek poem by Anacreon (in "The White-Haired Boy").[20] Love of music and poetry not only led her to an appreciation of ballad singing but had—twenty years before—helped her choose a husband. Ralph Flanders, she discovered, enjoyed reciting verse as much as she did.

In the years following their 1911 marriage, besides being busy with domestic life and raising three children, she also gave home musicales, organized a local orchestra, was active in the Altrurian (women's) club, and played the piano in children's recitals. In 1927, her first book of poems, *Looking out of Jimmie,* was published.[21] By 1930, she was ready for new challenges. When the time came, she would focus all of her energies toward collecting ballads. Her husband, who was very supportive, said that when she decided to do something, she had a "whim of iron."

Flanders approached collecting with the mindset of a manager. First she consulted the top person in the field. She went to Washington, D.C., where she met with Robert Winslow Gordon, head of the Archive of Folksongs at the Library of Congress. He told her about his collecting experiences and emphasized that it was essential to record every song—even song fragments. Next, she hired a temporary assistant. George Brown, from Boston, had been the conductor for the Springfield orchestra. He knew nothing about folk music but needed a job and could transcribe tunes. Finally, she contacted the media with news of the collection. She wrote letters to all the Vermont newspapers, describing the project as a state-wide effort and asking people to help her by sending in songs or providing the names of people she should meet who like to sing.

That first summer's work was successful but she had certain advantages. Because of her prominent family, she was known to many people. The newspaper publicity had sparked interest in the project, but while she looked for singers in the Springfield area, they also came to her. On the street or in the post office, she was often approached by strangers who would ask if she would like to hear songs or if she'd like the name of someone she should meet.

Brown's summer was not as successful. Flanders had sent him to towns close to West River, the oldest settled area in Vermont where generations of families had lived and farms had been passed down from father to son. But Brown was only in his twenties and a flatlander at that. His first efforts were disastrous. People didn't answer his calls or slammed the door in his face. Obviously he had to change his approach, so he invented a new collecting technique. He'd go into a country store, sit on a cracker barrel near the front, and, after a sufficient pause (essential for Vermonters), work himself into conversation with the locals. When he mentioned that he was from out of state and was working on a project for the governor of Vermont, their ears perked up. By the time he got off the barrel, Brown usually had the names of several potential singers.

One day he was directed to the house of Josiah Kennison and his luck changed dramatically. The old man was lying on a couch in his home, suffering from what appeared to be a hangover. He had been a scissors grinder, mender of clocks and locks, barker at village fairs, and small-time farmer; but he was also a goldmine for old songs.[22] Kennison was flattered to be asked to sing and contributed a number of rare songs. To record some of them, he rode his horse and buggy over Rattlesnake Mountain to Flanders's home in Springfield. The wax cylinder recordings made in those first months gave an indication of the types of songs that would make up the entire Flanders Ballad Collection—ancient Child ballads such as "Lord Randal" or the "House Carpenter"; broadsides such as "Caroline of Edinburgh Town" brought over by the settlers; and native songs like "On Springfield Mountain" and "The Sword of Bunker Hill" which were deeply rooted in American soil.

The committee assignment was completed in several months and Brown returned to Boston, but by that time Flanders had developed a passion for the song hunt. There was the fascination of the discovery of "a continued story of which you do not know its beginning. You drop into a situation or experiences that have been going on without you."[23] Then there was the experience and unexpected rewards of meeting all different types of people, finding that "there are few byroads that do not have some association, few noncommittal doorways which, opened by perfect strangers, have not given momentous experiences in texts and tunes."[24] Each song had its own story: how she found the singer—the drive, the scenery, frequently getting lost and meeting helpful strangers; once there, carefully observing the informant's face as he shared his recollections, songs, and family history; and, finally, the homework of putting the recording into historical context and identifying its genre and origin. She joked that she'd developed an allergy to ballads—every time she was around them, she caught them.[25] Soon she was following up leads in all the New England states.

During the 1930s, Flanders continued making field trips—often bringing along her sister, her best friend, or her daughter, Elizabeth, to keep her company. However, events in her personal life clouded the collecting progress. Besides health problems of her own, the family sustained major losses: her parents and Ralph's and her brother-in-law all passed away within a three-year period. When she could, she kept adding to the collection. Flanders was keenly aware that once radio music came to these rural homes, people would be less inclined to sing what had been handed down to them. While she believed Vermont was still rich with traditional music, she recognized that if it was to be preserved, the fieldwork had to be done quickly before the older generation died and took their songs to the grave.

Besides making recordings, she also wanted to balance her research with scholarship and learn to identify songs through their histories. Springfield was not far from Dartmouth, so she drove up and made use of the college library. There she studied balladry from the classic sources—from Bishop Thomas Percy's *Reliques of Ancient English Poetry* (1765) and Sir Walter Scott's *Minstrelsy of the Scottish Borders* (1802) to Francis James Child's *The English and Scottish Popular Ballads* (1882–1898) and Cecil Sharp's *English Folk-Songs from the Southern Appalachians* (1917).[26]

In the meantime, Phillips Barry had learned about Helen Hartness Flanders's collecting and wanted to meet her. His visit to Springfield marked the beginning of an important friendship. He not only became her mentor, he also encouraged her to concentrate on finding the oldest Child ballads. Over the next seven years, letters flew back and forth between Springfield and Cambridge—Flanders reporting new finds, and in the next mail Barry writing back with information about ballad origins, singing styles, and where certain songs had been previously collected. A good example of his guidance concerned one of Flanders's most prolific singers. Mrs. Sullivan was born in County Clare, Ireland. Since Barry knew which songs had been collected in that area, he was able to suggest certain songs that Mrs. Sullivan might remember from her childhood. She said later of Barry, "He fairly brought me up in knowing what I was finding the earliest years of my fieldwork."[27]

In 1930, Flanders joined in the Folk Song Society of the Northeast and became friends with Fannie Hardy Eckstorm. The next year, she was made vice president. Barry published a paper (in the *Bulletin of the Folklore Society of the Northeast*) on Child ballad number 10, "Two Sisters."[28] The ballad tells how one sister murdered the other because both of them liked the same man. His study was in part inspired by a new variant that Flanders had recorded from a Polish immigrant in Springfield, Vermont, in 1934. Most versions of "Two Sisters" previously found in New England originated from the British Isles, but Mrs. Stankiewicz's recording was unique because she sang it in Polish.

Helen Hartness Flanders's initial plan was to collect exclusively in Vermont. Then one day, Barry told her about a singer in New Hampshire. Flanders wondered if perhaps she ought to kidnap the man to get him into Vermont, but in the end, it was she who crossed the bridge over the state line.[29] She remarked that "ballads know no borders."[30] The New Hampshire man, Orlon Merrill, was part Native American. She recorded twenty-seven of his songs, including Child ballads and lumber camps songs. His close encounters with death in earlier days when he was a guide, trapper, and woodsman vividly influenced his singing.[31]

Besides collecting, Mrs. Flanders wrote articles, gave interviews, spoke on the radio, and gave lectures about ballads—not only in New England but in many other states. These presentations were a big hit at granges, schools, women's clubs, and various other community organizations. She brought singers who had previously recorded to illustrate the songs she discussed. When she invited members of the audience to share songs from their families, nearly anything could happen. Sometimes her husband would stand up, unannounced, and sing something he had learned from his father. On one occasion, a guest singer arrived rather "under the influence." When it was his turn to perform, he sang songs he had never previously recorded, and each one was more risqué than the last. As the audience grew more and more uneasy, she gracefully interrupted and suggested that there remained just enough time left for him to play a tune on the fiddle.[32]

For several years, she wrote a weekly ballad column, which appeared in several New England newspapers. Beginning with titles like "Vermont Folksongs—The Green Willow Tree," she would describe her informant and how they met, thereafter printing the song text. She asked readers whether they knew different versions and, as a result of these articles, many contributions were sent by mail.

Vermont Folk-Songs and Ballads (1932), coauthored with George Brown, included texts and transcriptions of 120 songs.[33] It was an overview of the first year's collecting, but it also presented the lives of Vermonters through their music. The song "Fair Charlotte," for example, represented the cold weather genre of snowstorm ballads. This book was followed by *The New Green Mountain Songster* (1939), coauthored with Phillips Barry, George Brown, and Flanders's daughter, Elizabeth Ballard, who both collected and transcribed tunes for her mother.[34]

In 1934, Helen Hartness Flanders represented Vermont at the first National Folk Festival held in St. Louis and brought Elmer George as her special guest to perform songs he had learned in the woods as a young lumberman. (George nearly missed his stage appearance when he disappeared to get cough medicine; upon his return sometime later, he was in extremely high spirits.) Flanders went on to serve on the National Committee of the National Folk Festival along with the director, Sarah Gertrude Knott, and other prominent names in the folk world including Bascom Lamar Lunsford, George Korson, Benjamin A. Botkin, Arthur Kyle Davis, Frances Densmore, Zora Neale Hurston, George Pullen Jackson, G. L. Kittredge, and Vance Randolph.

Lecture fees paid only a fraction of Flanders's expenses, but she was determined to continue and used her own financial resources to make it possible. In her home, she carefully filed papers in notebooks and cabinets and sometimes hired a part-time secretary to assist with correspondence and typing. While she planned her visits to singers carefully, the collecting results were often dictated by road conditions. In New England, driving was usually safe from April to November, but the winter months and "mud season" (the spring thaw) were set aside for writing, reflection, and research. It was then that she worked on long-term goals for the collection and plans for future books.

Flanders had maintained contact with Library of Congress Archive of Folk Culture from the start of her efforts. In the late 1930s, the foremost names in American folksong were John Lomax and his son, Alan, who had been collecting songs in many areas of the country. Through their connections at the Library, they had access to the best available recording equipment. The Lomaxes had not yet come to New England, but Flanders knew it was a matter of time before they would cross into what she considered her territory. Anticipating this, she invited Alan Lomax to come visit her home in Vermont with the intention to go out collecting.

In November of 1939, for nine days, the two of them traveled around the state with a recorder from the library, jointly collecting from her best singers. One of Lomax's collecting techniques, she found out later, was to offer a "toot" or two from his bottle (to relax the singer). Unfortunately, not everyone he met found this in good taste. Although Flanders and Lomax corresponded sporadically for years, it was not an easy relationship. She had very firm restrictions for keeping the collection under her control.[35] No one was to use her recordings without permission. She was incensed to discover, by accident, that Lomax had given out copies of field recordings to someone who used them on a lecture tour in South America without the knowledge that they came from the Flanders Ballad Collection.[36] As a consequence, she never fully trusted Lomax.

In 1940, Flanders hired an assistant, Marguerite Olney, who had a degree in music, was a good researcher, could transcribe tunes, and enjoyed meeting people. The two women visited the field on occasion and, in this way, Olney learned the techniques of collecting. By this time, the collection had outgrown her house. Flanders's plan was to eventually embed the collection in an educational institution so that students and scholars could hear the recordings and learn about their folksong heritage. In 1941, the Flanders Ballad Collection was donated to Middlebury College. Olney, as curator on campus, set up the collection rooms, assisted professors who wanted to include folk songs in their course programs, and occasionally gave lectures herself. Eventually, she took over much of the fieldwork.

Unfortunately, the collection was donated to Middlebury without an endowment, and money was a problem from the start. Flanders made the rounds of various foundations trying to get support but was unsuccessful. Due to budget constraints at Middlebury, Mrs. Flanders paid two-thirds of Miss Olney's salary for twenty years. Despite all this, *Ballads Migrant in New England*, coauthored by Flanders and Olney, was published in 1953.[37]

From 1944 to 1946, her husband was president of the Federal Reserve Bank in Boston. She continued to collect (especially in Maine and Rhode Island), give talks, and work on books. Then in 1946, Ralph Flanders was elected to be a senator from Vermont and the couple moved to Washington, D.C. Helen Hartness Flanders was a rarity, something of a phenomenon—no senator's wife had ever done anything like what she was doing. But nothing held her back: in government and diplomatic circles, she was never too shy to talk about ballad collecting.

In 1948, Flanders was invited to give a lecture in the Coolidge Auditorium at the Library of Congress—the first event of its kind ever to take place. The evening's topic was "British Ballads Found in New England," and sharing the stage were three elderly men, dressed in their Sunday best, who had never traveled so far from home or appeared before such a distinguished audience. Flanders introduced "Mr. Elmer George of North Calais, Vermont, who with members of his family can sit around and sing all night without repeating a song; Mr. Asa Davis, who treasures many songs known to his Irish forbearers; and Mr. Charles Finnemore, from Aroonstock County, Maine, whose ballads were learned among river-drivers on the East Branch of the Penobscot."[38] Flanders gave lively and scholarly descriptions of the interchange of themes and tales that emerged with the migrations. There was an overflow audience and response was extremely enthusiastic. That event gave enormous exposure to the Flanders Ballad Collection and to New England folk music in general, and it is still considered a milestone in the history of the Folk Archives.[39]

By the late 1950s, most of the singers who had participated in the ballad lectures had died. The active years of collecting were waning, and by 1960 had ended. Flanders was nearly seventy and in fragile health, but she had one last project to complete: a scholarly study of all the Child ballads in the Flanders Ballad Collection. This four-volume series, *Ancient Ballads Traditionally Sung in New England*, was published between 1958 and 1963, with folklorist Tristram Coffin providing critical analyses and Bruno Nettl contributing annotations on the music.[40]

In over thirty years, almost five hundred singers and fiddlers from Vermont, New Hampshire, Maine, Connecticut, Massachusetts, Rhode Island, and New York State had made recordings for the Flanders Ballad Collection. Most were between sixty and eighty years old, and all but a handful sang unaccompanied. They represented every imaginable occupation—mill worker, nurse, river driver, housewife, doctor, cemetery guardian, farmer, carpenter, sailor, school child, and minister. Most had families that originated elsewhere—Ireland, Scotland, England, Nova Scotia, Quebec, Poland, Russia—and they spoke with great pride about their traditions and family histories.[41] The nearly 4,500 songs were collected in kitchens, front parlors, at the bedsides of the dying, at a school construction site, on the grounds of a town fair, in "God's Little Acre" cemetery, up in a plum tree, and even in Mrs. Flanders's car. Thousands of additional song texts, mostly transcribed by hand, were sent in from people all over the United States. In all, there are over nine thousand songs in the collection.

Helen Hartness Flanders had pedigree, wealth, and free time—in ballad terms, she was "a lady of high degree." But rather than lead a life of leisure, she coupled her strong interests in music and poetry, and amassed the largest treasury of New England folk songs. The Helen Hartness Flanders Ballad Collection is housed at Middlebury College in Middlebury, Vermont. The American Folklife Center at the Library of Congress has a complete copy of the field recordings.

ELOISE HUBBARD LINSCOTT (1897–1978)

Eloise Hubbard Linscott was drawn into collecting through her maternal instinct. Mrs. Linscott wanted to give her son John a book containing all the folk songs she had known as a child. She searched libraries and stores and wrote to publishers, and when she didn't find what she wanted, she decided to write the book herself. *Folksongs of Old New England* (1939) remains today one of the most popular books for people who enjoy traditional music.[42]

Eloise Hubbard Linscott had grown up singing and swapping songs; her mother sang to her and her mother's grandmother had sung to her children. She, like Eckstorm, went out on excursions with her father, a physician who covered rural areas of eastern Massachusetts. During his medical "rounds," he not only monitored the heart rates of his patients but often lingered to socialize and hear their favorite songs and stories. For over forty years, her family operated a camp in New Hampshire. Summertime meant hard work but also plenty of singing and dancing. Everyone had responsibilities. It was Linscott's job to teach folk songs to the children.

After graduation from Radcliffe, where she was an English literature major, in 1920 she married businessman Charles Linscott, and the couple settled in Needham, Massachusetts, where Eloise became a full-time homemaker. She enjoyed making New England clam chowder and Johnny Cake, tending to the wildflower and herb gardens in back of her house, running a roadside vegetable stand in the summers, and participating in her son's activities. Like other housewives, she socialized by getting involved with community activities. She was four feet eleven inches tall, vivacious and neighborly—someone who was easy to get to know.

She began to work on her book around 1926, when she was twenty-nine years old. She went to libraries and learned more about folk music, and then wrote down all her mother's songs.[43] When her husband didn't need the car and her mother-in-law could babysit, Linscott took to the road in search of songs. Her collecting kit consisted of a notebook and a pencil; only later was she able to acquire a Dictaphone recorder. This arrangement worked well and Linscott prided herself that fieldwork never jeopardized her duties at home.

She first visited her relatives in eastern Massachusetts and wrote down all the songs they remembered. They also gave her names of other people who knew folk songs, and suddenly what had started as a family project began to mushroom. Eventually, she was making trips into New Hampshire, Connecticut, Vermont, and Maine. In all, she collected approximately 2,500 songs.

Linscott worked hard when she was on the road, sometimes traveling two or three hundred miles a day. One singer remembered that her visit was like being in the presence of a tornado: she whizzed in, quickly set up her equipment, demanded quiet in the room while he sang, and dashed away once the collecting was done.[44] On other occasions, when she wasn't rushed, she'd help a family finish the chores—hoeing beans or churning butter—so there'd be more time for singing.

Linscott kept good notes on her field adventures. On one wintry trip into the hills of Vermont, she was wrapped up in a buffalo robe and a shawl, being driven by her host in his "air conditioned" Model T Ford over "the back road while a whirling snowstorm covered the landscape and us."[45] The most unusual place where she recorded songs was in a stable operated by a horse trader whose business methods frequently drew the attention of the local police. When she first arrived, the man claimed he was too sick to sing, but after moistening his throat with "a little firewater," he had recovered enough to sing for five hours. Linscott recorded twenty-two of his songs.

She wrote that, "One of the prolific singers was Mrs. Carrie B. Grover of Gorham, Maine. What she didn't sing, she played on a fiddle from a repertoire of more than 400 family songs. And when Aunt Carrie couldn't finish singing 'The Oaks of James Dearning' because 'it ain't fitten',' her husband willingly sang the rest of it."[46]

Another informant, William J. Sherrard of Munsonville, New Hampshire, was born in Ireland. He was described as

> A deep water man of thirty years and first mate of square-rigger days, he recalls tales, yarns and songs of the windjammers as they sailed the oceans of the world. The chanteys he sings come alive with a roar and meaning that cannot be put on paper. He flings the whiplash of the cat o'nine tails into the rhythm, and one hears the wild scream of the wind as the crew scramble to don their "souls and bodies." His chanteys are... the heartbeat of a great ship as she rolls while the wind sighs in the rigging.[47]

Linscott arranged for him to perform at the National Folk Festival to great acclaim.

Despite all her dedication and energy, Linscott did not enjoy the opportunities that the other collectors were offered and this often led to frustration and bitterness. She worked by herself and for herself. She was not associated with a university or institution and not active in the American Folklore Society or the Folksong Society of the Northeast. Without such connections, the Library of Congress would not lend its recording equipment. Unlike the other "ladies of the Northeast," Linscott had no financial backing. In fact, it was said that funding for collecting expenses came from one source: money she had squirreled away in a tin can that had previously held Ocean Spray cranberries.

In a funding request letter to the Rockefeller Foundation—which was rejected—she wrote, "I am not much of a scholar; just a woman of New England heritage—with a home and family my first consideration; but a tremendous desire to keep this music . . . for always."[48] When she applied for a Guggenheim fellowship, she was rejected again. Linscott, in general, did not correspond or mingle with other scholars. She did, however, meet Phillips Barry. He encouraged her folk song project and invited her to make use of his library; he also helped with editing and contributed songs from his own collection to be used in her book. Although Linscott and Flanders were in touch, there was a rivalry between them over who had territorial rights to collect in certain areas of New England.

In his introduction to *Folksongs of Old New England*, collector James Madison Carpenter wrote, "Here are songs for almost every palate: semi popular songs, treasured by past generations; comical songs, lumbermen's songs, sea chanteys and; songs with a strictly New England flavor; and finally, there were a fair number of Child ballads, 'the aristocrats of folksong.'"[49] The book provides the basics for someone beginning to learn about folksongs. In the section of dance tunes, there was a glossary of dance terms; for each song—sea chantey, ballad, or folk song—she included information about the informant and about the type of song it represents. "Fiddle Dee Dee," she wrote, is a ballad in which animals behave like humans, and such songs were very popular in the sixteenth and seventeenth centuries.[50]

Folksongs of Old New England is divided into four sections: game songs, dances, chanteys, and folk songs and ballads—each with a simple piano accompaniment. There are twenty-eight singing games with simple directions, diagrams, and notes. "London Bridge," she pointed out, can be traced to prisoner-taking on a bridge and similar medieval tales about the devil, while "Inty, Minty, Tippity, Fig" represents the genre of counting out games. Among the thirty-five country dances (with fiddle accompaniment, directions, calls, and charts) are "Boston Fancy" and "Maid in the Pump Room." There are seventeen sea chanteys and sailors' work songs, such as "Haul Away Joe" and "Reuben Renzo," and seventy-seven folk songs and ballads, which include classic Child ballads as well as other songs like "Tittery Nan" and "Willikins and Dinah" of the "read 'em-and-weep" variety.

Folksongs of Old New England established Linscott's name as a collector, yet when she learned there was an equipment loan program at the Library of Congress and asked to borrow a disc recording machine, Alan Lomax—head of the Archive of American Folk Song—was reluctant to help her. She kept hounding him until he finally changed his mind. In fall of 1941, she went on a two-week collecting tour with Library of Congress equipment. It was an ambitious schedule, but when she returned she delivered to Lomax thirty-six glass-based discs with field notes and transcriptions.

Linscott, like Flanders, gave talks at various music societies, camps, women's clubs, and arts groups. Her presentations were very popular. She and her guest singer or fiddler came dressed up in colonial costumes. Sometimes Linscott sang, and on occasion taught the audience a song.

In the 1940s, she became involved with the National Folk Festival and helped coordinate performers who would represent New England. Through her volunteer work, she developed a warm friendship with Sarah Gertrude Knott, founder of the National Folk Festival, and corresponded with her for several years.

Linscott was not able to interest any editor in subsequent publications, so *Folksongs of Old New England* would be her only book. She was frustrated that she didn't gain more recognition, but she made her mark in other ways. If someone was needed to spend a weekend teaching and judging square dancing, she was the one they called. She was also instrumental in organizing regional folk festivals, including one in the Boston Arena and another at the Boston Public Garden. Eloise Hubbard Linscott was dedicated to bringing people to folk events and promoting traditional music within their communities. She was people's collector. The Eloise Hubbard Linscott Collection is at the American Folklife Center in the Library of Congress.

By the late 1920s, when women were bobbing their hair, going to college, driving cars, and voting for the president, many worked as secretaries, nurses, and teachers. Fannie Hardy Eckstorm, Mary Winslow Smyth, Helen Hartness Flanders, and Eloise Hubbard Linscott burst out of that mold and reinvented themselves as songcatchers. Their mission was to preserve the New England folksong heritage for posterity.

As the rate of change in American culture has reached blinding speed, the collections these four women amassed give us a clear, steady view back into the daily lives of New Englanders who created so much of the framework we build on today—the language, landscape, affiliations, and pioneering spirit. Singing, once a vital part daily life, is living history. Working in a field previously dominated by men—several from Harvard University—these grassroots ladies of the Northeast enlisted their contemporaries to help locate and record songs which still lingered in the memories of a generation born in the nineteenth century. Fannie Hardy Eckstorm, Mary Winslow Smyth, Helen Hartness Flanders, and Eloise Hubbard Linscott not only recorded this music for the New Englanders of the future; they put the "woman's touch" into collecting.

NOTES

1. Fannie Hardy Eckstorm, *The Penobscot Man* (Freeport, NY: Books for Libraries Press, 1904).
2. Roland Palmer Gray, *Songs and Ballads of Maine Lumberjacks* (Cambridge: Harvard University Press, 1924).
3. Letter, Eckstorm to Smyth, 20 August 1925. Brewer, Maine, Accession 118 Box 2, Phillips Barry Collection, Houghton Library, Harvard University, Cambridge, Massachusetts.
4. Fannie Hardy Eckstorm and Mary Winslow Smyth, *The Minstrelsy of Maine: Folksongs and Ballads of the Woods and the Coast* (Boston: Houghton Mifflin, 1927).
5. Eckstorm and Smyth, *Minstrelsy of Maine*, 3.
6. Eckstorm and Smyth, *Minstrelsy of Maine*, 340.
7. Eckstorm and Smyth, *Minstrelsy of Maine*, 170.
8. Eckstorm and Smyth, *Minstrelsy of Maine*, 202.
9. Eckstorm and Smyth, *Minstrelsy of Maine*, 75.
10. Phillips Barry, Fanny Hardy Eckstorm, and Mary Smyth, *British Ballads from Maine: The Development of Popular Songs with Texts and Airs* (New Haven, CT: Yale University Press, 1929).
11. Eckstorm made all the arrangements for these trips, including locating the informants.
12. Pauleena MacDougall, "Understanding the Hearts of the People: Fannie Hardy Eckstorm and Phillips Barry," *The Folklore Historian* 2001, 17–28.
13. Barry, Eckstorm, and Smyth, *British Ballads*, 419.
14. Constitution of the Folk Song Society of the Northeast. This statement appeared on the first page of the *Bulletin of the Folk Song Society of the Northeast* 1 (1930).
15. Letter, Fannie Hardy Eckstorm to Helen Hartness Flanders, 6 August 1940, Brewer, Maine, held in the Helen Hartness Flanders Ballad Collection at Middlebury, Vermont.
16. MacDougall, "Understanding," 17–28.
17. The Committee on Traditions and Ideals was part of the Governor's Commission on Country Life, intended to assess the state of the state. Other subcommittees studied areas such as dairy production, religious forces, and farm forestry.
18. The song was also known as "Katy Cruel."
19. Helen Hartness Flanders and Marguerite Olney, *Ballads Migrant in New England* (New York: Farrar, Straus and Young, 1953), 28.
20. Flanders and Olney, *Ballads*, 179.
21. Helen Hartness Flanders, *Looking out of Jimmie* (New York: Dutton, 1927).
22. George Brown, field notes. A copy was sent to me by Stephen Green, who interviewed Brown in 1982.
23. Helen Hartness Flanders, 1948 (unpublished article), Helen Hartness Flanders Ballad Collection.
24. Helen Hartness Flanders, "Confessions of a Ballad Collector," 1946 (unpublished article), Helen Hartness Flanders Ballad Collection.
25. Helen Hartness Flanders, Notes, Helen Hartness Flanders Ballad Collection.
26. Bishop Thomas Percy, *Reliques of Ancient English Poetry* (self published, 1765); Francis James Child, *The English and Scottish Popular Ballads* (Boston: Houghton Mifflin,

1882–1898); Cecil Sharp and Olive Dame Campbell, *English Folk-Songs from the Southern Appalachians* (New York: Putnam, 1917).

27. Letter, Helen Hartness Flanders to Dr. Michael, 8 November 1958, Helen Hartness Flanders Ballad Collection.

28. Phillips Barry, "Polish Ballad: Trzy Siostry," *Bulletin of the Folk Song Society of the Northeast* 10 (1935): 2–5; Phillips Barry, "Polish Ballad: Trzy Siostry," *Bulletin of the Folk Song Society of the Northeast* 11 (1935): 2–4.

29. Helen Hartness Flanders, notes about Orlon Merrell, Helen Hartness Flanders Ballad Collection.

30. Helen Hartness Flanders, notes, Helen Hartness Flanders Ballad Collection.

31. Helen Hartness Flanders, from a series of ballad articles in the *Springfield Reporter*, 1931.

32. Helen Hartness Flanders, "The Quest for Vermont Ballads," *Proceedings of the Vermont Historical Society* 7, (June 1939): 2.

33. Helen Hartness Flanders and George Brown, *Vermont Folk-Songs and Ballads* (Brattleboro, VT: Stephen Daye Press, 1932).

34. Helen Hartness Flanders, E. F. Ballard, G. Brown, and P. Barry, *The New Green Mountain Songster* (New Haven: Yale University Press, 1939).

35. Flanders wanted first claim to her collected songs for use in publications and lectures. Her restrictions were so tight that many scholars were intimidated to use the collection.

36. Dr. Carleton Sprague Smith of the New York Public Library was identified as the person who received the recording from Lomax. See also letter from Flanders to Legal Authority for Author's League of America, 20 April 1942, Helen Hartness Flanders Ballad Collection.

37. Helen Hartness Flanders and Marguerite Olney, *Ballads Migrant in New England* (New York: Farrar, Straus, and Young, 1953).

38. Helen Hartness Flanders, text of Library of Congress Lecture (unpublished), 1948.

39. An audio recording of the lecture is available at the Helen Hartness Flanders Ballad Collection at Middlebury College and at the American Folklife Center of the Library of Congress.

40. Helen Hartness Flanders, *Ancient Ballads Traditionally Sung in New England, Volumes 1–4* (Philadelphia: University of Pennsylvania Press, 1960–1965).

41. There were also several singers with mixed Native American background.

42. Eloise Hubbard Linscott, *Folksongs of Old New England* (New York: Macmillan, 1939).

43. She really wanted to go to Harvard University's Widener Library, but gender kept her from getting a library card.

44. Iree Monsier, "The Memory Man," *Rockland Maine Courier Gazette*, 19 December 1941.

45. Letter, Eloise Hubbard Linscott to Rosa E. Hutchinson at MacMillan Company, 22 June 1938, Eloise Hubbard Linscott Collection at the American Folklife Center at the Library of Congress.

46. Eloise Hubbard Linscott, *Folk Songs of Old New England*, 2nd ed. (North Haven, CT: Archon Books, Shoe String Press, 1962), vii.

47. Linscott, *Folk Songs*, viii.

48. Letter, Eloise Hubbard Linscott to Rockefeller Foundation in New York City, 28 May 1940, Eloise Hubbard Linscott Collection.

49. Linscott, *Folk Songs*, vii.

50. Linscott, *Folk Songs*, 196.

EIGHT

Four Songcatchers in Eastern Canada

I. Sheldon Posen

In the spring of 1920, Elisabeth Bristol of New York City arrived by skiff in the tiny community of Sally's Cove on the northwest coast of Newfoundland. Bristol was twenty-four years old, three years out of Vassar College, and she had volunteered to teach for the summer at the local school. She spent her first evening at her lodgings receiving people who dropped by to "see the teacher." As she settled into bed afterwards, something magical happened. "There floated in on the fragrant air," Bristol wrote home,

> the most beautifully haunting melody I think I have ever heard, sung by three or four rough heavy boys' voices, swelling out on the climaxes and indistinguishable in between. I hopped up and peeped out in time to see them swaying along in rhythm clumping in their rubber boots. This is Sally's Cove, unless I am mistaken, wild, rough, and untrained, but with a most moving melody.[1]

With this introduction to Newfoundland song, Bristol—we know her now by her married name, Greenleaf—was shortly to take her place as one of four major folk song collectors on Canada's east coast in the first four decades of the twentieth century.[2] The others were Nova Scotians W. Roy Mackenzie and Helen Creighton, and an Englishwoman, Maud Karpeles. (Grace Yarrow Mansfield, Greenleaf's musicologist collaborator and fellow American, and Helen Senior, Creighton's English music transcriber, are honorary members of this group.) They were, in fact, the first systematic collectors of folk songs anywhere in English Canada. They worked separately and, in some cases, years apart. But their mission in the small fishing villages and rural settlements they visited was more or less the same: to seek out traditional songs in the repertoires of local "folk" singers and get them down on paper.

Since these collectors were come-from-away strangers to the communities they chose to work in, they all faced the same daunting task: to discover singers they didn't know and persuade them to perform songs they either hadn't sung in years, or normally sang only in the presence of close family, friends, or fellow workers in carefully negotiated social interactions.[3] Harder still, the researchers had to persuade the singers—this was mostly in the days before electronic recording devices—to perform the songs again and again, until the text could be transcribed and, if the collector was interested and musically capable, the song's melody line written down.[4] It was a patience-sapping process for collector and singer alike, and we owe much to the perseverance of the former and the generosity of the latter that so many songs from that time and place have come down to us.

If it had been just songs these four collectors had documented, we should have reason enough to be grateful. For all the shortcomings some of these pioneers have been accused of—inadequate musical transcription, edited or collated texts, or worst of all, not collecting what a modern folklorist would have collected—they gave to academic folklore, and to music in general, a repertoire of song and ballad that would otherwise simply not be here. But more than that: two of the collectors—Greenleaf and Mackenzie—came to the field with an unusual regard for singing as a valuable social act, and an affectionate esteem for the men and women who took part in it. This attitude shines through their work and in many ways makes it transcendent in the discipline. Their books give us a world of songs, singers, and singing—how it worked and what it meant—that is, not just the map, but some of the territory as well.

W. ROY MACKENZIE

W. Roy Mackenzie's groundbreaking *Quest of the Ballad* (1919) was the first detailed personal account of folksong collecting anywhere in North America—nothing short of a how-to book for other collectors.[5] And his second work, *Ballads and Sea Songs from Nova Scotia* (1929), provided a benchmark collection for many researchers that followed him.[6]

Mackenzie came to his task with impeccable academic credentials. He had studied the ballad at Harvard with Professor George Lyman Kittredge, student of Francis James Child—the renowned scholar who had compiled what has been regarded as the great reference work on the subject.[7] But Mackenzie seems to have been a lover of folksong long before he reached Cambridge—he was in fact something of a boy folklorist. He was born into a middle-class ship-building family in River John, Nova Scotia, in 1883.[8] As a lad, he sought out old men who had ballads to perform, hanging around their workshops and cabins and listening to them sing. He learned to perform some of his favorites—a resource that would come in handy during his fieldwork as an adult.

As an undergraduate at Dalhousie University in Halifax (he graduated in 1902), Mackenzie read through Child's famous collection and realized that its ballads were similar to those he had heard in his youth. He decided it was necessary "to preserve some local versions of the genuine old stock," and so went searching for his old singing acquaintances in River John to transcribe their ballads.[9] With a novice's rigid orthodoxy, Mackenzie initially considered only the old Child-type ballads worthy of his attention. After a year's classes at Harvard, though, he returned to Nova Scotia and applied the more flexible principles he had learned at Kittredge's knee—"no popular version of any sort of ballad, ancient or modern, can be regarded as common or unclean."[10] Besides writing down the songs he heard, he also wound up field testing then-current scholarly paradigms about balladry, tradition, and "the folk." The result was an innovative look at local singing history which, with Kittredge's encouragement, he published as articles in the *Journal of American Folklore*, and later, in much expanded form, in *Quest of the Ballad*.[11] The songs themselves were given their own book ten years later.[12]

Whichever of Mackenzie's works the modern reader reads, he or she must come to terms with his writing style. By the time he wrote *Quest*, Mackenzie was a professor of English at Washington University in St. Louis. From this lofty height he looks back abashed, almost apologetic, on his youthful tastes and propensities:

> I have always been addicted to what is frequently described as "low company." Since I was reared in a Nova Scotia seaport town, where the grades of society go down as low as heart could desire, I had for years ample opportunity of satisfying this base-born predilection to the full.[13]

As if to compensate for a professor of English having consorted with such riff-raff as old seafarers and cottage dwellers, Mackenzie lays on a prose style that is highfalutin' in the extreme to the modern ear. Many of his phrases seem downright pretentious in a Nova Scotian, even one that's been to Harvard: "A modest enough beginning to my labors, in good sooth";[14] "Both Dave and Sandy had vigorously survived the allotted period of the life of man";[15] "'S blood, there is something in this more than natural, if philosophy could find it out."[16]

Such literary allusions and five-dollar phrases may first strike the reader as a distancing strategy—a backhanded way for Mackenzie to show up his informants as rural characters and rustic rubes. But eventually one realizes that they are simply a style that, like a tangled verbal undergrowth, can be brushed aside to reach the verdant, sunlit groves within (goodness, it's catching). Moreover, the overwrought passages often end in humorous deflation:

> It is the trade of the ballad-collector to walk up to roaring lions chained in caves and to attack fortified cities whose walls perchance will tumble at the blast of a trumpet; therefore I did not hesitate at the prospect of storming the little house, up over the hill, which immured the grim and mysterious figure of old Ann Thompson.[17]

What ultimately redeems Mackenzie's overwriting is a healthy dose of self-parody, coupled with a good-humoured love of the songs and a genuine, wryly expressed fondness and respect for the old folk who had preserved them. His style may even grow on the reader. For instance, Mackenzie had constantly to bridge the class divide between himself and his informants. He tells of being icily met by "a certain old, savage, man-eating tiger in the shape of a north-shore fisherman by the name of Sandy Macdonald."[18] Macdonald disdainfully allows as how Mackenzie must be fabulously wealthy. Abruptly parrying the remark, Mackenzie demonstrates their common humanity by proceeding as many a (male) Maritimes guest might in another's house: he offers Mr. Macdonald liquor, but in the most amusing, backhanded way:

> I was moved to remark unto Sandy that when traveling in the rain I frequently carried a pocket-vessel containing a well-known Scottish restorative, as an antidote to the grosser forms of dampness. My information elicited another stentorian avowal . . . : "Ha!" roared my host, "and, by the Lord, ye're a gentleman too!—Sit down," he added, "and I'll do what I can for ye."[19]

Mackenzie must have been a charmer: he did nothing so much as "court" his informants, both male and female, with a lover's patience and a wooer's cunning. Some he wheedled, others he teased, some he befriended, others he just foxed and won over. Ann Thompson met his requests to sing with steely-eyed silence. Even her daughter could not persuade her to perform: the older woman was afraid that the stranger would return to the village and make fun of her "settin' around on her bare feet singin' foolish old songs."[20] So she had her daughter bring out a book of old songs from the house for him to copy, saying, "They're a blame sight better than any I could give him."[21] The songs in the book were the likes of "Swanee River" and "Old Black Joe." Mackenzie said to her, "There are plenty of songs better than these, and they've never been written in books either."[22] And he sang her two stanzas of "The Plains of Waterloo." She rose to the bait: "So ye know that one, do ye? Well, there's plenty more like ye that knows it too, but I have a song about Waterloo that I'll be ye never heard from anyone but me!"[23] And she sang him a unique version of "Waterloo," boasting afterwards that no one could sing it differently because no one else knew it. She then invited him into her cottage to sing some more, joking to her daughter, "I s'pose I'd better put on me boots an' me silk stockin's before I go to set up in the parlor with him."[24]

Watching Mackenzie at work, we realize he was a natural ethnographer, one perhaps ahead of his time. His descriptions of singing take us deeper into the process than folklorists would plumb for decades. On one occasion, "Old Bob" Langille took a rest and his sister Maggie sang. Mackenzie is keenly aware that Bob continues to participate:

> This time it was Bob's turn to act the part of bystander and to evince a sympathetic interest in the progress of events. He became more and more wrought up as the heroine's fortunes darkened, and his excitement grew overpowering as the singer described poor Mary's grief when the perfidious William prepared to execute his master-stroke of villainy [i.e., tells her he's been digging her grave "the whole of last night"]. This was too much for human endurance. "The damn scoundrel!" roared Bob, "I wisht I hed him be the throat fer a minute or two!" Then, with a renewed sense of the pathos of the situation, "Ah, the pore guyrl! I can't keep the tears out o' me eyes when I think of her!"[25]

What Mackenzie is depicting, of course, is not only the depth of feeling with which singers and listeners regarded their songs but the fact that there is a communication system at work, in which listeners are as important to the process as the singers. He states the principle explicitly:

> It is only when a ballad is rendered by a singer of the old school in the presence of one or more listeners who have by chance survived with him that the full significance of ballad-singing can be realized. The total effect is infinitely greater than that suggested by the unanimated ballad which is transmitted to the printed page, or even by the words with the music. It is both of these plus the emotion of singer and listeners, an emotion manifested by the latter, something in ejaculatory comments, and sometimes in an unconscious or excited joining of forces with the singer in the rendition of a line or refrain.[26]

So sensitive is Mackenzie to audience–performer dynamics that he also knows when an element is absent, and shows how his informants are expert enough to compensate:

> If I had been a listener of the good old-fashioned sort I could not have sat gazing silently and impassively at the singer who [singing of a British victory at sea] was making this passionate appeal to my loyalty and manliness. This lack of the proper response in me put upon old Bob the constraint of piecing up my imperfections in himself, and, as he delivered the last word of the brave chorus, he opened his eyes, glared upon me with an access of patriotic fervor, and bellowed, "They never was afraid yit, me boy!"[27]

We have to admire the breadth of Mackenzie's inquiry and be grateful for what he thought was important to tell us. Easter Ann Langille sang him two ballads she'd learned from her father, George. How did she learn them? Mackenzie tells us. George was a vain man, proud of a fine mane of coal-black hair. As he grew older and gray hairs appeared among the black,

> He would summon his daughter to stand behind his chair and pluck out these pallid intruders, while in payment for the service he would sing these her two favourite old songs. The white hairs reappeared and the songs were repeated until, without any effort to acquire them for her own use, the daughter had unconsciously come to the point where she could sing them herself.[28]

That is ethnography!

Mackenzie is refreshingly aware of the difference between the *act* of collecting and *writing* about it. To keep *Quest* readable, he admits that he wrote it as if he had been the sole person in the field. In fact, he says, he often went out on his collecting jaunts with his wife Ethel or his cousin — for very practical reasons: each companion made the visits more "sociable" and rendered Mackenzie's figure as a lone male less threatening. Moreover, Mrs. Mackenzie helped him (this was an idea of Mackenzie's devising) by writing down alternate lines as the singers sang, cutting down on the number of repetitions required to complete the transcription. But it was awkward to write about his research companions, so he framed the telling around a single collector.[29]

Reading the two books, *Quest* and *Ballads*, one realizes how much is missing if songs and headnotes — the contents of *Ballads* — are the sole results of a collector's labor. Essential to scholarship as a collection like *Ballads* is, how much more vivid, how much more connected it is to human experience, with *Quest* as its companion. The photographs of informants are in *Quest*, not *Ballads*. And while there are no photographs of Mackenzie himself in either book, we get a few physical details.[30] He was thin ("she was much more concerned about some remedies for my lean and depleted appearance than about the pedantries of ballad-lore"), and he smoked a pipe ("The husband was further adding to the domesticity of the scene with a comforting pipe of Pictou twist, the most concentrated narcotic in existence; so, in order not to infringe on the harmony of the scene, I put my own pipe into operation before entering upon a discussion of the weather and the briefness of human existence").[31]

We also learn about Mackenzie the proud songcatcher. There's no hint in *Ballads*, for instance, that "Van Dieman's Land" was the first song he collected, but it's there in *Quest*:

> After a short period of studying . . . he closed his eyes, leaned back in his chair, and proceeded to rasp out in a very hoarse voice a ballad which I should like to present in full — partly because, as I learned subsequently, it once enjoyed a wide popularity in the community, and partly because it has in my eyes a large extrinsic interest as being the first ballad that I set to paper.[32]

Mackenzie writes about songs and singers with wonder and admiration, but *Quest* is tinged with a certain melancholy. For one thing, Mackenzie, ever the honest ethnographer, admits to how dispiriting it was making cold calls and being rebuffed. There were times, he says, he'd have been glad to let the project lapse had his wife not prodded him to continue. Another source of gloom was his feeling that he was on a hopeless salvage mission, a sense of witnessing the end of a once-vital tradition. Through the ravages of Protestant orthodoxy and the pace of modern life, the singing he'd loved since boyhood was on its way out, he felt, and the songs he was writing down would soon be heard no more. In fact, they had at least several decades more to go, but Mackenzie was not there to hear them. His two books marked the end of his involvement with folksong, except as a model to those who came after him. At the end of his career he retired to Nova Scotia, and when Helen Creighton visited him in the early 1950s, a few years before he died, she found he had kept none of his folksong field notes or transcriptions. For all intents and purposes, he had long since declared his folksong revels ended, burned his manuscripts, and embraced a new academic life that required he abandon the "low company" of folksong for the pursuit of Shakespeare and the lofty, well-tilled fields of English literature.

ELISABETH BRISTOL GREENLEAF

If anyone has found more magic in folk songs than Elisabeth Greenleaf, or gotten more of a kick out of collecting them, that person has not surfaced in eighty years. Greenleaf's letters home from Newfoundland (there were three trips) and every page of her published song collection are suffused with the light of her special, glowing presence. Greenleaf took delight in students, hosts, friends, acquaintances, strangers—everyone and everything she encountered during her Newfoundland enterprise. Nothing and no one, it seems, could staunch the flow of her enthusiasm; everywhere was the potential for enchantment, no experience was wasted. Was she going to have to spend ten days in a tiny community till the boat came to take her to her first posting? No problem: she went on outings with a local trapper and guide ("if he is a good sample, I am crazy about them"); trekked into the hills with a bird expert and learned to recognize the song of the Wilson snipe ("a hollow, woodwind sound, difficult to locate"); found lady-slipper and pitcher plants; watched a beaver "swim around, slap the water with his tail, gnaw off a plant and eat it and in general behave as if he were showing off to us."[33] Life was an adventure, life was a lark.

An interest in music and the world around her had been part of Greenleaf's life since childhood. Her father was a professor of biology (science was in her blood, one might say), and her schooling in New York

City (where she had been born in 1895) had included music: she could notate a melody as it was being played or sung. At Vassar College, she majored in both subjects. She studied the ballad as literature and attended a lecture by song collecting pioneer John Lomax. She loved to sing, and she played the university student's hot instrument of the day, the ukulele—she had arrived with one on her first trip to Newfoundland, to help occupy her spare time when her supply of novels ran out.

It was not song collecting that had brought Greenleaf to Newfoundland in 1920, but teaching. She had volunteered for duties at a summer school in the tiny west coast community of Sally's Cove. She taught children during the day and adult literacy classes in the evenings. But Newfoundland song found her—and her ears and heart were primed to listen. As proof, it could be mentioned that she collected a song on her journey even before she reached the island. It was a bird song! On the train to Sydney, Nova Scotia, she had befriended a group of ornithologists heading for the arctic. In Sydney, they invited her on a "bird hunting" trip. She wrote home: "The number and sweetness of the songs delights and excites me. While you are seeking the water-thrush, whose poised melody allures you, some other little warbler starts up right in your ear apparently, and you don't know which way to turn."[34] In her diary can be found the notes of the fox sparrow's song.[35]

Greenleaf's first encounter with Newfoundland song, sung by the boys outside her bedroom window (described at the beginning of this chapter) was rivalled in its powerful effect on her by another instance that same summer. After a long day's teaching she returned to her lodgings where her landlord, Uncle Dan Endacott, offered to sing her a song while she ate. It was a local ballad about two fishermen who survived twelve days in heavy seas before being rescued. Of the performance she wrote: "I sat stunned as the meaning of it all came over me. This man could neither read nor write. He was recounting the history of an event in the only way he could be sure of remembering it, and I felt like a Saxon princess to whom her minstrel sung a new lay of Beowulf."[36]

Greenleaf saw no disconnect between native Newfoundland ballads and their ancient antecedents: she instinctively recognized the continuity in form and function between old and new. This was to be the key factor in her collecting and publishing the broad range of Newfoundland song that came her way. In so doing, she validated the island's ongoing creative tradition—one of her great gifts and legacies as a song collector.

By the time Greenleaf left Newfoundland at the end of her first summer, she was deeply invested in the community: she went to dances, picnics, and weddings, played baseball, and wrote home excitedly that there might be a baby named for her![37] She was enamoured of the songs she heard, sung not just by Uncle Dan but by her students and their parents. She was not yet transcribing these in formal sessions, but she learned many that she heard. She was also flowering as an ethnographer:

she collected the riddles beloved of her pupils to use as a teaching aid, and wrote letters home that were essentially field notes:

> I must say a word about the manner in which the ballads are sung. In the first place, it is always conventional for the singer to offer excuses, but when he is finally persuaded he usually sits on the floor, clears his throat, spits energetically and sings leaning his head back on the wall, with his stubby pipe in his hand and his eyes closed. His voice rises with the action of the song, but suddenly he breaks off, opens his eyes and finishes the line in a speaking voice or mumble.[38]

At summer's end, Greenleaf was so enthralled by the songs and the singing she'd encountered that she went back to Vassar and told members of the staff about them. When she announced her intention to return and teach the next summer, they encouraged her to undertake some focused collecting. This she did: in Sally's Cove in 1921, she garnered some thirty songs, taken down in the time-honored fashion, in longhand as her informants repeated the song over and over. She also wrote out any melody lines she was able to absorb in the process, using her ukulele to confirm the notes.

She returned to New York, and life took a different turn. Miss Bristol became Mrs. Greenleaf and had a son, Robert. But in 1929, the lure of Newfoundland and its songs reasserted itself. Greenleaf arranged for funding from the Vassar Folklore Foundation and teamed up with a Vassar graduate musician ten years her junior, Grace Yarrow Mansfield, whose job it would be to transcribe the melodies they heard while Greenleaf wrote down the words. Playful as ever, Greenleaf dubbed their enterprise "the Vassar College folklore expedition to Newfoundland."[39]

From the beginning of July to the end of August, 1929, the two women voyaged around the island counterclockwise, from four to eight o'clock, as it were. They started in St. John's in the southeast and ended at the Port au Port Peninsula on the opposite, southwest coast. They travelled by steamer, calling in at Twillingate on the east coast, Fortune Harbour and Fleur de Lys on the north coast, then Flower's Cove on the other side of the Great Northern Peninsula. Every place they stayed, they made side trips to nearby communities and sought out the good singers. Often they had audiences of thirty or more family and community members crowding into kitchens to watch the collecting process. They collected some of their best songs on board the steamers from captains, crew members, and fellow passengers.

The collectors made a favorable impression wherever they went. Sometimes it was due to their high spirits, as when Mansfield jumped overboard and swam alongside the docked vessel, or to their enthusiasm to give as good as they got: Greenleaf induced or added momentum to singing sessions by trading songs with the Newfoundlanders, putting to use her repertoire from her college days or acquired ten years before in

Sally's Cove. (Back in 1921, she had had only her college songs to rely on. On one occasion, doing her best to come up with a long ballad-like song, she had sung Percy French's popular comical fight saga, "Abdul Abulbul Ameer," only to find that her listeners "viewed the situation as a tragedy and there were tears in eyes" as the duelling belligerents killed each other. They implored her for copies; it was a great lesson in Newfoundland song aesthetics.)[40]

The routine during their outport stays was to collect as many songs as they could before supper—fifteen on a good day—then spend from seven to eleven in the evening putting the songs together. Mansfield would sing the melodies from her on-the-spot transcriptions, and Greenleaf would suggest alternatives and corrections based on her memory of the performances. Mansfield did her best with the tunes, but sometimes found it tough going where singing styles were particularly ornamental or creative. Greenleaf described one instance in Fortune Harbour with typical good humor, as they tried to transcribe the singing of James Day in a kitchen "packed to capacity" with onlookers:

> Under the stimulus of the breathless appreciation, Mr. Day became a creator, treating words, tune, and time with lofty freedom. The listeners enjoyed themselves hugely, but upon the recorders descended a sense of inadequacy (reflected in their notes), as they heard a new phrase struck off fresh from the mint whenever they meekly asked for a repetition of some phrase missed in the excitement.[41]

One of Greenleaf's letters home provides a sense of how sensitized she was during the collecting, how aware of her relationship with her informants. On a steamer, the two women had a session with Manuel Roberts, one of the crew:

> Capt. Gullage and several of the officers were sitting with us ... and watching us write down the words and music. People liked to see my pencil scoot across the note-book, while Grace's ability to write down the music seemed to them almost miraculous. "Look well, b'ys," said a man once, "for you never seed anything to equal it. Them scratches is the h'air."[42]

When Roberts had finished, he asked Greenleaf to sing a song she had learned ten years before in Sally's Cove, about a daring rescue of passengers by improvised rope tow from the *S. S. Ethie*, which the crew had purposely run aground to keep it from sinking during a winter storm. As she began to sing, Greenleaf realized that the captain of her steamer, sitting right there, and some of his men, had actually been on the *Ethie*:

> Capt. Gullage was her first mate then and held the wheel while they ran her ashore and several others of the officers and crew had also been through the wreck, displaying in the highest degree the Newfoundland virtues of steadfast calm courage and resource in time of danger.... So

> I had one of the great thrills of the trip singing this story with its chief heroes listening.[43]

In a moving way, she quotes lines from the song and intersperses her observations of the men and their comments as they listened. A tape recorder could not have made it more vivid. She was clearly very affected by the experience:

The glass indicated a wild raging storm
And about nine o'clock the storm did come on—
(Slow but emphatic nods from the officers.)
And the great waves all round her like mountains did rise
And the crew all stood staring with fear in their eyes—
("Indeed yes—not one of us expected to see the sun rise again"—this from Capt. Gullage.)
Walter Young been our purser, as you may understand
Volunteered for to guide her safely into the land
(All eyes turned to Mr. Young quietly sitting in a corner. He is a thickset, kindly man. Only an occasional expression in his steady gray eyes indicates his nerve and ability.)
And the people on the shore saw the ship in distress
And rushed to the spot for to help do their best.
And then we were landed in a rude bo'sun's chair
(Capt. Gullage tied the knots which held every person secure. His hands were swollen like thole-pins in the cold, so he could hardly move the fingers, but every knot held.)

> "'Tis a good song," said Manuel, "and you sing it grand," he added politely. But I was thinking the thrill of the occasion was in the presence of those quiet, unboastful men, whose attitude toward the events of that night seems to be merely deep gratitude to God.[44]

Harvard University Press published Greenleaf and Mansfield's collection *Ballads and Sea Songs of Newfoundland* in 1933.[45] There are 189 numbered entries—ballads, songs, dance tunes, fragments, including materials Greenleaf had transcribed on her second Newfoundland trip. The tunes to some ninety-one of the songs also appear, and not at the back (as in Mackenzie's collection), but on the same page as their texts, a structure that Greenleaf had to fight for by threatening to take the manuscript to Yale.[46] The dance tunes (which *are* at the end of the book) are a bonus unheard of in song collections of the time. The texts are true to what had been taken down in the field: no interpolations or corrections, and dialects intact. The work joined the canon of North American folksong collections, along with Mackenzie's before it, to be cited in Laws and every major collection since.

Greenleaf continued to teach and write, but like Mackenzie, she never published on folksong after her major work was done. She died in 1980. Copies of her letters and journals are in Memorial University's Folklore and Language Archives. But anyone who spends time with *Ballads and*

Sea Songs of Newfoundland will encounter, more than in any song collection before or since (other than perhaps the oeuvre of Ozark folklorist Vance Randolph), a collector enjoying contact with a tradition she clearly respects, practiced by people she clearly loves. About "The Fishermen of Newfoundland," she wrote, "This is the first song Uncle Dan Endacott sang me, and as such will always hold a unique place in my affections. In the line, 'Snatched from the jaws of death,' Uncle Dan, like so many Newfoundlanders, pronounced the last word as if it were 'debt.' I always listened for it with private joy." [47]

Such notes reflect a lively listener and an appreciative observer, and—I don't know how else to convey this—it is clear in various places that we are reading the remarks of a sparkling, intelligent woman who has spent long hours of appreciative scholarly attention on Newfoundland males and male culture: "It was truly a pleasure to watch [Sam Roberts] dance. He had beautiful muscular control, and a great variety of steps, and grace, rhythm, and life in every movement." [48]

Greenleaf's eye—what she notices—is patently female, and her written voice that of a loving daughter, niece, or woman friend. Of "The Ghostly Lover," she wrote, "The tune expresses grief, resignation, and passion, just as the lines do, and from my experience with Newfoundlanders, I should say the song represents quite accurately the attitude of the women toward the loss of their men." [49]

Greenleaf's being a woman worked for her in the field in various ways, and her generous intellect and spirit kept what she wrote about women and men light and non-polemical. So while she was able to draw information from her female informants that a male collector might not, she maintained an amicable balance in representing the two sexes: "Aunt Fanny Jane Endacott thought this word ['beauty' in the line, 'For beauty's a flower that reigns o'er us all'] should be duty, but I am afraid the men won't agree with her." [50]

That said, every so often one comes upon Greenleaf-the-graduate-of-Vassar in which the sensibility of women is the norm. The view of the world so constructed comes across occasionally as a political one. In her summary of the plot of "Lord Ateman," a version of Child 53, she tells how the Turkish lady, after saving Lord Ateman's life and receiving his promise of marriage, goes to the lord's castle years later when he is about to marry another. What happens next in the ballad is that the lord relents and is true to his word. But the way Greenleaf puts it is: "*To the glory and honor of men*, Lord Ateman at once welcomes the Turkish lady and sends the other lady home" [51] (my italics).

In this regard, Greenleaf's choice of a final song in the book, appearing just before the "Dance Tunes" section, is perhaps a telling one: it is "Women's the Joy and the Pride of the Land," a fulsome paean to the joys of marriage and the woman's role, taken down from the singing of Thomas Endacott, Sally's Cove, on the 1929 voyage:

No pleasure is found in a lifetime of roving;
Young man, take a partner and join hand in hand;
Believe me, there's nothing can equal a woman,
For women's the joy and the pride of the land.[52]

It has no commentary other than its privileged place in the book, the last song sung before the dancing begins.

MAUD KARPELES

In the world of Newfoundland folksong, Maud Karpeles will likely be forever linked with Elisabeth Greenleaf—and doomed to stand in her shadow. Greenleaf, every folklore graduate student learns, found the sunshine in Newfoundland; Karpeles, the fog, the cold, and the rain. Decades later, Karpeles's island enterprise is seen less as a courageous, one-woman project that produced a major published collection of British ballads in Newfoundland, than as a stark lesson in how not to conduct fieldwork.[53] One has to work hard not to view Karpeles and the vivacious Greenleaf through the same lens, let alone assign them relative merit. Both were foreign women who came to the island to collect folk songs; one year their visits were actually within two months of each other (they never actually met). Both also wrote vividly about their experiences in their books, diaries, and letters home.

But linking the two does Karpeles no favours and is in many ways unfair. She was a different person than Greenleaf: nine years older (forty-three in 1929), of a more serious frame of mind and outlook, and on a song-finding mission that reflected a personal quest, not to mention a scholarly paradigm quite different from Greenleaf's. Moreover, where Greenleaf seemed to sparkle whatever happened in the field, Karpeles was the opposite—dismayed by the physical conditions, stymied by delayed trains and steamers, put off by the Vassar expedition itself, and repeatedly disappointed by informants who could not offer her the kind of song she had come to find. She was frank about it in her notebooks, and reading them creates the impression of a certain bitterness and rigidity in the writer.

But Karpeles's daily trials masked the overall success of her enterprise, even to her: at the end of each of her two trips (in the fall of 1929 and the summer of 1930), she was pleasantly surprised with the size and quality of her harvest. And where no one song recovered by Greenleaf ever entered the national, let alone international, canon of English folksong, one of Karpeles's—"She's Like the Swallow"—did. (Perhaps it was a matter of having friends in high musical places, as English composer Ralph Vaughan Williams, who arranged and promoted the song, clearly was—but the fact is Karpeles brought back a gem that caught his ear.)

Maud Karpeles was born in London in 1886, the daughter of a Jewish businessman (her religious background was a significant factor in her career during the 1930s).[54] At age twenty, she was sent to study piano in Berlin. Within a few years, she was teaching dance to children in Canning Town, East London. The English folksong and dance revival was on the rise, led by music educator Cecil Sharp, who was combing the countryside for local forms of dance, writing them down, teaching them in schools, and judging their performance in competitions. In May of 1909, Maud and her sister Helen watched Sharp in action at the Shakespeare Festival in Stratford. They were enchanted both by the dancing and the man. The following September, they attended Sharp's Morris dance classes in the Chelsea Polytechnic Institute. They quickly formed a folk dance club of fellow enthusiasts, mostly young women. Under Sharp's supervision, they gave public performances and began to train other dancers as well. In 1911, the sisters were instrumental in planning and organizing the establishment by Sharp of the English Folk Dance Society "to preserve and promote the practice of English folk-dances in their true traditional form."[55] Helen was made Honorary Secretary, and in 1912, Maud became Sharp's personal aide and secretary. The pair's names, work, and lives would be entwined thereafter.

To understand Karpeles as a solo collector in Newfoundland, one must know about Sharp in North America. The outbreak of World War I put the folk dance society's activities on hold, and Sharp accepted an offer to work on a New York theatre production. When it was done, he stayed on and virtually relocated his English folk dance activities to the United States. He established an American branch of the society, taught folk dance courses and organized folk pageants in cities and colleges in the northeast and Midwest. In chronic poor health, he brought Karpeles across the Atlantic to help him.

Among the many Americans inspired by Sharp's work was a Mrs. Olive Dame Campbell, who brought Sharp a sample of songs she had collected while teaching in the Appalachians. Sharp was intrigued by the existence in that backwoods setting of old versions of British traditional songs and ballads unknown at home. In late July of 1916, he took Karpeles for a collecting expedition to North Carolina to look for more. Her job was to write down the words while he tackled the tunes. They found the travel difficult but the locals welcoming and their repertoire up to expectations: in just over two months, the two collectors documented some four hundred song variants. The next year, Sharp and Karpeles spent nineteen weeks in Kentucky, Tennessee, and North Carolina, and nearly as long in Virginia in 1918. Their harvest was extremely rich—in all, some 1,500 tunes.

Sharp then cast his eye on Newfoundland. He assumed that, as in the Appalachians or even more so, the island would be a well-stocked storehouse of old English song. A hoped-for trip never materialized: he could not get funding, and in any case, the war ended and he and Karpeles returned home to resuscitate the folk dance society. Sharp resumed his activities with the same vigour and dedication as ever—teaching, lecturing, and collecting in the countryside—with Maud at his side. He did not forget Newfoundland and made plans to go, but his health was failing. Sharp died in 1924.

Karpeles was devastated. She wrote that she felt she had been left "groping in a sunless world . . . very lonely and helpless."[56] For the next five years, she threw herself into her work, promoting the society, raising funds for its headquarters ("Cecil Sharp House"), and doing desultory collecting on her own—Morris dances in Worcestershire, sword dances in the north, mumming and country dance tunes in Gloucestershire and Devon, country dances in Northumberland.

In 1929, Karpeles accepted an invitation to direct a folk music summer school in Massachusetts and in the fall to tour the country with a dance team. She had two months to spare between the two, and decided to spend them collecting in Newfoundland. She did so out of a sense of obligation to Sharp, as part of a promise she had made to him, shortly before he died, to carry on his work. It was up to her to save whatever was left of the British traditional repertoire in Newfoundland before it was lost.

There was also a sense in which Karpeles saw Newfoundland as something of a proving ground for herself. She had always worked with her old mentor. Her solo ventures into the field during the years since his death had given her a chance to work up her notational skills and her overall confidence as a lone field-worker. When she landed in St. John's on 9 September 1929, she was both determined and full of trepidation.[57] Karpeles travelled for seven weeks and visited some forty villages, mostly on the east coast, with a quick sojourn to the north (including Fortune Harbour, where Greenleaf and Mansfield had been two months before); she noted songs from 104 singers. She returned the following summer and spent the same number of weeks, this time visiting communities on the south coast. In all, she noted 191 versions of ninety-one songs.

Karpeles's field diaries and letters home offer frank assessments of pretty much everything she encountered. Her judgments can be withering: the "wonderful sense of humour" and "good eye for the ridiculous" cherished in her by others either fails her or does not come across.[58] Read today, her letters and diaries make her seem crabby and pinched, "St. John's is quite the shabbiest town I have ever seen. It is really rather pathetic, especially as they are all so proud of it."[59]

Reading between the lines can make it worse. Even a rare rave about the surroundings is marred by the subsequent picture of a relatively wealthy, foreign woman thoughtlessly taking working people away from their subsistence living so they can sing her songs they may not have or that she may not want:

> Island Cove entrancingly beautiful, the view of Conception Bay from the hill just took my breath away.... People all out in their "gardens" digging potatoes. Most friendly people.... Aunt Salina Combs, an old lady of 90 ... was hard at work digging potatoes. After some persuasion she consented to come back to her cottage, and started off by jumping over the stone wall as nimbly as a young girl. I got no songs from her but Aunt Sally gave me some. They did not stay long because in a hurry to get back to their potatoes.[60]

In some ways, her collecting experience mirrored that of Greenleaf and Mansfield, but one comes to expect that anything positive in her description must share space with the negative, "Called on Joanie Ryan ... Got her to sing and with utmost difficulty took down tune and words. The room gradually filled with men, women and children, and before I had finished there must have been about a dozen people there—all highly interested and entertained."[61]

Karpeles's experience in Appalachia had not prepared her for Newfoundland, and her song paradigm—what she believed was worthwhile to write down—was too narrow to do justice to the island's song traditions. Instead of the relatively isolated, geographically circumscribed, and musically conservative singers of Appalachia, Karpeles encountered a sea-going people in close touch with the Mother Country (Newfoundland was then a colony of England) and their maritime neighbours in "the Boston states." The island's culture was alive to every musical genre and song entertainment the modern English-speaking world offered. More important, it was home to a creative musical tradition that produced songs about the lives and experiences of Newfoundlanders. These songs were widely known, much loved, and not perceived to be different from or inferior to the songs that had come over from Britain and been sung in the fishing villages for generations—the ones Karpeles had come to find.

To Karpeles, these songs—popular ballads, sentimental ditties, and the glory of the Newfoundland song making tradition: accounts of wrecks and fishing disasters—were interference to a very weak signal of worth and beauty that she was tracking. She felt quite justified in passing on them:

> The proportion of authentic folk songs is small compared with the general repertory. In addition to the composed songs of an earlier generation, songs are constantly being made up about contemporary events such as exploits at sea, shipwrecks, etc. These are often set to a well-known "Come-all-ye" type of tune. They usually have but little aesthetic value and since my interest lay in songs that represent an older tradition I did not note any of them.[62]

Her disappointment is palpable. Her notebooks are full of references to her rejections of what was offered by singers: "Saw several people ... but no songs, at least none that I want."[63] "Joe White most obligingly sang me song after song, but none any use. A few folk-songs among them, but he has no tunes: has evidently been affected by his sister's organ accompaniments."[64] "A dismal evening listening to jazz and sentimental drawing room ballads."[65] "The songs have all gone from Trepassey."[66]

These are words to make many modern folklorists want to shake her. They are annoying because not only was Karpeles turning down what would be wonderfully valuable material today; but her field experience was so clearly the cause, for no reason we can now approve, of mutual frustration—for Karpeles, who sensed her time was running out and that she was making little headway, even though (to modern eyes) the good stuff was all around her; and for her hosts, who liked her and tried to please her, but could not: "Evidently a lot of songs about, but they have got covered up by the new songs and most people have to dig into their memories to recall them. I am creating a great impression by the number of songs I 'know,' i.e. those I don't want."[67]

It might be said that in terms of its duration and public visibility, Maud Karpeles's time in Newfoundland was a minor part of her career. She was already something of a star in the first English folksong revival when she arrived on the island, and after returning home she led a long life (she died in 1976) studying and promoting folksong, in which Newfoundland figured relatively little. The initial publication of her island materials in 1934 was just thirty songs, including "She's Like the Swallow," in a two-volume songbook, each song with piano accompaniment. A major publication from the oeuvre didn't occur for nearly forty years: *Folk Songs from Newfoundland*, containing eighty-nine songs, appeared in 1970, the same year she travelled once more to Newfoundland, this time to accept an honorary doctorate from Memorial University.[68]

But Karpeles's Newfoundland experience resonated throughout the rest of her life. Her diaries were not the whole story, nor the end of it. She had written, "It would be impossible to find a kindlier or friendlier people than the Newfoundlanders."[69] She made close friends among her informants and intermediaries (teachers and other contacts who were her entry into the communities). She kept in touch with some over the years, and tried to contact several when she returned in 1970, at the age of eighty-four, for her honorary degree. And she would always be the collector of "She's Like the Swallow."

Where her voyages to the island had a wider impact was in the self confidence Karpeles had gained by undertaking them at all and carrying them to a successful conclusion. She had demonstrated her loyalty to Sharp by pursuing his dream alone in a strange land and under the most trying conditions; she had held true to the ideals he had set forth and come back with the goods. In some ways, her Newfoundland experience may have laid the foundation for her subsequent work—the publication of *English Folk Songs from the Southern Appalachians* plus a major biography of Sharp, administration of the English Folk Dance and Song Society, and later, formation of the International Folk Music Council.[70]

For the comparison between Karpeles and Greenleaf to be complete, this one additional difference must be cited: unlike Greenleaf, Karpeles's life was folk dance and song, and Newfoundland did not culminate it, but invigorated it, and propelled it forward.

HELEN CREIGHTON

If (and it's a big "if") the average English-speaking Canadian is able to identify one folklorist, Canadian or otherwise, it is likely Helen Creighton. Creighton's reputation is partly due to the unrivalled number of items she collected in her lifetime—more than four thousand songs, mostly in English but also in French, Gaelic, Micmac, German, and Dutch, plus shipwreck and pirates' treasure tales, ghost stories, legends, superstitions, and folk cures. It is also a product of her longevity. Creighton began collecting in 1928, published her first book of songs in 1932 (there would eventually be some dozen folklore books in all), and continued to produce for more than fifty years—long enough to capture folklore materials in every medium from pen on paper to Dictaphone, acetate disks, audio tape, film, broadcast microphone, and television camera.[71]

Creighton was the first of the major pre-1940 song collectors in English Canada—really the only one—to make her livelihood as a popular folklorist. She collected traditional materials in more or less traditional settings from more or less traditional informants, then used the materials as the basis of a publishing, lecturing, and broadcasting career aimed at the general public. Early on, she was conscious of the dearth of English Canadian folk materials on radio, in films, in books: what there was came from the United States and Great Britain. Creighton's highly focused drive to collect folklore materials and place them before the public was informed by this central fact. It probably lay at the heart of her success as a "folklore entrepreneur."[72]

That success did not take place overnight nor without many setbacks and disappointments. Creighton was not robust: she had recurring bouts of nervous exhaustion when she could do nothing but rest. It also fell to her, since she was unmarried and living at home, to take responsibility for the care of her aging parents. In addition, it wasn't until at least two and a half decades after she started working that a nexus of media interest and public acceptance made it possible to carve a career out of folklore. Despite these hurdles, Creighton eventually made her mark, not only with the publicly appealing quality of her product (not to mention its sheer volume), but by dint of tireless networking and self promotion, vigilant protection of her turf and informants, and constant grooming of her reputation as the authority in her area.

She also had extraordinary luck. Creighton lived through an era when oral arts practiced in, say, fishermen's kitchens, changed from being insider lore that was ignored or disparaged by outsiders, to that of a valued body of materials popularly regarded as Our Heritage. This transformation was particularly visible in Canada's Maritime provinces beginning in the 1980s, when regional pride movements arose, relying heavily on the promotion of local culture. Pioneers such as Creighton who had collected and published heritage materials were honored as its preservers. (It may fairly be said that Creighton had a hand in bringing about and shaping this change—her selection and presentation of folk materials helped paint a rosy picture of a romantic folklore past that was highly attractive to mainstream North America in the second half of the twentieth century; it remains part of the popular concept of folklore today.)[73]

By the time Creighton died in 1989, at the age of ninety, she was a Maritimes celebrity and a national institution, "Canada's First Lady of Folklore."[74] The materials she had collected were standard issue in school textbooks and on long playing records, and a Halifax folk festival was established in her honor. In Nova Scotia, she was revered as the collector of the song considered the province's unofficial anthem, "The Nova Scotia Song," better known (ironically) from the first words of its chorus, "Farewell to Nova Scotia."

Other than that song, Creighton became her own best-known product, featured in magazine articles, documentary films, and television specials. The shift in public attention from the materials Creighton had collected to the collector herself can be traced in the titles over the years of Canadian classical and popular compositions based on her collections: 1953—*The Broken Ring* (opera); 1958—*Sea Gallows* (ballet); 1970—*Two Maritime Aquarelles*; 1977—*Maritime Folk Song Medley*; 1980—*The Collector* (a musical about her); 1987—*Tribute to Helen Creighton*; 1991—*Homage to Helen*.

Creighton was something of a controversial figure among her fellow folklorists. Many academics regarded her as a "popularizer" who compromised the materials she published and presented them with inadequate contextual information and no analysis.[75] She also had little interest in the role perceived by many at the time of folksong in promoting social justice: to her, folksong was comforting evidence of social order, not an instrument for overthrowing it.[76] On the other hand, her popularity was recognized as good for the discipline: she was endorsed by folk arts professionals—archivists, festival organizers, museum and library staff, grants officers—whose activities depended on the public's esteem for heritage materials. The Rockefeller Foundation and the Canada Council gave her grants, and she enjoyed the support of institutions such as the Archive of American Folk Song at the Library of Congress (Alan Lomax was a particular champion) and the National Museum of Canada (now the Canadian Museum of Civilization) where Marius Barbeau and Carmen Roy sponsored her work for many years. Revival singers from the 1950s to the present day ransacked her books and recordings for material and made her a patron saint.

The foundation for Creighton's career was laid by 1940. She was born in Dartmouth, Nova Scotia, across the harbor from Halifax in 1899, the youngest of six children. Her father was a food broker and the family, while not among the wealthiest in the city, was well enough placed that throughout her life Creighton could call on members of the highest echelons of society for endorsement and recommendations. However, she was expected by her family to make her own way, so while her father paid for her education, she spent her twenties searching for a vocation that would make her financially independent and justify his "investment."

Her career path was full of twists and turns, most of them dead ends in social service: driver for a Red Cross rural outreach program, social work training in Toronto, client screening in a home for unwed mothers, teaching at an American school in Mexico. It was during the last of these that she started writing articles and sending them off to magazines and newspapers back home. *Maclean's* published an item on bullfighting, and Creighton was launched as a freelance journalist. She returned to Dartmouth in 1925 and, along with writing articles and verse, she became "Aunt Helen" on a local radio station and read her own children's stories.

In 1926 she moved to Ottawa and published pieces in the prestigious publication *Saturday Night*, mostly on Nova Scotia subjects. Since what was exotically "Maritimes" seemed to sell, she returned home after a year to find new local material. In 1928, she went to see Henry Monroe, the province's superintendent for education, and asked for advice. Monroe was a local song buff and showed her a copy of an exciting new publication, W. Roy Mackenzie's *Ballads and Sea Songs of Nova Scotia*.[77] He suggested to Creighton that she do what Mackenzie had done: "If you could find only one ballad," he said, "your fortune would be made."[78] He gave her the book to study.

A few days later, Creighton and some friends picnicked on a beach near her home and encountered a local man, Mike Matthews. Creighton, in freelance mode, asked if there was buried treasure about. Matthews told her there were old people living nearby who talked about such things and who could "tell you stories and sing you songs as well." "What kind of songs?" she asked. "Pirate songs." "Well," wrote Creighton later in her autobiography, "if the stories were too incredible, I could write about men who still sang pirate songs."[79] Matthews gave her names and directions to a point at "the end of the land," and Creighton wrote, "A great new door had been opened and . . . the Eastern Passage road had become my path of destiny."[80]

Over the next months, Creighton met singers and wrote down their songs. She was working within ten miles of where she lived, so many recognized her as "Aunt Helen" of radio fame—a useful means of entrée.

"My folk singers," as she came to refer to them, were farmer-fisher folk. They included Mrs. Thomas Osborne, Enos Hartlan, and her big find, Ben Henneberry, who lived on Devil's Island at the mouth of Halifax Harbour. So large was Henneberry's repertoire (he eventually gave her ninety songs, including one with seventy-eight verses), Creighton arranged to board with an island family so she could visit with him every day. She had him sing in the morning as he mended nets in his shed, then again every evening after supper in his kitchen. Their evening sessions were often attended by his family and by neighbors. Other singers dropped by her lodgings and sang for her and her hosts far into the night. She collected one hundred songs in a single week. Devil's Island was, in one of her favorite and oft-used phrases, a "gold mine."

Creighton worked in the time-honored way, writing down the words as the singers performed. Once that was done, she worked out the tunes on a melodeon she wheeled from place to place on a hand barrow; the singers and anyone else who was present helped. She learned that, with her limited expertise, her music transcription had better be a collaborative process: early on she played her worked out version of the tune for "The Turkish Lady" to Enos Hartlan who had sung it for her, then asked if he liked it: "Yes," he replied with complete honesty, "it's a fine tune, a fine tune, but it's not 'The Turkish Lady.'"[81] As soon as she could, Creighton switched to electric recording media and the result was a dramatic increase in product: "I wondered if a Dictaphone might help, and tried one out on the Hartlans where I got twenty-six songs at a sitting that might have yielded six before."[82]

By 1931, Creighton had a "sizeable collection" of songs.[83] Her first sale of material was six "pirate songs" at ten dollars apiece to J. Murray Gibbon, publicity agent for the Canadian Pacific Railway, who was promoting travel by organizing folk festivals around the country.[84] The issue of informants' copyright or performance ownership was not addressed by Creighton on this occasion or at any time during a lifetime of putting out popular products based on informants' materials. "Her" singers, she felt, were custodians of a heritage that belonged to all, and they had offered her the songs out of friendship and a shared sense of their importance. Whatever income she derived paid not for the songs she felt, but for the long hours she had spent and the expenses she had borne in collecting them.[85]

Three years into her project, Creighton had many songs on paper but little confidence in dealing with them for publication. She applied to experts for help. In a lucky train of events, her membership in the Canadian Authors Association led her to ballad scholar John Robins, a professor of English at Victoria College, University of Toronto. He made available a workroom at the college and his own reference library, and coached her in writing headnotes. Likewise, the songs' music was put in order by three stars of the contemporary Toronto music scene: Healey Willan, Campbell McInnes, and Ernest (later Sir Ernest) MacMillan.

The upshot was acceptance of the manuscript by a major Toronto publisher and an attractive and accessible book, *Songs and Ballads from Nova Scotia*.[86] (The title was grander perhaps than was warranted, since most of the songs came from the Dartmouth area; then again, Mackenzie had done the same with the songs from the environs of River John.) Reviews were positive, and Henry Monroe, who had set Creighton on her folk song collecting path four years before, bought 250 copies for Nova Scotia schools.

In the summer of 1932, Creighton met Doreen Senior, a visiting English Folk Dance and Song Society instructor hired by a local summer school. Senior eagerly accepted Creighton's invitation to accompany her on her collecting trips and take charge of transcribing the tunes. Senior helped shape Creighton's developing ideas about what a folk song was — very much in the Cecil Sharp mode. It was therefore fortunate that they even bothered to collect the now famous "Farewell to Nova Scotia," since "we didn't realize anything locally composed could have that much value, and anyhow Doreen didn't consider it a folk song."[87]

The picture Creighton draws of collecting this particular song is an informative one. Creighton frequently mentions picnic lunches eaten during her collecting trips. She brought food for two reasons: first, she preferred not to impose on new informants who would be courtesy-bound to feed her. And second, her sanitation standards made her reluctant to accept some individuals' hospitality (she writes of "fine day" houses, meaning those with questionable cleanliness she would save to collect from in good weather, so at lunchtime she could picnic outside).[88] On this particular occasion, she and Senior had just spent the day with two informants and eaten two picnic meals, the second — Nova Scotia weather being what it is — in the rain. They entered the home of Mrs. Dennis Greenough, a new informant, soaking wet. "Why didn't you use our kitchen?" was Mrs. Greenough's hospitable question.[89] At her invitation, the two researchers sat on chairs with feet in the oven to dry their socks and warm their toes. In that position, they took down words and music as Mrs. Greenough sang through her songs.[90] Perhaps with one's feet in one's host's oven, one cannot graciously turn down any song the host chooses to sing, even if it is local.

For the rest of the 1930s, Creighton tried to establish herself professionally and financially. Sales of her book languished, but she continued collecting, financed largely by her parents. She started to take down tales and beliefs as well as song lyrics, and kept lists of informants to return to with Senior during the summer. In 1937, she tried to get the Associated Screen News interested in making a feature about her work, "the survival of the songs through [the singers], and the use to which songs can be put in the present day" — meaning, for the film, their performance "by a glee club group at the apple blossom festival at Kentville, or in a selected school group."[91]

A major breakthrough occurred the same year when she accepted an offer to give a lecture-concert series in New York, with local singers performing songs from her collection. It was an artistic, if not a financial, success, and it led to an innovative series of lecture-concerts on national CBC radio, hosted by Creighton, in 1938. The series ran for two years. The twenty programs were broadcast live from Halifax and featured some of her informants—the first time traditional singers appeared on national Canadian radio. Covering all tastes, however, Creighton had professional singers begin and end the show with other songs she had collected. These were evidently greeted with dismay by the original informants listening at home. Friends and family by the radio with them demanded they perform the song after the broadcast and do it "right."[92]

By the end of the decade, Creighton still was not making much money, but her name was getting around as the person to go to in the area for her sort of material. A dialect researcher came to record her informants' speech; two New York stage entertainers arranged to meet one of her singers for material and inspiration. When they photographed Dennis Smith and his wife, she was wearing a long cotton dress and boots, dust cap, and a shawl, and he a brown waistcoat. The entertainers returned to New York and sang their songs in similar clothing.

The summer of 1939 was the last Creighton partnered in the field with Doreen Senior, who returned to England just before the war. They had collected a considerable number of songs over some five summers. That fall, Creighton accepted an offer from University of King's College in Halifax to act as its dean of women. She spent the first two years of the war in that role.

The departure of Senior and the arrival of Creighton's first steady job (she would leave the college at the end of 1941) marked the end of an early stage in Creighton's career as a folklorist. The final curtain fell with the appearance in 1940 of *Twelve Folk Songs from Nova Scotia*.[93] This was a selection of items collected by her and Senior, published in England, edited by Senior. It was very much a publication in the tradition of Sharp and Vaughan Williams, a soft cover folio of songs arranged for piano by Senior. Senior kept an introduction by Creighton intact, but omitted the headnotes for the individual songs which, Creighton felt later, ruined the book. The difficulties of transatlantic collaboration in wartime were blamed. (Creighton published the major part of their joint collection in Canada nine years later under the title *Traditional Songs from Nova Scotia*; again, both names were on the cover, but to her collaborator's dismay, Creighton did not solicit her approval on the rendering of the music.)[94]

In 1940, the great triumphs of Creighton's career still lay ahead of her: her training was incomplete, her publishing had just begun, and her broadcast work was still in its infancy. But in her first dozen years as a folklorist she had marked her territory, found the greatest of her folk song informants, established her methodology, and tasted the first fruits of public recognition for her efforts.

And she was ready to meet other folklorists—as she did at the Indiana University Folklore Institute in 1942—as a veteran field researcher, published author, and folklore broadcaster, a song collector in the tradition of Mackenzie and Sharp. At the Institute, Creighton traded field stories and talked about some of her methods. One of her favorites was to prime a singer who was not coming up with the "right type of song" by asking, "Do you know the one about the milk white steed?"[95] (This question had once prompted a man to reply, "No, but I know one about a little page boy," whereupon he sang a twenty-seven-verse ballad.)[96] Alan Lomax, she reports, found it "very funny" to think of her "approaching a burly fisherman" and asking about milk white steeds.[97] Creighton maintained that if *that* failed, she had "learned to ask if they know one with broadswords in it, or one that began, 'As I walked out one May morning.'"[98] Lomax offered her the use of a Library of Congress recording machine.

AFTERWORD: LINES OF CONNECTION

McKay wrote in his introduction to *Quest of the Ballad* that, for practical reasons as a writer, he would describe his experiences in the rest of the book as if he had been on his own, rather than with his wife or cousin as had often been the case.[99] Similarly, I have left it to the end to say that there are one or two interesting lines of connection between Mackenzie, Greenleaf, Karpeles, and Creighton that extend in some cases beyond 1940 which add some extra dimension to what might otherwise be mistakenly regarded as separate stories.

First, there is a line of classic ballad scholarship—drawn in the United States from Child and Kittredge through to Mackenzie and Greenleaf (Kittredge had taught one of them, and published both collectors' volumes), and in England from Sharp through to Karpeles. Both lines later meet, via Mackenzie, on one side of the Atlantic and via Doreen Senior on the other side of the Atlantic, in Creighton. But this is too abstract: the fact is, the collectors were more or less aware of each other's work, and some came into actual contact. The world of early twentieth-century song collecting was too small for it to be otherwise.

Mackenzie's books had influenced Creighton, of course—they had pushed her into her career and given her early standards to emulate—and she made a point of meeting him in the early 1950s, after he had retired to Nova Scotia. The two even paid a little visit to Mackenzie's last living informant, an old woman who had sung for him as a little girl.[100]

Greenleaf too had been influenced by Mackenzie's work and was in touch with him in the early 1930s—enough to share a little joke about

Kittredge. Greenleaf disapproved of the way Kittredge had tacked the tunes on to the end of Mackenzie's book, and in a conversation with Mackenzie, asked: "'Tell me, Professor Mackenzie, can Kittredge carry a tune?' to which Mackenzie gave a telling reply, 'If he has a very large basket!'"[101]

Greenleaf made sure that her book did not meet the same fate as Mackenzie's: she insisted to the president of Vassar College, who insisted to Kittredge, that the words and music appear on the same pages—one of the first scholarly folksong books that did so.[102]

Karpeles and Greenleaf were famously too close in their Newfoundland experience for Karpeles's comfort. The Englishwoman had felt "depressed and helpless" during her first trip to Newfoundland on hearing that: "I've been forestalled by 2 American women who spent three months here this summer and took down hundreds of songs. One is a Mrs. Greenleaf from New York."[103] But Karpeles subsequently published a favorable review[104] of Greenleaf and Mansfield's collection: it contained "very, very good stuff," she said, and an excellent introduction.[105] On the other hand, she pointed out that the book featured "many popular songs which are not folksongs," and that "no attempt was made to at least put them in a different category"—no surprise there.[106]

What is less well known is the connection between Karpeles and Creighton. When Creighton was preparing her first collection for publication in 1931, she appealed to Karpeles for direction—like her, a woman and an independent researcher, but well established in the field. Karpeles generously wrote back, "Keep in touch with what you are doing, and if you ever find that the field of research is bigger than you can tackle, let me know, and I will try to come along and do what I can."[107] The two women developed a long distance friendship. During World War II and into the 1950s, when Britain was still rationing food, Creighton sent Karpeles care packages. In 1959, the two women met for the first time and attended an international folk tale conference together.[108] Later, Karpeles wrote a warm letter of congratulation to Creighton on the publication of *A Life in Folklore*, which said, "You are a wonder and I am filled with admiration."[109]

NOTES

1. Isabelle Peere, "Elisabeth Greenleaf: An Appraisal," in *Canadian Folk Music Journal* 13 (1985): 20–31, 24.

2. There were, of course, other collectors of song in Newfoundland and Maritimes Canada whose relatively small collections belie their significance to the field. See Arthur Huff Fauset, *Folklore from Nova Scotia* (New York: American Folk-Lore Society, 1931), and Neil V. Rosenberg, "The Gerald S. Doyle Songsters and the Politics of Newfoundland Folksong," in *Canadian Folklore canadien* 13:1 (1991): 45–57.

3. For more on social interaction and song, see Sheldon Posen, "Coaxing" in Pauleena MacDougall and David Taylor, *Northeast Folklore: Essays in Honor of Edward D. Ives* (Orono, ME: The University of Maine Press and The Maine Folklife Center, 2000), 137–152.

4. It is disconcerting for the modern reader to encounter in these collections, as he or she frequently does, the word "recorded" meaning, "taken down on paper." There is always a small frisson of excitement, followed by a letdown as the true meaning asserts itself: There is no disk, no cylinder. What you see "recorded" on the page is what there was, and is.

5. W. Roy Mackenzie, *The Quest of the Ballad* (Princeton, NJ: Princeton University Press, 1919).

6. W. Roy Mackenzie, *Ballads and Sea Songs from Nova Scotia* (Cambridge, MA: Harvard University Press, 1928).

7. Francis James Child, *The English and Scottish Popular Ballads* (Boston: Houghton Mifflin, 1882–1898).

8. For further biographical information, see Martin Lovelace, "W. Roy Mackenzie as a Collector of Folksongs," *Canadian Folk Music Journal* 5 (1977): 5–11.

9. Mackenzie, *Quest*, 63.

10. Mackenzie, *Quest*, 65.

11. W. Roy Mackenzie, "Ballad Singing in Nova Scotia," *Journal of American Folklore* 22 (July–September 1909): 327–331; W. Roy Mackenzie, "Three Ballads from Nova Scotia," *Journal of American Folklore* 23 (July–September 1910): 371–380; W. Roy Mackenzie, "Ballads from Nova Scotia," *Journal of American Folklore* 25 (April–June 1912): 182–187; Mackenzie, *Quest*.

12. Mackenzie, *Ballads*.

13. Mackenzie, *Quest*, 33.

14. Mackenzie, *Quest*, 40.

15. Mackenzie, *Quest*, 112.

16. Mackenzie, *Ballads and Sea Songs from Nova Scotia*, xxiii.

17. Mackenzie, *Quest*, 27.

18. Mackenzie, *Quest*, 22.

19. Mackenzie, *Quest*, 22.

20. Mackenzie, *Quest*, 27–32.

21. Mackenzie, *Quest*, 27–32.

22. Mackenzie, *Quest*, 27–32.

23. Mackenzie, *Quest*, 27–32.

24. Mackenzie, *Quest*, 27–32.

25. Mackenzie, *Quest*, 59.

26. Mackenzie, *Quest*, 41.

27. Mackenzie, *Quest*, 50.

28. Mackenzie, *Quest*, 90–91.

29. Mackenzie, *Quest*, xi.

30. Happily, photographs of Mackenzie do exist. A particularly nice one with his wife and Helen Creighton, circa 1951, appears in Helen Creighton, *Helen Creighton: A Life in Folklore* (Toronto: McGraw-Hill Ryerson Limited, 1975), 86; and, much clearer, in Clary Croft, *Helen Creighton: Canada's First Lady of Folklore* (Halifax: Nimbus Publishing Limited, 1999), 126. There are also somewhat less accessible images among Mackenzie's papers at Washington University in St. Louis and in his obituary in the *St. Louis Post-Dispatch* (30 September 1957). All show a broad, chiselled face with a strong, wide mouth, prominent chin, high forehead, and hair combed up and back like a fright wig, which seems to have inspired students to nickname him "Fuzzy." My thanks to Brad Short, Music Librarian, and Sonya McDonald, University Archivist, Washington University in St. Louis, for copies of the clipping and university photo.

31. Mackenzie, *Quest*, 37.

32. Mackenzie, *Quest*, 39.

33. R. D. Madison, ed., *Newfoundland Summers: The Ballad Collecting of Elisabeth Bristol Greenleaf* (Westerly, RI: The Utter Company, 1982), 4–5.
34. Peere, "Elisabeth Greenleaf," 21–22.
35. Madison, *Newfoundland Summers*, 4–5.
36. Madison, *Newfoundland Summers*, 7. The source of this quote is held at the Memorial University of Newfoundland Folklore and Language Archive, Ms., 82–189, from a draft of her article *Newfoundland Days*, as sent to a *Scribner's* editor.
37. Peere, "Elisabeth Greenleaf," 24.
38. Madison, *Newfoundland Summers*, 7.
39. Greenleaf, Elisabeth Bristol and Grace Yarrow Mansfield, eds., *Ballads and Sea Songs of Newfoundland* (Cambridge, MA: Harvard University Press, 1933), xx.
40. Neil V. Rosenberg and Anna Kearney Guigné, "Foreword," in *Ballads and Sea Songs of Newfoundland, A Facsimile of the 1933 Edition* (St. John's, Newfoundland: Memorial University of Newfoundland, 2004), xv.
41. Rosenberg and Guigné, *Ballads and Sea Songs*, 95.
42. Madison, *Newfoundland Summers*, 11.
43. Madison, *Newfoundland Summers*, 11.
44. Madison, *Newfoundland Summers*, 12–13.
45. Rosenberg and Guigné, *Ballads and Sea Songs*.
46. Peere, "Elisabeth Greenleaf," 27.
47. Rosenberg and Guigné, *Ballads and Sea Songs*, 287.
48. Rosenberg and Guigné, *Ballads and Sea Songs*, 323.
49. Rosenberg and Guigné, *Ballads and Sea Songs*, 77.
50. Rosenberg and Guigné, *Ballads and Sea Songs*, 74.
51. Rosenberg and Guigné, *Ballads and Sea Songs*, 17.
52. Rosenberg and Guigné, *Ballads and Sea Songs*, 372.
53. Carpenter, Peere, Lovelace, and Narvaez all compare Karpeles and Greenleaf to the former's detriment. David Gregory mounts a well-articulated defense of Karpeles which resonates throughout the present chapter. According to Boyes, Karpeles seems to be routinely and unfairly disparaged in England as well: see her remarks, 173–175. Carole Henderson Carpenter, "Forty Years Later: Maud Karpeles in Newfoundland" in Kenneth S. Goldstein and Neil V. Rosenberg, eds., *Folklore Studies in Honour of Herbert Halpert* (St. John's, Newfoundland: Memorial University, 1980), 111–124; Peere, "Elisabeth Greenleaf"; Martin Lovelace, "Unnatural Selection: Maud Karpeles's Newfoundland Field Diaries" in Ian Russell and David Atkinson, eds., *Folk Song: Tradition, Revival, and Re-Creation* (Aberdeen: The Elphinstone Institute, University of Aberdeen, 2004), 284–298; Peter Narvaez, "Newfoundland and Vernacular Song" in Will Straw and Stacey Johnson, et al., eds., *Popular Music—Style and Identity* (Montreal: The Centre for Research on Canadian Cultural Industries and Institutions, 1995), 215–219; David Gregory, "Maud Karpeles, Newfoundland, and the Crisis of the Folksong Revival 1924–1935," in *Newfoundland Studies* 16:2 (2000): 151–165; Georgina Boyes, "'The lady that is with you . . . ': Maud Pauline Karpeles (1885–1976) and the Folk Revival," in Georgina Boyes, ed., *Step Change: New Views on Traditional Dance* (London: Francis Boutle Publishers, 2001), 171–195.
54. Boyes makes the case that Karpeles was squeezed out of the society she had helped found by a fascist element that objected to her being female and of Jewish ancestry.
55. David Manning, ed., *Vaughan Williams on Music* (New York: Oxford University Press, 2008), 240.
56. Gregory, "Maud Karpeles," 152.
57. Gregory, "Maud Karpeles," 153.
58. Boyes, "'The lady," 192.
59. Lovelace, "Unnatural Selection," 286.
60. Lovelace, "Unnatural Selection," 292–293.
61. Gregory, "Maud Karpeles," 156.

62. Maud Karpeles, *Folk Songs from Newfoundland* (Hamden, CT: Archon Books, 1970), 18. In a footnote, she directs those interested in native Newfoundland songs to Greenleaf and Mansfield, and to the Doyle songsters.
63. Lovelace, "Unnatural Selection," 291.
64. Lovelace, "Unnatural Selection," 291.
65. Lovelace, "Unnatural Selection," 292.
66. Gregory, "Maud Karpeles," 159.
67. Gregory, "Maud Karpeles," 156.
68. Maud Karpeles (coll. and ed.), *Folk Songs from Newfoundland* (London: Oxford University Press, 1934); reprinted as Maud Karpeles, *Folk Songs from Newfoundland* (Hamden, CT: Archon Books, 1970).
69. Karpeles, *Folk Songs* (1934), iii.
70. Maud Karpeles, *English Folk Songs from the Southern Appalachians. Collected by Cecil J. Sharp*, 2 volumes (London: Oxford University Press, 1932); Maud Karpeles and A. H. Fox Strangeways, *Cecil Sharp: His Life and Work* (London: Oxford University Press, 1933).
71. Helen Creighton, *Songs and Ballads from Nova Scotia* (Toronto: J. M. Dent and Sons, Limited, 1932).
72. The term is McKay's: Ian McKay, *The Quest of the Folk: Antimodernism and Cultural Selection in Twentieth-Century Nova Scotia* (Montreal: McGill-Queen's University Press, 1994).
73. Argued cogently and at some length in McKay, *Quest*, 99–144.
74. The phrase is used by Croft as a subtitle for his biography of Creighton: Clary Croft, *Helen Creighton: Canada's First Lady of Folklore* (Halifax: Nimbus Publishing Limited, 1999).
75. McKay, *Quest*, 139.
76. McKay, *Quest*, 139.
77. Mackenzie, *Ballads*.
78. Helen Creighton, *Helen Creighton: A Life in Folklore* (Toronto: McGraw-Hill Ryerson Limited, 1975), 49.
79. Creighton, *Helen Creighton*, 50.
80. Creighton, *Helen Creighton*, 50.
81. Creighton, *Helen Creighton*, 53.
82. Creighton, *Helen Creighton*, 60.
83. Creighton, *Helen Creighton*, 60.
84. See Janet Elizabeth McNaughton, "John Murray Gibbon and the Inter-war Folk Festivals," *Journal of Canadian Folklore* (1982): 66–73.
85. McKay, *Quest*, 138.
86. Creighton, *Songs and Ballads*.
87. Creighton, *Helen Creighton*, 86.
88. Creighton, *Helen Creighton*, 68–69.
89. Creighton, *Helen Creighton*, 86.
90. Creighton, *Helen Creighton*, 86.
91. McKay, *Quest*, 76.
92. Creighton, *Helen Creighton*, 112.
93. Helen Creighton with Doreen Senior. *Twelve Folk Songs from Nova Scotia* (London: Novello and Company, Ltd., 1940).
94. McKay, *Quest*, 82.
95. Creighton, *Helen Creighton*, 126.
96. Creighton, *Helen Creighton*, 126.
97. Creighton, *Helen Creighton*, 126.
98. Creighton, *Helen Creighton*, 126.
99. McKay, *Quest*.
100. Croft, *Helen Creighton*, 240.
101. Peere, "Elisabeth Greenleaf," 27.
102. Carpenter, "Forty Years," 5.

103. Peere, "Elisabeth Greenleaf," 26.
104. Gregory, "Maud Karpeles," 160.
105. Carpenter, "Forty Years," 119.
106. Peere, "Elisabeth Greenleaf," 28.
107. Croft, *Helen Creighton*, 40.
108. Croft, *Helen Creighton*, 152.
109. Croft, *Helen Creighton*, 191.

NINE

The Lomaxes

Matthew Barton

> It was in 1933 in the summer when the Depression had put a good man in the White House and wiped out the Lomax family financially. My father went back into the ballad field and that shows that sometimes, good things can grow out of painful events. We had a second hand Model A Ford, and there was John A. Lomax who had been trained by [Barrett] Wendell and there was Alan Lomax who was a junior in the University of Texas and who was full of George Bernard Shaw and Charles Beard and the intensive study of cultural anthropology, and Karl Marx and Weblin [Max Weber] and especially Charles Pearse [Charles Sanders Peirce], the main thinker in the theory of science in the United States.
>
> And I went along on this trip to see what sense could be made out of what my father had been singing to me all these years. — Alan Lomax[1]

Alan Lomax's career as a songcatcher began when he hit the road with his father John A. Lomax in 1933, helping him to collect material to finish a folk song anthology. John Avery Lomax (1867–1948) had been a prominent figure in American folksong scholarship since publishing *Cowboy Songs and other Frontier Ballads* in 1910 but had made his living since then as a teacher and banker in Texas, where he and his first wife raised their four children.[2] The Depression year of 1933 found him an unemployed widower, with his reputation as a folklorist his most bankable asset.

The book, eventually entitled *American Ballads and Folksong*, would draw from earlier work in the field, including his own, and be enhanced with new material that John and Alan would record in the South on a three-hundred-plus-pound aluminum disc recorder then still in the design phase.[3] The machine was to be paid for by the Music Division of the

Library of Congress, home of the Archive of American Folksong, started as part of the Library's Music Division by Robert Winslow Gordon in the more prosperous year of 1928. Music Division chief Carl Engel, among others, had grown impatient with the visionary but idiosyncratic scholar and field recorder, whose outside funding had run out. Gordon had never managed to convey the scope and significance of his work to those at the Library whom he needed most to impress, and their misperception of him was probably reinforced by the fact that he had published virtually nothing during his time there.

John Lomax, fresh from a successful speaking tour and eager to hit the road again to finish his book, must have looked very good indeed. He would soon replace Gordon, acquire the title of Honorary Curator of the Archive of American Folksong, and prove himself not only an able field recorder but a resourceful fundraiser as well, bringing in donations from the Carnegie and Rockefeller foundations and others to support further fieldwork. For the first four years, he would not receive more than reimbursement for his expenses and a token payment from the Library, but he gained a base from which he and Alan would be able to work for years to come.

The Lomaxes' new recorder embossed grooves on noisy aluminum discs, which still captured greater fidelity and permitted longer recording times than the cylinders most field recorders had used up to that point. Big as it was, it still fit in the back of the Lomaxes' Ford, the seat having been removed, and could run off the car's battery when local power supplies were unreliable or nonexistent. However, it was not yet ready when John and Alan set out in the early summer of 1933, so they used a wind-up cylinder recorder until the finished machine could be shipped to them. With it, they made a series of recordings in Texas, including several at Sugarland Penitentiary, the first of many sessions with black inmates in the segregated prisons of the South, where John Lomax had conjectured that old folkways might persist among isolated black prisoners. Later in the summer they took the disk recorder into the field, recording at more prisons, including Parchman Farm in Mississippi and Angola, Louisiana, where they met and recorded the great songster Huddie Ledbetter, better known as "Lead Belly."

When they returned to Washington at the end of the summer, they brought with them a mere twenty-five cylinders and fifteen aluminum discs. With these they staged a "recording concert" for a group of scholars assembled by Herbert Putnam, the Librarian of Congress. One by one, the Lomaxes played back the highlights of their work to date, including the powerful first recordings of African-American work songs sung in southern prisons, such as "Go Down Old Hannah," and "Rosie." Lomax remembered later that "nothing quite happened at the end of it," recalling "And then they all got up and stood as a group. And from that moment on there was no more worry about the administrative future of the Archive, because everybody who counted was there and everybody heard it and heard the importance."[4]

One cylinder, now lost, captured a performance that Alan Lomax would describe repeatedly, for the next sixty years and more, as the turning point in his young life. It was recorded in a plantation church in the Brazos Bottoms of Texas. The building was filled with black sharecroppers:

> After we'd recorded some spirituals they said "we want to hear old Blue, bring old Blue up!" So old Blue came up. And you remember we had limited money and limited materials, so we wanted to hear the songs before we recorded because we had only a few cylinders. And so we said "would you sing the song?" and Blue said "No. I want to sing the song just like I composed it the first time." And he wouldn't give and he sang finally, into the horn:
>
> > *Poor farmer, poor farmer, poor farmer*
> > *They get all the farmer make . . .*
> >
> > *His hat is full of patches*
> > *And his clothes is full of holes*
> > *Stooping down picking cotton*
> > *Off the bottom bolls*
> >
> > *Poor farmer, poor farmer, poor farmer*
> > *They get all the farmer make . . .*
>
> By the time the playback was ended there was riotous applause. The plantation manager had disappeared from the back of the church, but I had received my instructions and so had my father about what our purpose really was, which was not to bring the material to this room to you scholars, not to develop new theories about the development of American culture but to get room on the air for the people who were voiceless in this country.[5]

The material they played for Putnam and the others also showed that they had moved beyond the narrow category of ballads so beloved by Engel and others and into a much wider range of songs and folklore. For Alan, it turned out that seeing "what sense could be made" of it all also meant making sense of the country and its people, in a mission of cultural patriotism:

> We were able to reassure, so America could believe in itself, the way that my father believed and had taught me to believe, so that the whole range of American versifying and singing could be in one book. There wasn't room for 25 versions of *John Henry*. Instead, I spent a delightful week making a composite of everything that everybody had collected about John Henry. And what I'm proud of is that song was the first song in our book. We didn't begin with *Barbara Allen* or with an Appalachian lyric, we began with a song that says "a man ain't nothin' but a

> man." Probably the finest of all our ballads. And that had been the purpose of our trip .... That's how *American Ballads and Folksongs* was born. But its aim was to go beyond scholarship and do a job of revelation for the whole of the country. By this time Weblin [Weber] and Charles Pearse [Peirce] were over in a corner for me and I was completely and passionately tied to my father's purpose which was to make these revelations for, and to reassure Americans that it was alright to be a westerner, or a lumberjack or a lady who washed dishes in Peoria. Everybody counted.[6]

Indeed, among the book's most enduring attributes is its attention to the lives of the informants who contributed to it and its understanding of the importance that singing and song making held for them. One may question Alan's estimation of the book's achievements today, but it was well received at the time, and in it a road map for the next several years of Lomax field recording can be discerned, when they would record extensively in every region and from every genre and tradition covered in their book, as well as many others.

The recording session with Blue also foreshadowed what would be a growing gulf between Alan's social views and his father's. Father and son shared many aesthetic, intellectual, and emotional traits but not their sociopolitical outlook. Moreover, John Lomax was dismissive of what he saw as his teenaged son's naiveté about race relations in the South, and later said in his autobiography that "at every opportunity" on their early field trips to segregated prisons, the inmates "told Alan and me their pitiful stories. Alan seemed to want to set them all free."[7] For John, a man like Blue was a fine singer with a hard lot in life, and he'd help him if he could. For Alan, though, Blue was a symbol of all that was wrong in the country. John Henry Faulk, a Texas writer, humorist and broadcaster who knew both men well said:

> [John] Lomax was unquestionably a genius ... a man of a magnificent mind [but] he never put the two and two together. He never questioned the system ... lynching was the inevitable result of such a system ... and while he disapproved of it very profoundly—I would, this is the way I would analyze the situation. He'll never say, "Well the system itself creates this." He would just say, "These are the aberrations of lawless people."[8]

But eighteen-year-old Alan's views would mature and develop in ways that his sixty-seven-year-old father's would not and could not. His desire to understand and redress the social injustice he saw would become a consuming passion that informed his work for the rest of his life and lead to some of his most important fieldwork in his last years at the Library of Congress.

In the meantime, John and Alan's joint fieldwork continued. The French and Spanish field recordings in their songbook had been drawn from outside sources, but by the summer of 1934, John and Alan were making French and Spanish field recordings of their own in Louisiana and Texas. Later that year, John visited several more Southern prisons with the recently paroled Lead Belly as his driver, and as a kind of second fieldworker when a musical demonstration of the sort of material he was looking for was expedient. At Cummins State Farm in Arkansas, they recorded inmate Kelly Pace and a group of prisoners singing "Rock Island Line," which Lead Belly later added to his repertoire.[9]

Initially, the Lomaxes looked in the places where they thought old songs might still be sung, such as isolated rural communities and racially segregated prisons. Their interest was not limited to old songs, which they indeed found, but extended to the people—old and young—who sang them and the new songs that some were making. In the process they documented styles and genres they had not expected to find. Some were continuations of traditions thought defunct or near-dead, such as the African-American work songs still being sung in Southern prisons. Others were emerging, such as the nascent zydeco melodies and rhythms that Alan recorded from Louisiana ring-dancers in 1934.

Although both John and Alan are often portrayed as arch-conservatives and folk purists hostile to any song that betrayed foreign, commercial, or modern influences, they recorded the new material and forms frequently and repeatedly in their fieldwork, though not necessarily performances that were simply copied note-for-note, word-for-word from radio and records. John Lomax, after all, had made his name with American cowboy songs—a form that only emerged after the Civil War—and reflected the myriad influences brought to it by the cowboys themselves, men of varied backgrounds who came from all over, sharing no one class, skin color, or even language, but with common vocations and experiences. The "functionalist" approach to field recording, which held that new, emergent forms of folklore and folksong needed to be collected and studied as much as the old, had not yet been articulated by B. A. Botkin, Herbert Halpert, Alan Lomax, and others. But in the introduction to *American Ballads and Folksongs*, the Lomaxes, citing Robert Winslow Gordon and others, held that "American folk-song examples are greater in number, and . . . folk-song production is more active in America than in any other country that is preserving this form of literature."[10]

Since these recordings, which were dated and annotated, were being deposited in a public archive, they could serve as the basis for songbooks aimed at a broad audience and still be available for scholars and others to study. The Lomaxes were consciously developing an archive, not just of songs but performances as well. Some of them were brilliant, but most would never find a home in a songbook or any other published outlet.

The practice of recording also enabled more accurate transcription of words, melodies, and the intricacies and complexities of folk performance styles. Initially, this was applied mainly to the transcription of accents and dialects in songs, with notes on actual performance limited notes on how to approach the material, such as this caveat for a cowboy song, "The above note and time values can but poorly, approximately, and arbitrarily reproduce the cowboy's chant; its freedom of motion, unusual disposition of accent, and rising and falling of the voice are never twice the same."[11]

The Lomaxes never entirely succeeded in creating a generally accessible mass-market songbook that disseminated both traditional lyrics and performance style. The note above may have been written by transcriptionist Mary E. Gresham, who also said in the introduction "there was no way of expressing the indefinable variations of pitch and intonation which are fundamental characteristics of Negro singing."[12] Still, the Lomaxes kept searching for a solution, and George Herzog's transcriptions for their next book, Negro Folksongs as Sung by Leadbelly tried to capture his phrasing with standard notation augmented by symbols indicating pitch variation.[13] For the Lomaxes' 1941 songbook Our Singing Country, composer Ruth Crawford Seeger's precise transcriptions often amount to insightful commentary and analyses of the songs, but they are hard to sing off the page and reveal levels of structure and rhythmic sophistication that even the Lomaxes hadn't expected—including "a work song in 5/4 meter, a Cajun tune consistently in 10/8 throughout, a Ravel-like banjo accompaniment, a ballad of archaic tonal texture, a Bahaman part-song of contrapuntal bareness."[14]

It is in this context that the fieldwork of the Lomaxes is best understood: a broad, continually developing effort to record and popularize what Alan called "the truly original creation of the American people," and not a search for great individual artists or songs.[15] For every Lead Belly or Woody Guthrie they recorded who continues to influence American music there is a Henry Truvillion—the Texas levee camp and railroad worker who filled dozens of discs with unique stories and songs—whose influence is yet to be felt. For every "Bonaparte's Retreat" now heard around the world in Aaron Copland's orchestral arrangement, there are the dance melodies played by Serbian-American autoworker Ilija Sanovic of Detroit in 1938 on a flute he fashioned from a scavenged automobile part—music that probably went unheard for decades until Alan played it for an audience at a Library of Congress symposium in 1978, and which still await a broader audience.[16]

In 1935, Alan pursued some comparably little-known but nonetheless vital work when he went into the field without his father for the first time. That summer, he traveled to the Georgia Sea Islands and Florida with Zora Neale Hurston and Mary Elisabeth Barnicle. Hurston was the guide for the first part of the trip, on which recordings ranged from the recollections of former slave Wallace Quarterman, older forms of game songs, chanties, field hollers, and ring shouts that showed strong African retentions, as well as more recent blues guitar styles.[17] Evidence of Alan's compulsive love of field recording surfaced for the first time in Florida, where they recorded a "fire dance" as performed by a group of migrant workers from the Bahamas. He and Barnicle decided to continue the field trip in the Bahamas. There they recorded over 150 discs, more than they made in Georgia and Florida combined. Included were the four-part "anthems" sung by sponge fishermen, string bands, story songs, and even a Bahamian version of the bawdy Child ballad known variously as "Our Goodman" and "Three Nights Drunk."

In 1937, the Archive of American Folksong received for the first time a direct appropriation from Congress. It was used, in part, to make Alan a full-time salaried employee of the Library of Congress. As Assistant in Charge of the Archive of American Folksong, he now answered to Harold Spivacke, the new head of the Music Division. Spivacke was a more active collaborator than Carl Engel—even accompanying John Lomax on a field trip to a Tennessee prison in 1936—and soon widened the scope of the Archive's fieldwork: "He pulled me back away from my absolute fascination with the South and said 'Alan you've got to get to the rest of the country.'"[18]

Spivacke called for a long-term, more systematized approach. In a letter to the Librarian of Congress requesting funds to support Alan's two-month field trip to eastern Kentucky in the fall of 1937, he wrote:

> Our collection of songs of the southern whites is far from complete, however, and those to be found west of Mississippi, in the middle west, and the northeastern section of the country, practically unrepresented.
>
> To make a systematic survey of this vast area would be too great an undertaking for the Archive with its present equipment. But the same result may be accomplished by carefully planning its activities during the next few years. If the Archive were to dispatch recording expeditions to strategic points, it would soon build up a cross section of the country's singing and at the same time encourage private collectors in territory surrounding those points to contribute their own. The interest thus displayed by the Library, as well as the contacts made by the Library's representative, should go a long way in accomplishing this result.[19]

There had been some earlier work with other collectors and institutions, as well as some acquisitions of outside field recordings, but collaboration and outreach now became a frequent and vital means of building the Archive's collection. John Lomax, whose conservative Republican politics set him apart in the Washington of Franklin D. Roosevelt, somewhat ironically proved adept at partnering with such New Deal programs as the Federal Writer's Project and the Historical Records Survey as he continued and expanded his Southern field work. Beginning in 1937, he served as director of the Works Progress Administration's Slave Narrative project.

Other New Deal era agencies that partnered with the Archive included the Farm Securities Administration, the Resettlement Administration, the Federal Music Project, and the Federal Theatre Project. Further collaboration resulted from an equipment loan program, a highly effective means of encouraging outside research and recording while further enhancing the holding of the Archive. A recording laboratory was eventually established in the Music Division, and acquisitions of recordings from outside collectors were enabled by the ability to duplicate their discs and cylinders. Spivacke's letter does not mention universities, but they would also be important partners in the next few years, when UCLA cosponsored Sidney Robertson Cowell's multiethnic fieldwork in California and Juan Rael of Stanford University documented Spanish folk music in the New Mexico and Colorado with equipment provided by the Archive of Folksong.[20]

In Kentucky, and on several subsequent field trips, Lomax traveled and worked with his new wife Elizabeth. Frequently, she operated the recording equipment, took notes, and occasionally did interviews, especially when Alan thought that an informant might be more comfortable talking to a woman.[21] The next major field trip came in April of 1938, when the couple made a three-week journey through Ohio and Indiana. Alan's reports to Spivacke were becoming ever more detailed and impassioned, moving well beyond standard geographical and biographical data on the informants, even when the subject was not musical, as in this account of an incident after a session on a rainy night in Alton, Indiana, with a white ballad singer named Oscar Parks:

> By the time we were loaded up and on our way, the road was clay soup and on the third hill we slithered into the ditch and the more we backed, the deeper we sank. There was not a light in sight, no raincoats in the party, and a cold wind was blowing through the rain. By the time I walked the mile back to Oscar's house without a light, I was covered with mud. Mr. Parks and his oldest son got up cheerfully enough and went back to the car with me to see if they could run it out of the ditch on planks.
>
> We called on the nearest neighbor, an old bachelor who lived just down the hill from the place the car had run off the road, and all of us waded about, knee deep in the mud, an hour or two trying to get the car out, but to no avail. About two o'clock in the morning we decided to call for a wrecker, and there was another mile walk through the mud to the telephone, with our lantern by this time nearly out of oil. (There was only one available lantern in the neighborhood.) The telephone was in the house of two brothers, tall, lean farmers they were, who had been sitting up for weeks of nights. The third brother had gone mad some time before and they were trying to keep him in bed and see that he didn't hurt himself. Late as the hour was and cheerless as they were, they shouted over the party line for minutes, trying to get a truck to come to our help, but everybody was too comfortably asleep.

Finally Oscar and I gave the wrecker up and it then occurred to Oscar that there was a man in the neighborhood who had a yoke of oxen which he said could "pull a mountain down if you hitched them to it." We found, however, that when we had shouted the man out of his bed that the left-off-ox had had the glanders or something or other and couldn't come out on such a wild night. Nothing for it then, but to spend the night on the road, so we locked the car and having told the Parks's good-night, went down the hill to sit up around the old bachelor's stove.

It turned out he wasn't really a bachelor at all. He had worked on the section gang near Evansville all his life, had finally got to be section boss and then, wearying of the railroad and the city, he had thrown up his job and bought this little farm on the knobs of Crawford County. As soon as the money was in the other man's pocket, he discovered that the property was loaded with such a debt that he could never pay it. The land, too, had turned out to be fit only for chickens and after several lean years in the wretched log cabin in this scrubby backwoods, the missus had finally taken her children and gone back to live with her daughter in Evansville. Her husband had decided to quit, too, and was daily expecting the truck that was to take him up country a few miles to work in the timber business. At sixty, he had to look forward to spending the rest of his life at hard day labor.

This big, sad, kindly man had only one bed in the house, and since he couldn't put us up properly, he refused to lie in it himself and all four of us—Brewster [Paul Brewster, of the Indiana branch of the Writers' Project], Elizabeth, the lorn [lone] bachelor and myself sat around his little wooden stove all night and nodded. About five in the morning he gave us bitter coffee, hunks of fried salt pork and some canned peaches in the four chipped dishes that he had and we ate as much of it as we could stomach and then smiled away our hunger; we hadn't really eaten since the morning before.

The more Elizabeth and I see of back-country America, the more we are amazed at how the fine people who exist in it stand their wretched lives at all.[22]

Around this time, at the recommendation of BBC Washington correspondent Alistair Cooke and others, Lomax went to hear pianist Jelly Roll Morton at the small club he co-owned, The Jungle Inn. Before long, Morton—the self-proclaimed originator of jazz—had proposed that he should record for the Library of Congress. Initially, Lomax may have felt that Morton could be documented properly in a single session. If so, he changed his mind very quickly. Morton, he said

> was thoroughly prepared. He'd thought about the whole thing. And we had a few minutes' conversation and I knew I had a winner and I had my own plot and I knew he had his plot and I ran up the Coolidge Auditorium stairs to Harold [Spivacke] and I said "Harold, I want to have a guarantee of a hundred discs." And he said "What?" . . . and I said "Yeah, we're going to do the history of New Orleans Jazz." Now I

didn't particularly like jazz, because it was always buttin' my music off the air and ruining the chances for the kind of thing I believed in, so I decided to see how much folklore Jelly Roll had in him, and that was my plot. And his plot was to make sure that the place of New Orleans in the history of American music would be clearly and forever stated and he did that in a simply brilliant way.[23]

By the time these sessions began in May of 1938, Morton was regarded, even among the jazz intelligentsia, as something of anachronism: an eccentric braggart playing in a New Orleans idiom long since swept away in the Swing Era. Scholars continue to question Lomax's approach and its results, but the Morton sessions remain a unique document: more than eight hours of singing, playing, storytelling, and oral history recorded on some fifty-four acetate discs.[24] Whatever their faults, it must be remembered that no one else had so much time for Morton, who would die less than three years later. When Lomax queried record producer and jazz authority John Hammond[25] about Morton, for instance, he received this reply:

My own views about Jelly are somewhat mixed: I realize that some of his compositions are historically very important and that he exerted more than a minor influence on American popular music. But frankly, I have never enjoyed his piano playing at all. He has always seemed heavy-handed and stodgy, with a faulty ear that permitted atrocious chord sequences that would never occur to the great genuine unschooled blues artists like [Meade] Lux Lewis, Albert Ammons, Pete Johnson, Jimmy [James P.] Johnson, and the scores of other natural folk artists one can find in the backwoods of this country.

Do forgive me for my bluntness here. It is quite possible that I may be wrong or prejudiced; but I have never been able to get excited about Jelly as either an artist or a person. Most of the Negro blues artists that I have known have been great, warm, unostentatious people, and it may be that Jelly's personality rubbed me the wrong way. But I felt the same way about his music even before I met him.[26]

The next major project was another departure from the past. Later that summer, Alan prefaced ten weeks of field work in Michigan with this announcement:

This recording is being made at Clairepoint, Michigan, on the outskirts of Detroit, August 5, 1938. The section here is almost totally Serbian. In the shadow of the Chrysler plant you find the Serbians still playing their native shepherd's flutes and the *gusla*, singing the heroic ballads of the old days in Serbia.[27]

Both John and Alan had done a considerable amount of non-English language field recording by this time. John Lomax made numerous Spanish recordings in Texas, though he spoke little or no Spanish. Most recently, Alan had recorded French and German material that spring in

Indiana and some bits of Creole French from Jelly Roll Morton. There had even been a four-month recording project in Haiti the previous year. This trip was something else again, though. From late summer into the fall, Alan recorded all over lower Michigan, the Upper Peninsula, and Beaver Island. Throughout the state he worked in both older and newly established ethnic communities, recording performances that displayed generations of fusion and assimilation as well as some that reflected little or no change from their counterparts in Europe. English, Irish, Serbian, Slovenian, Rumanian, Polish, French-Canadian, Finnish, Italian, Croatian, Hungarian, Norwegian, and German performance were recorded over the course of August, September, and October.

By now, Alan was even more compulsive about field recording, following up on leads gained in the field wherever possible, and frequently sending urgent missives to Spivacke when he ran out of recording supplies or funds. This admonition received in Michigan is not unique in their correspondence:

> Dear Alan:
> I am sorry to hear that you have had so much trouble and that you have had to cut down on your food. This is inexcusable as I thought I had impressed on you many times before that it is not the Library's wish to see you drive yourself to death. I wrote you all this when you were in Kentucky and thought you had learned your lesson. But I see that you haven't. You should plan ahead and play safe. If you find yourself short of money, it is foolish to move very far until you have received some money.[28]

On Beaver Island in Lake Michigan, Alan worked with Great Lakes folklorist Ivan H. Walton, who had been collecting songs with pen and paper in the region for many years and introduced Lomax to many of his best informants.[29] Professor E. C. Beck, who had contributed lumberjack songs to *American Ballads and Folksongs,* was another collaborator during the Michigan fieldwork. In his preparations, Lomax also consulted with Sidney Robertson Cowell, who had done European-American field recording in the Midwest for the Resettlement Administration in partnership with the Archive in 1936 and 1937, but for the most part he was on his own.

Throughout most of 1939 and 1940, Alan divided his time between graduate studies in New York and official duties in Washington, where he continued to record singers at the Library of Congress. Unexpectedly, his major activity in New York became radio broadcasting when CBS invited him to join *The American School of the Air,* a daily half-hour program for students. Each day had a different theme, such as history or science. The Tuesday programs were devoted to music. This had usually been classical music, but in October, 1939 Alan started performing and presenting folk music. Not much earlier he had scorned radio:

> I thought this was a joke. I didn't know that anybody could be seriously interested in working on the radio, a pile of crap. Then I heard [Norman] Corwin's broadcast and I did a flip. I realized that radio was great art of the time . . . well I took the job, partly because Nick [Nicholas Ray][30] encouraged me and said it would be an opportunity. He was always a good writer, he had a sense of theatre and drama, so it was with his encouragement that I learned how to write a script. It was the first time that America had ever heard itself, and it went into all the schools.[31]

By this time, Alan was an experienced public performer, though often in academic settings such as lectures and conferences. He had also presented a program of traditional music at the White House that June in front of the Roosevelts and the King and Queen of England. At first, CBS expected him to do most of the singing and talking. Whenever possible, though, he showcased others. Elmer George, a Vermont lumberjack-turned-car salesman whom Lomax met through his fieldwork with New England folklorist Helen Hartness Flanders, was brought down to New York for one show. Kentucky midwife, labor organizer, and balladeer Aunt Molly Jackson, now a New York resident, appeared on two programs. One week, Lomax hosted the show from Galax, Virginia, and the Bogtrotters, a string band first recorded there by his father in 1937, played for half an hour.

Frequent guests also included a class of folk artists that Lomax characterized as "model singers"—professional performers from various backgrounds able to reshape traditional music in a way that a mass audience would enjoy. They included Lead Belly, Josh White, Burl Ives, and Pete Seeger. Woody Guthrie also got his first national exposure on the *School of the Air* a few weeks after meeting Lomax in New York and subsequently making his first Library of Congress recordings in Washington.

While in New York, Alan added many significant recordings to the Archive. There was a sea chantey session with Capt. Richard Maitland at the sailor's home in Snug Harbor, Staten Island, as well as lengthy sessions with Aunt Molly Jackson. He made further Library of Congress recordings of Lead Belly, and set up, supervised, and annotated commercial recording sessions for him with Musicraft and RCA. He found New York a rich and untapped area for field recording, as he wrote to folklorist Joanna Colcord:

> For sometime I have been interested in initiating a project in New York City to record the folk songs of the foreign minorities there. There are fine singers there in every language and dialect in the world probably, and there are also a number of people competent to give counsel, direction and advice to such a project. At this time, especially, it seems to me, America should make clear her concern for the cultural riches of the peoples whom she has welcomed into her borders, and no better evidence of this interest could be given than a project launched in New

York City to record and to make available in all sorts of ways the songs of the national minorities there.[32]

Lomax left CBS in the spring of 1941, free to concentrate on several new projects but mindful that the United States might soon be at war. Poet Archibald MacLeish was now Librarian of Congress and had started the Radio Research Project, which drew on the Library's resources to produce programs designed to educate Americans about the history of their free nation in a time when freedom was under fire around the world. So far, this had taken the form of radio plays about important but little known people and incidents in American history, such as the *Hidden History* series hosted by Alexander Woolcott. Folklore and folk songs played an occasional role in these broadcasts, but Alan wanted a more active role for the Archive. He proposed to MacLeish a documentary series based on new field recordings that would demonstrate "a new function for radio; that of letting the people explain themselves and their lives to the entire nation."[33]

Most of the fieldwork was done in the summer of 1941, using sound recording vans financed by the Rockefeller Foundation. With his assistant Jerome Weisner[34] and Radio Research Project Editor Joseph Liss, Alan collected interview and music material for two of the programs: *Mr. Ledford and the TVA* (recorded in Harris County, Georgia) and *Mountain Festival* (recorded at an Asheville, North Carolina, folk festival hosted by Bascam Lamar Lunsford). Weisner, Liss, and others made recordings for other programs in Delaware, Maryland, a migrant labor camp in Oklahoma, and in a traveling carnival that visited Washington, D.C. Folk music was recorded and prominently featured, but the programs were mainly built around interviews with ordinary people about their lives, homes, work, and their thoughts about the war in Europe. The final program originated in Wilmington, North Carolina, and was the work of Joseph Liss's playwright friend Arthur Miller, not yet famous for *All My Sons* (1947) and *Death of a Salesman* (1949). On the day that Miller set out from Washington with sound engineer John Langenegger, Lomax protested to Project Director Phillip Cohen that he lacked the experience and understanding to do good fieldwork, but later acknowledged that Miller's Wilmington program was the best of all.[35]

Work on the series was not yet finished when Pearl Harbor was attacked on 7 December 1941. In short order, Lomax contacted fieldworkers for the series and others affiliated with the Archive throughout the country, and asked them to hit the streets to record the reactions of ordinary Americans to this event; these recordings became the basis of another radio program, as well as unique historical documents.[36]

In 1941, the first album of Library of Congress field recordings was made available to the public, if only in a short press run aimed primarily at libraries—*Anglo-American Ballads*, edited and annotated by Alan.[37]

This began a series that would eventually grow to over seventy albums and include many of Alan and John's field recordings, though Alan only prepared five for release during his tenure at the Library.[38] The fourth, *Afro-American Blues and Game Songs*, included two performances by a young blues singer and guitarist named McKinley Morganfield, who would be better known as Muddy Waters, recorded in the summer of 1941, during Alan's first southern fieldwork in nearly three years, and part of a large collaboration with Fisk University, the pioneering black college in Nashville, Tennessee.[39]

Alan had first corresponded with Harold C. Schmidt, the white head of Fisk University's music department, in 1939. Schmidt was interested in using the Archive's resources as the basis of a public program on African-American music, though nothing seems to have come of it until Alan visited Fisk in April of 1941 to take part in their seventy-fifth anniversary celebration. While there, he met with Schmidt, Fisk president Thomas E. Jones, sociology department head Charles S. Johnson, and Fisk music teacher and composer John W. Work III. Johnson, an innovative African-American sociologist, and his associates had just published *Growing Up in the Black Belt*, a classic and still vital survey of eight predominantly black southern counties, most of them dominated by cotton production.[40] Johnson and his associates, including sociologist Lewis Wade Jones of Fisk, studied southern black life at the county level with field interviews and a variety of statistics, though not sound recordings. Although *Growing Up in the Black Belt* was concerned with the social, economic, educational, emotional, and psychological issues of younger African-Americans in these counties, and not with folk music or folk culture, it provided an ideal platform on which to build a study that combined the interview and statistical methods with field recordings, and Lomax suggested that one of the eight counties examined for it be the location of such an endeavor, to be undertaken jointly by the Archive of American Folksong and Fisk University.[41] Coahoma County, Mississippi, was eventually chosen, a once-isolated cotton producing area in the Mississippi Delta experiencing rapid urbanization and mechanization but still dominated by the plantation system.

Although it took some time to choose Coahoma, Alan would have needed little encouragement to record there. His views of the consequences of racism and segregation, and well as their significance in African-American folk culture, had developed apace with his fieldwork throughout the 1930s, and the confluence of musical, economic, and social factors in the Delta was particularly interesting to him. In October 1938, Sampson Pittman, a Delta bluesman and veteran of the Mississippi Delta levee camps, had told him of a world where "white people don't break the law, they make it. You had to be black to break the law."[42] Two years later, following a series of exceptionally rewarding recording sessions in the Delta, John Lomax declared, "I believe this to be the richest unexplored field for folk song and folklore in these United States."[43] Good as his father's Delta recordings were, Alan was eager to do his own and delve into the culture and context of the music in ways that John Lomax would not. The functionalist concept of folklore was well articulated by this time, and Alan and other proponents perceived a complex, interdependent network of sociological and aesthetic factors at work among the folk that they were recording.

Most of the recording for the new project, some forty hours or more, would be done by Alan and Lewis Wade Jones during an intense four weeks in July and August 1942. Fisk graduate students Samuel Adams and Ulysses Jackson worked separately, conducting further field interviews. Copies of the recordings were given to John Work for transcription. Summer heat, wartime tensions, and the open hostility of some local whites made this a difficult project. In 1940, a plantation boss nearby had suspected the older, deeply conservative John Lomax of being a troublemaking labor organizer, and Alan and the others now faced similar reactions and worse.

In the late summer of 1941, a preliminary trip of a week or so was undertaken in Coahoma County with Elizabeth, Dr. Johnson, Lewis Wade Jones, and John Work in late August and early September.[44] As had been his habit in the past, Lomax followed every lead as far as he could. Eager to get back in the field, he arrived in Coahoma before the others and quickly located bluesman Son House. When Lomax queried House about his one-time student Robert Johnson, House mentioned a young player who lived nearby, McKinley Morganfield. Soon after, Alan, Elizabeth, and John Work were recording him.

There were other notable blues sessions with House, David "Honeyboy" Edwards, Willie Brown, and others. But blues was just one form recorded for the comprehensive project. Also documented were early spiritual styles at a plantation church, a middle class black choir at a Baptist Convention, young groups singing in the emerging Gospel quartet style, sermons, children's game songs, ballads (including an African-American variant of the ubiquitous "Our Goodman"), work songs, gamblers' songs, and much more. Interviews were recorded as well, including a lengthy session with Charles Haffer, a blind author and publisher of fascinating hymns that drew parallels between scripture and current events; and also interviews on more mundane matters that were still important to the study. Earthy, ribald sessions of toasts and tall tales filled other discs.

Early in the trip, Turner Junior Johnson, a blind street musician whom Alan recorded told him of the music he'd heard as a boy in the hill country outside of Coahoma, and Alan and Lewis Jones trekked to the hills for a last field recording session in mid-August. They arrived in the evening, in time to record a string band led by fiddler Sid Hemphill:

> That wild, sad, braying fiddle of his rolled around in my head until late that night. Next morning I was feeling quite ill. I had had enough of the field—too much dust, too much sun, too much irony. I was washed up and longing to get the hell away.[45]

These recordings added to the slim stock of recordings in this genre by African-American musicians. But Sid Hemphill and his friends would play music yet more rare the next day, when their fife and drum band entertained at a local picnic—a quintessentially American aggregation playing a unique fusion of African and American styles in a remote corner of the South. Alan Lomax surely knew it was unlike anything recorded to date, but years later admitted that he could not fully grasp what he was hearing:

> I wish I could say the next hours were a joyous and replenishing experience. I wish I could say that on August 15 at Sledge, Mississippi, the black farmers of the Mississippi repossessed the earth with their laughter and their dancing. Actually, hardly anyone had come to the picnic, and I was too inexperienced to appreciate the treasure Lewis Jones and I had discovered. Sid's music represented an early phase of African-American music, kept alive in the Mississippi backwoods. As we have looked more deeply into the tradition of northeast Mississippi Hill country, we have found instruments styles, and dancing that link the black South to the black Caribbean, and no question of it, the dance of Africa itself.
>
> That afternoon in the Funky Fives I had only an inkling of all this. I was half sick and there was nothing to eat and nothing to drink except for the local brand of firewater.[46]

Twenty-seven-year-old weary frustration may have been intensified by the realization that he had only six weeks left in his career at the Library of Congress. He would leave to take a job with the Office of War Information on 1 October and was later inducted into the Army, leaving this and many other projects unfinished.[47] Even now there was still more fieldwork to do on the way back to Washington, including an all-day session in Birmingham, Alabama, at a Sacred Harp singing convention and recordings with mountain music Renaissance man Hobart Smith in Saltville, Virginia. Alan's father was in Texas, making his last field trip for the Archive in the same state where they had begun. They had recorded more than they could have ever foreseen in 1933, and the Archive now held nearly seven thousand discs recorded by the two men and their colleagues. For Alan there would be much more to come in the ensuing decades, but he had only begun to find "what sense could be made" of all he had seen, heard recorded, and taken to heart.

NOTES

1. Transcribed from recordings of Alan Lomax's remarks at the Fiftieth Anniversary Symposium for the Archive of American Folksong, Library of Congress, Washington, DC, 16 November 1978 (AFS 20,105 and 20,106), American Folklife Center, Library of Congress, Washington, DC. All quotes from Alan Lomax, unless otherwise noted, are from his remarks at this event.
2. John A. Lomax, *Cowboy Songs and Other Frontier Ballads* (New York: Sturgis and Walton Co., 1910).
3. John A. Lomax and Alan Lomax, *American Ballads and Folk Songs* (New York: Macmillan, 1934).
4. Alan Lomax, remarks, 16 November 1978.
5. Alan Lomax, remarks, 16 November 1978.
6. Alan Lomax, remarks, 16 November 1978. This was also the basis for the co-compositional copyright registrations the Lomaxes made with Lead Belly in their next book, John A. Lomax and Alan Lomax, *Negro Folksongs*. The creation of composite song texts was controversial with folksong scholars, but the practice was certainly widespread among the folk themselves.
7. John A. Lomax, *Adventures of a Ballad Hunter* (New York: Macmillan, 1947), 113.
8. John Henry Faulk, quoted in James McNutt, "John Henry Faulk: An Interview" *Folklife Annual* (1987): 126. American Folklife Center, Library of Congress, Washington DC. Faulk also did field recording for the Library in black churches and from former slaves in Texas in the early 1940s.
9. The details of John Lomax's troubled and controversial relationship with Lead Belly are beyond the scope of this essay. They have been recounted many times elsewhere, most thoroughly in Charles Wolfe and Kip Lornell, *The Life and Legend of Leadbelly* (New York: Da Capo Press, 1999).
10. John A. and Alan Lomax, *American Ballads*, xxv.
11. John A. and Alan Lomax, *American Ballads*, 381. This is from the notes to the song, "Cowboy to Pitching Bronco."
12. John A. and Alan Lomax, *American Ballads*, xxiv.
13. John A. and Alan Lomax, *Negro Folksongs as Sung by Leadbelly* (New York: Macmillan, 1936).
14. Ruth Crawford Seeger, "Music Preface," in John A. and Alan Lomax, *Our Singing Country* (New York: Macmillan, 1941), xviii.
15. John A. and Alan Lomax, *American Ballads*.
16. Copland appears to have used Ruth Crawford Seeger's transcription from *Our Singing Country* as the basis for his setting.
17. The interview with Quartermain can be heard at http://memory.loc.gov/ammem/collections/voices/title.html.
18. Alan Lomax, remarks, 16 November 1978.
19. Harold Spivacke, memorandum to M. A. Roberts, acting Librarian of Congress, 14 August 1937, Alan and Elizabeth Lomax Kentucky Collection (AFC 1937/001), correspondence folder, American Folklife Center, Library of Congress, Washington, DC.
20. Cowell's Calfornia fieldwork is available online at http://memory.loc.gov/ammem/afcchtml/cowhome.html. Rael's fieldwork is available at http://memory.loc.gov/ammem/rghtml/rghome.html.
21. John Lomax had a similar working relationship with his second wife, Ruby Terrill Lomax.
22. Alan Lomax, from *Journal of the Indiana Field Trip, March 26 to April 16, 1938*. Entry for 5 April, 41–42. Alan Lomax Ohio and Indiana Collection, American Folklife Center, Library of Congress, Washington, DC.
23. Alan Lomax, remarks, 16 November 1978.
24. By this time, the Archive had switched to the quieter, more sensitive, and more portable Presto acetate disc recorders.

25. Hammond and Lomax had not met in person at this point. Their association would lead to Alan making recordings in New York that December with the pianists mentioned by Hammond in this letter.

26. John Hammond, letter to Alan Lomax dated 18 June 1938, correspondence files of the American Folklife Center, Library of Congress, Washington, DC.

27. Transcribed from disc AFS 2238 A1, in the collection of the Archive of Folk Culture, American Folklife Center, Library of Congress, Washington, DC.

28. Harold Spivacke, letter to Alan Lomax dated 16 September 1938, General Delivery, Escanaba, Michigan. John A. and Alan Lomax Manuscript Collection (AFC 1933/01), American Folklife Center, Library of Congress, Washington, DC.

29. In 1940, Walton would get to make recordings of his own with equipment supplied by the Library of Congress.

30. Ray, a lifelong friend, is now best known as the director of such films as *Rebel Without a Cause* (1955). The two also collaborated on *Back Where I Come From*, a thrice-weekly fifteen-minute folk music radio show aimed at an older audience that featured Woody Guthrie, Burl Ives, the Golden Gate Quartet, Josh White, and others, in late 1940 and early 1941.

31. Bernard Eisenschitz, *Nicholas Ray: An American Journey* (London: Faber and Faber, 1993): 52.

32. Alan Lomax, letter to Joanna Colcord, the Russell Sage Foundation, dated 19 July 1941. Ronald D. Cohen, ed., *Alan Lomax, Assistant in Charge: The Library of Congress Letters, 1935–1945* (Jackson: University Press of Mississippi, 2011), 232.

33. Alan Lomax, Report on the Radio Research Project, circa January 1942. Papers of the Radio Research Project, Recorded Sound Reference Center, Motion Picture, Broadcast, and Recorded Sound Division, Library of Congress, Washington, DC.

34. Weisner was later a science advisor to Presidents Kennedy and Johnson and was eventually president of M.I.T.

35. For a more thorough account of Miller's work on the Radio Research project, see Matthew Barton, "Arthur Miller: A View from the Field," *Folklife Center News* (Winter/Spring 2005): 3–5. Available online at http://www.loc.gov/folklife/news/pdf/afcnews-winterspring-2005.pdf.

36. These recordings are now available online as part of the web presentation "After the Day of Infamy" at http://memory.loc.gov/ammem/afcphhtml/afcphhome.html.

37. Alan Lomax, ed. *Anglo-American Ballads* (AFS L1), Library of Congress Archive of Folk Songs (1942).

38. Gaining permissions from performers and subsequently making payments inevitably slowed down the production process. There had been no consistent protocol for paying in the field, though payments were often made, sometimes after a field trip. For these commercially available albums, performers were always sought out for permissions and payments.

39. Alan Lomax, ed. *Afro-American Blues and Game Songs* (AFS L4), Library of Congress Archive of Folk Songs (1942).

40. Charles S. Johnson, *Growing up in the Black Belt* (Washington, DC: American Council on Education, 1941).

41. This scenario is very different from the one put forth by Robert Winslow Gordon and Bruce Nemerov, eds., in *Lost Delta Found: Rediscovering the Fisk University—Library of Congress Coahoma County Study, 1941–1942* (Nashville: Vanderbilt University Press, 2005), a collection of project writings by several of the Fisk participants. They hold that a proposal made by John Work was the basis for the eventual Coahoma study, for which Lomax denied him credit in the book, Alan Lomax, *The Land Where the Blues Began* (New York: Pantheon, 1941). But Work had wanted to go to Natchez, two hundred miles south of Coahoma, to collect songs he conjectured had been written about a catastrophic 1940 fire, a project very different from the broad survey eventually undertaken in Coahoma. In a 24 July 1941 letter to Lomax, Work himself wrote "As I understand *your* proposal, it stipulated Dr. Johnson's selecting an area, (or areas), previously studied by him for the recording to be done." (Emphasis added.)

This letter can be viewed at http://memory.loc.gov/ammem/ftvhtml/ftvhome.html, under Manuscripts.) Work had submitted his Natchez proposal to the Julius Rosenwald Foundation in New York for funding and been turned down. Gordon and Nemerov offer no evidence that it was ever proposed to Lomax or anyone else at the Library of Congress. In his letter to Spivacke about the April 1941 meeting at Fisk, Lomax makes no mention of such a proposal. Natchez was also far from any county studied for *Growing Up in the Black Belt*. If it was discussed, Lomax might have been uninterested because John and Ruby T. Lomax had been to Natchez a few months earlier and found local expression to have actually have been diminished by the trauma of the fire. Work had made some field recordings on his own in and around Nashville, and as far afield as Dothan, Alabama, where he had recorded black shape note singers. Gordon and Nemerov also hold that Lomax actively prevented him from being a field recorder for the project, but that Lomax's choice of Lewis Wade Jones as coworker in Coahoma made considerable sense, as Jones knew Coahoma well from his work with Johnson and was steeped in Johnson's methodology, having worked for Johnson since 1932 as a research assistant and field study supervisor. Lomax proposed that Work continue his Nashville fieldwork, and to this end provided him with recording discs and professional repairs for Fisk's disc recorder.

42. Alan Lomax, remarks, 16 November 1978.

43. John Lomax, from a report filed on his 1940 Southern Field Recording trip. Description of AFS discs 4015 and 4016, recorded at the Roger Williams Plantation "six miles west of Drew [Mississippi]." Collection of the American Folklife Center, Library of Congress, Washington, DC.

44. Johnson's interview with a former slave George Johnson made on this trip can be heard at http://memory.loc.gov/ammem/collections/voices/title.html.

45. Alan Lomax, *The Land Where the Blues Began*, 317–318.

46. Lomax, *The Land Where the Blues Began*, 318.

47. No agreement was reached on how a field study should be written. Jones and Work wrote manuscripts, and Adams used the study as the basis for his graduate thesis, later publishing a truncated form of it under the title "The Acculturation of the Delta Negro" in *Social Forces* 26:2 (December 1947), without mentioning the project or even Fisk University in it. Alan eventually included accounts of many of his experiences on the project in *The Land Where the Blues Began*, in the context of his African-American fieldwork from 1933 to 1978.

TEN
Robert Winslow Gordon

Paul J. Stamler

PREFATORY NOTE

The life of Robert Winslow Gordon (1888–1961) did not arrange itself in neat chronological order, as his most important projects had a tendency to run concurrently or overlap. That makes writing a coherent account of his life difficult. In this chapter, I've tried to be chronological in my organization and have also presented much of the story thematically. I suspect he would have done the same.

Gordon left remarkably little published material outside of his *Adventure* columns (which are still not readily accessible), his slim volume on *Mademoiselle from Armentières* (1935), and his *New York Times* essays.[1] With limited primary sources from which to work, any discussion of Gordon must rely strongly on the excellent biography by Debora Kodish, *Good Friends and Bad Enemies* (1986).[2]

EARLY DAYS

Robert Winslow Gordon was born on 2 September 1888 in Boyer, Maine. His father, a carpenter and cabinet maker, had gone west in the latter days of the Gold Rush, arriving in San Francisco in 1855. Gordon may have picked up his interest in traditional music and folklore from hearing his father's stories of the gold fields. Gordon's biographer, Debora Kodish, describes his mother as "emotionally needy," and suggests Gordon may have inherited that trait from her along with his father's adventurous spirit.[3] It was a spirit which dovetailed with that era of "Muscular Christianity."

Precocious and bright, Robert Winslow Gordon won scholarships to the prestigious Phillips-Exeter Academy and then to Harvard University, where he made *Phi Beta Kappa* in his undergraduate years. At Harvard, he studied with Frances James Child's successors—George Lyman Kittredge (1860–1941), Barrett Wendell (1855–1921), and Francis Gummere (1895–1979).[4] From his earliest days, Gordon was fascinated by the burgeoning technology of the time, particularly photography and sound recording; he would bring those interests to bear on his work in folklore. At Harvard, he built wax cylinder recording equipment and developed his interest in the songs he heard during excursions to working-class bars and immigrant slum communities. Such excursions were popular with such fellow students as John Dos Passos, T. S. Eliot, and e. e. cummings; Gordon shared their interest in working-class culture, but not the political and cultural radicalism to which that interest led many of them.[5]

Competitive, ambitious, and perfectionistic, Gordon wanted to "do for American folk song what Child had done for the English and Scottish Popular Ballad."[6] He began work on a doctoral dissertation on the Scottish collector Peter Buchan, with the aim of proving the "untrustworthiness and inauthenticity of Buchan's ballads."[7] Characteristically, he gathered huge quantities of evidence, but if he wrote anything, it has not survived. He would never finish the dissertation.

In 1918, Gordon left Harvard for an appointment in the department of English at the University of California, Berkeley, just as Charles Seeger was being effectively forced off the faculty due to his antiwar position.[8] Along with the usual courses assigned to new faculty, he taught graduate courses on English and Scottish ballads—courses that proved popular and inspiring to his students.[9] From the beginning, he got along badly at Berkeley; his behavior didn't fit into the standard faculty mold and neither did his appearance in that more formal time: "Once, one of his colleagues in Berkeley's English department urged him to do something about his rather slovenly appearance. Gordon answered sharply that he was not paid for the way he looked."[10] Another source of irritation on the campus of the not-yet-free-swinging university was the fact that most of Gordon's publications appeared not in academic journals but in the pages of a mass-circulation pulp magazine.

OLD SONGS THAT MEN HAVE SUNG

In the flowering of pulp magazines that occurred after World War I, *Adventure* was one of the classier specimens. Ron Goulart in his book on pulp magazines, *Cheap Thrills* (1972), called it "the aristocrat of the cheap magazine."[11] Robust, nativist, and a promoter of "manly" character, *Ad-*

venture published rugged tales (fiction and nonfiction) and encouraged the formation of local "Camp Fire Clubs" among their readers to promote wholesome, outdoorsy activities.[12]

The idea of a column devoted to "old songs" was not new; *Railroad Man's Magazine* and *Sea Stories*, among others, had long-running features on the songs of their respective fields. *Adventure*'s editor, Arthur Sullivant Hoffman, followed suit—spinning off "Old Songs That Men Have Sung" from the "Ask *Adventure*" column. Hoffman wanted a feature that would provoke strong interaction with readers (he was also probably mindful of the fact that most folk songs were not covered by copyright), but his first hosts, including folklorists John Lomax and H. M. Belden and the poet Robert Frothingham, proved unsatisfactory. They seem to have been primarily interested in using the magazine to solicit material without responding to readers in return.[13]

In 1923, Hoffman asked Gordon to take over the column. Gordon responded enthusiastically; he saw the "Old Songs" column as an opportunity to collect a broad variety of folk songs from a wide cross-section of Americans and thus create a folk song collection that was comprehensive and heterogeneous rather than focused on a particular region, ethnic group, or type of material. In his biographer's words, Gordon hoped to learn songs from "a considerably larger number of people than he could ever hope to reach by personal contact alone. . . . He was hoping to construct a great machine to do an immense job."[14]

To that end, Gordon employed a method he would return to over and over: decentralizing the collecting process. *Adventure*'s two million readers would serve as both informants and collectors, while he functioned as editor, theoretician, analyst, and facilitator. His interest in raw collecting was matched by a passion similar to Cecil Sharp's for understanding the processes by which folk songs changed, evolved, and spread, and he hoped the column would provoke a sufficient diversity of responses for him to make progress on theoretical questions. He wrote to one of his reader/correspondents, D. G. Newell, thanking him for his help in "enabling me to run down the history and the changes in the song ['Springfield Mountain']. And that is really one of my major interests. I want to add my bit toward discovering just how the songs of the folk originate and how they 'live,' for they really do live and grow like human beings."[15] In this work, he was one of the early practitioners of the "historic-geographic" method of folk song analysis.[16]

As Kodish suggests, Gordon was a trifle optimistic in this hope, as his readership was by no means as universal as he supposed. Nonetheless, in his nearly five years at the helm of the column he managed to amass a remarkable selection of songs and variants. He carried on a voluminous correspondence with readers, abetted by the magazine's practice of paying fifty cents for each letter answered. In the end, he wrote some four thousand letters during his tenure, which his biographer has analyzed extensively.[17]

During his years at Berkeley, Gordon devoted much time and effort to both his own collecting and his work on *Adventure*, seeing the two endeavors as complementary. He made friends with Frank Kester, who as marine editor of the *Oakland Tribune* ran his own old-songs feature in his column "The Dogwatch." Gordon used this friendship to meet and record sailors, longshoremen, and hobos; from them he recorded a variety of songs and stories on an Edison wax cylinder recorder, including chanteys, religious songs, blues, Child ballads, and bawdy material—some 250 songs in all.[18] In using a recording machine rather than a notebook for his collecting, Gordon was something of a pioneer. While collectors such as Vaughan Williams, Grainger, and Bartók had used recorders two decades earlier, they had primarily been used in the United States only by ethnographers documenting the music and rituals of Native Americans.[19] With Kester, Gordon also founded a local Camp Fire Club that eventually incorporated, among other enthusiasts, three retired sea captains with firsthand knowledge of songs from the windjammer days. Led by the three captains, the group sang sea chanteys for regional "maritime clubs" and even appeared on an Oakland radio station.[20] One of the captains, Leighton Robinson, would later make classic recordings of chanteys for the Library of Congress.[21]

In the summer of 1924, Gordon's relationship with the University of California reached the point of divorce. After standing up for a close friend in a dispute with the department chair (and breaking into the files one night to retrieve a letter critical to the dispute, which he proceeded to read at a department meeting—shades of *Adventure*!), he was informed that following his 1924–1925 sabbatical he would not be rehired. While his extended family remained behind, he returned to Harvard with the intent of finishing his doctorate.[22]

IN THE FIELD

At Harvard, letting his dissertation lie fallow, Gordon planned an ambitious collecting trip, during which he hoped to generate three thousand or more cylinder recordings. He would begin in Asheville, North Carolina, in the folk song–rich Smoky Mountains; proceed to Darien, Georgia, to record African-American singers from the Sea Islands; travel across the southeast, up the Mississippi/Missouri rivers through the Dakotas and Canada; and finish in Newfoundland. In the end, only the first two stops would be completed.[23]

One of Gordon's goals for this expedition points out one of his blind spots: while he was notably ahead of most of his contemporaries in viewing Anglo-American and African-American folk music as a single, unified body of culture, the belief was based on the idea that the African-American segment of that body was essentially derivative, a borrowing from white people without significant African influences. He told correspondent E. M. Guest that on his marathon collecting effort he would "attempt to run down . . . white sources of negro spirituals."[24]

Gordon had difficulty raising support for the trip. He offered to let a radio station broadcast his recordings in return for funding, but was turned down. He offered Victor Records first refusal on issuing his material commercially along with his services as consultant on copyright issues, again in return for funding. Victor's staff expressed interest, but management narrowly voted the idea down.[25] (Meanwhile, Victor's legal department would, quite independently, request Gordon's expert assistance in a pending lawsuit, of which more later.)

He was slightly more successful in obtaining material support. After visiting Thomas Edison and huddling with his engineers, Gordon purchased a recording machine custom-built to his specifications and worked out an agreement allowing him to purchase blank cylinders at a discount. His approaches to the Ford Motor Company for the donation of a vehicle were unsuccessful despite Henry Ford's interest in traditional fiddle music, but they did agree to sell him a used car at cost, $270. Eastman Kodak also turned down his requests, but a dealer agreed to sell him equipment and film at cost. He had already obtained a Sheldon Fellowship from Harvard, and *Adventure* finally agreed to lend him $400. His most fruitful pitch was aimed at the *New York Times*; in 1925 they agreed to publish ten articles by Gordon on American folk music (he would eventually write fifteen) at the very generous rate of $100 apiece.[26]

Despite straitened family circumstances, and the illness of his wife and mother, he decided that henceforth he would earn his living strictly as a professional folklorist. In September 1925, he headed south.[27] After spending some time doing preliminary research at the Library of Congress (obtaining letters of endorsement from, among others, President Coolidge), and stopping to record material from two men involved in the "Old 97" controversy (see below), he began his work in Asheville, North Carolina. To keep costs down, and perhaps also to maintain his air of adventurous vigor, he set up housekeeping in a tent on the edge of town. He would move into town when the weather turned cold.[28]

His first contact in Asheville was Bascom Lamar Lunsford, a country lawyer and self-conscious folklore collector who had gathered extensive material in the region during an earlier career as a traveling seed salesman, and who had recently recorded several 78s for the Okeh label. Gordon recorded several cylinders of Lunsford's performances, and Lunsford acted as intermediary between Gordon and the mountain people, introducing Gordon to several informants.[29]

Short of money and nearly out of blank cylinders, Gordon obtained support from the Asheville Chamber of Commerce, which saw the area's musical traditions as a tourist attraction. He continued to collect, maintaining his practices of working through local intermediaries and collecting black material second hand from white singers who had learned them from blacks.[30] Unusually for an American collector, he recorded a wide variety of material, going beyond the usual focus on Child ballads to record fiddle tunes, lyric songs, and native American ballads.[31] His motivations—including a clear conviction that the material he sought was rapidly disappearing—can be gleaned from a letter he wrote to one of his *Adventure* correspondents, Esther Colin: "I'm not a fanatic at all, but I do think that a lot our fathers and grandfathers sung helped toward making good Americans. Much more than this modern jazz—which I detest. I hate to see the old songs and the old traditions drop out. And unless some fool like me saves them they soon will."[32]

At the end of 1925, Gordon moved on to Darien, Georgia (his wife's home town), to collect in the Sea Islands. He was profoundly excited by the African-American religious music he found, devoting a pair of *Times* articles to it.[33] Recording services in the church at St. Simon's Island, where the preacher asked the congregation to sing the oldest songs they remembered for their visitor, Gordon saw many features of the worship style as novel, although in fact they had been described by previous visitors.[34]

Favorite themes from Gordon's life are clearly evident in his Darien collecting. He adhered to a collective model for folk song composition: speaking of a singer of spirituals, he wrote, "He was not an 'author' in the ordinary sense, for he did not himself create new lines. He merely put together traditional lines in new forms, adding nothing on his own. . . . Without conscious method, and often by sheer accident, he attained combinations of striking effectiveness or equally striking incongruity."[35]

He expressed his belief that African-American music is essentially derivative, learned from white sources, in a vignette:

> The aged preacher mounts to the pulpit, a small bare table at the edge of the raised platform. Slowly and impressively he "lines out" a hymn just as he heard the white preacher do it seventy years ago when as a pickaninny he used to climb up into the high balcony at the rear of the white church. It is not a spiritual, but an old hymn of the camp-meeting type.[36]

He treated blacks very differently from the white mountaineers from whom he had collected in North Carolina. The latter he had approached with straightforward directness;[37] with black informants, however, he was indirect and often disingenuous:

> Direct statements and leading questions are to be avoided. . . . Often it may be a good plan to make a statement, giving as your authority some definite negro in a near-by district, and intimating that you are a bit in doubt as to the accuracy of your information. That spur almost never

fails. "Huh! W'ut dat nigger know? I axe you. Don't know nottin'."
And for the next five minutes your notebook fills rapidly with more
material for later checking.[38]

Finally, it's clear from Gordon's writings at this time that he saw no conflict between the work he was doing and the upholding of the "southern way of life" in all its inhumanity. In a letter to Fiswoode Tarleton, he stated, "I'm no 'nigger-lover' don't worry your head on that score! . . . I'm not going to turn against the South, or the whites of the south, and take away or help to take away anything that can serve them in holding in check the negroes . . . mainly my duty to the whites, not to the negroes."[39]

Gordon did not continue his epic collecting trip beyond Darien. He had found an embarrassment of riches there, and reading between the lines it's clear this was the happiest time in his life; he was finally doing the work he had always hoped to do. By mid-1927, however, he was out of money and unable to support his family or continue his collecting. On eight occasions he submitted manuscripts to publishers, but they were rejected—as was his idea for a nationally syndicated newspaper feature.[40] Finally, in September of 1927 a new editor at *Adventure* dropped the "Old Songs" column.

OLD 97 AND THE MADEMOISELLE

On two occasions, Gordon applied the techniques he had developed for the analysis of folksong evolution to concrete bits of popular culture. One was a smash hit record—perhaps the first million-seller in the world of commercial country music; the other was a song that circulated under the radar—a bawdy song known to virtually every doughboy who had served with the Allied Expeditionary Force during World War I.

The hit record was "Wreck of the Old 97," and Gordon's involvement came at the behest of Victor Records, which was enmeshed in a lawsuit concerning the song's authorship.[41] The story is too involved to discuss here in detail; however, a brief synopsis is in order. For the following information, I am indebted to Norm Cohen's exhaustive study of the song, referenced below. In 1903, the Southern Railway's fast mail train number 97 ran off a trestle in Monroe, Virginia, killing nine people, including the engineer and several crew members. Quickly, local singers began creating songs about the wreck, including North Carolina residents Charles Noell and Fred Lewey.[42]

In late 1923, Virginia singer Henry Whitter recorded "Wreck on the Southern Old 97" for the General Record Company's Okeh label; he had learned the words from Frank Burnett, who had heard Noell and Lewey singing on the street in 1904.[43] Whitter reset their lyrics to the tune of Henry Clay Work's popular "The Ship That Never Returned," which had already been used for several parodies and pastiches, including some with train wreck themes. Shortly after Whitter's recording, the song was cut by Ernest Thompson, George Reneau, Kelly Harrell, and Vernon Dalhart, all pioneers in recorded hillbilly music along with Riley Puckett, Ernest Stoneman, and Fiddlin' John Carson. It was Dalhart's record, however, that caused all the fuss; the flip side of Dalhart's Victor 78 was a cobbled-together piece called "The Prisoner's Song," and it sold well over a million copies. Dalhart, no believer in exclusive contracts, also cut "Old 97" for the Edison, Gennett, Grey Gull, and Emerson labels, and made a recording sold by various members of the American Record Company group.[44]

The first copyright on the song was registered in the name of Henry Whitter by the Okeh label; when they filed a claim against Victor for infringement, Victor settled out of court. Not long after, however, Virginian David Graves George claimed authorship, and after the failure of negotiations sued Victor in 1928.[45]

In the course of the Okeh/Whitter suit, Victor had consulted Gordon's expertise; he had visited Noell and Lewey, heard their stories and recorded their versions of the song. Victor asked for Gordon's help again in the George case; he spent two years gathering and analyzing material using the techniques he'd developed for his *Adventure* column. (He also suggested to Victor's attorneys the use of chemical tests on the carbon paper George had used, a suggestion which they adopted.) In 1931, Gordon testified at the trial that internal textual evidence indicated that George was not the author. Dalhart had misheard some of the words in Whitter's recording, incorporating the errors into his own best-selling version; Gordon showed that three out of Dalhart's four errors also appeared in George's text. Despite Gordon's testimony, in which he was permitted only to offer factual information and not expert conclusions, in 1933 the judge found for the plaintiff, ruling that George was indeed the author of "Old 97."[46] Reading Norm Cohen's summary, the assembled texts and Gordon's excerpted testimony, one is drawn inescapably to the conclusion that this was that rarest of events: a record company bested by a songwriter, rather than the other way around.

The bawdy song was "Mademoiselle from Armentières," or "Hinky-Dinky Parlez-vous," whose off-color couplets had been cheerfully sung by millions of American soldiers during the war. Gordon had been collecting bawdy songs (including this one) along with the rest of his material since his Berkeley days, assembling them into what he called his "Inferno" collection. He had good theoretical reasons; in Kodish's words, "He had realized early that because bawdy material was seldom printed, it was extremely helpful to his study of the origin and development of folksong."[47] Characteristically, he believed there had been a real mademoiselle on which the song was based, although given the activities detailed in the lyrics, she could not have lasted long.

Working in collaboration with Melbert Cary, Gordon employed a variation on his approach from the *Adventure* years: he published a booklet, aimed at ex-servicemen, seeking verses to the song. The effort was successful; by early 1933 they had amassed 498 distinct verses, a selection of which they issued in a privately printed volume, along with an analysis of the song's evolution.[48] The privately printed book, perhaps the best surviving example of Gordon's methods and approach, was arguably the first American folklore publication to print and analyze bawdy material without expurgation or bowdlerization. The book was aimed primarily at ex-doughboys, another milestone in that its intended audience was drawn from its source population, with the added purpose of helping to keep the song alive among its original singers.

"A HUNT ON HIDDEN TRAILS"

Gordon's articles for the *New York Times*, which overlapped his work in Darien and the beginning of his tenure at the Library of Congress, were perhaps the first comprehensive look at American folk music presented to a mass audience. (The other candidate for that honor, Sandburg's *American Songbag*, was published when Gordon was in mid-series. Gordon contributed material to that work, although his contributions were "changed beyond recognition".)[49] It's worth noting his topics for the *Times* (all titles are prefaced with "The Folk-Songs of America"):

1. "A Hunt on Hidden Trails" [overview] (2 January 1927)
2. "Among the Hills Our Folk-Songs Thrive" [Appalachian music] (9 January 1927)
3. "Work chanteys" [most or all are African American] (16 January 1927)
4. "The [Negro] Spirituals" (20 February 1927)
5. "Negro [religious] Shouts" (24 April 1927)
6. "Negro [religious] Chants" (8 May 1927)
7. "Outlaw ballads" (5 June 1927)
8. "Jail Ballads" (19 June 1927)
9. "Shanty-Boy Lays" [lumberjack songs] (28 August 1927)
10. "The Old Ballads" [Child ballads] (9 October 1927)
11. "Fiddle Tunes" [concentrates on those with words] (27 November 1927)
12. "Banjo tunes" [lyric songs] (1 January 1928)
13. "Nursery Ballads" [children's songs] (8 January 1928)
14. "In Pioneer Days" [songs of westward migration] (15 January 1928)
15. "Cowboy songs" (22 January 1928)

Articles 4, 5, and perhaps 6 were essentially reports on his current collecting work. Merge them into a single category of "Black religious songs," however, and you are left with an almost canonical organization for the popular presentation of American folk music, one that has been used many times since Gordon's articles, including Sandburg's *The American Songbag* (see chapter 12).

Gordon's articles are more than descriptive; they are a missionary's passionate advocacy for an art form he clearly finds compelling. They also, inevitably, reflect the attitudes Gordon brought to his work; the introductory overview is particularly revealing. Most notable is his initial attachment to a collective-creation model for songs, and his desire to find a synthesis between that model and an understanding of the role of individual songsmiths:

> Folk-song is not the product of an author. An author may have composed it, but it is not his; he is merely an incident, unimportant and soon forgotten. It is, in fact, no more the property of the author than is the oak the exclusive property of the soil and water in which it chanced to grow. . . . Some author was necessary, but almost any one would have served equally well. There would have been little appreciable difference in the resulting product. As a fact both the author element and the folk element are to be found in all folk-songs of civilized peoples today. Sometimes the folk element predominates to such a degree that the author element can scarcely be discovered. Usually the latter is discernible, though always of less importance. That we shall find author traits in some of the songs classified above need not worry us. It would be foolish for the seeker after gold to pick up only nuggets and ignore veins of gold-bearing quartz. Separation is a later task.[50]

It is ironic that only a few years later, Gordon would be testifying in court concerning a particular individual's authorship rights to "Old 97." His choice of a gold rush metaphor hearkens back to his father's adventures in the mining camps. He also explicitly details his dismissal of significant African influence in the music of black Americans:

> The negro of the South is perhaps our best folk-singer. . . . Some of his types—perhaps most of them—he derived in the beginning from the whites, for he is a marvelous assimilator. But in nearly every case he has so thoroughly made over the material that it would be unfair to say that it is not now his own. From the white man he took the old camp-meeting hymn and built upon it his spiritual. Most of the basic technique was already there: the refrain, the repetitions, the sequences of names, many of the actual words and expressions. At first the negro simply copied; then he began to build for himself.[51]

Gordon makes a strong case for going beyond his contemporaries' concentration on Child ballads:

> Scholars in general have vastly underrated the extent of the field. To study the ballad alone is not enough. The ballad is folk-song, but it is only one tiny division of folk-song. It contains its own special conventions, many of them due solely to the particular period and fashions under which it grew. Folk-song is not dead, it is being composed today. To approach any true doctrine of origins, to discover the laws of growth, we must include all available material.[52]

Indeed, Gordon pointedly does not discuss the Child ballads until the tenth article in the series. The theoretical underpinnings of his efforts, and the integration he sought of his work through *Adventure* and field collecting, come through clearly:

> The entire field needs to be marked out and surveyed and a census taken of the various types of folk-songs to be found in the different districts. Only then will it be possible to give any true definition of folk-song or to lay down with any certainty the laws that govern its growth. Just such a survey is being attempted at present by the writer; first, by the gradual building up of a nationwide group of correspondents fully in touch with the changing conditions in the various districts and ready to send in local songs; and, second, by a series of field trips.[53]

After outlining his grand plans for the field recording expedition, Gordon adds, "At least, that is the way the original plans read. Weather, roads and the abundance or scarcity of material in some of the districts have made certain minor changes advisable."[54] Indeed they had; in the midst of the series, Gordon lamented to correspondent Theodore Lancaster, "Wish I could be in a hundred places at once. This trying to gather all there is—everywhere keeps me humping all the time."[55] When the series ended, he was still working in Darien, having been there for over two years. He had lost the financial bedrock of his *Adventure* column, and failed to interest other funding sources, but he was now talking to the Library of Congress.

"A PRETERNATURALLY KEEN EYE FOR FLIES IN OINTMENT"

Beginning in early 1927, Gordon was in frequent contact with Carl Engel, director of the Music Division at the Library of Congress. After donating a complete collection of his *Adventure* columns to the Library, he broached the idea that a government agency—perhaps even the Library itself—could support his massive project.[56] Engel bit. In September 1927 he suggested that a private supporter could fund the project, or that the Carnegie Foundation and Victor Records might fund work under the auspices of the Library. He suggested the equivalent of an endowed chair at the library, or at the Curtis Institute of Music in Philadelphia, with Gordon occupying the post.[57]

Gordon apparently disliked this proposal, as it would cause him to lose possession of and control over the material he collected. Engel, meanwhile, had managed to raise funds for a stipend to support Gordon's work. In the end, Engel agreed to the creation of a national folk song archive in the Library itself, and in April of 1928 he announced to the press that the archive would be created, and that Gordon would be in charge.

It's clear that the two men had radically different visions of how the archive would be run. Gordon planned to continue with the mass-based, decentralized model of folksong collecting epitomized by his *Adventure* column, suggesting the formation of a loose network of independent, regional folksong societies. He also saw no reason to discontinue his fieldwork, and apart from a lecture at the Library a month after the announcement (several weeks before his appointment would become official), he remained in Darien and continued collecting. He also continued to write articles for the *Times* and kept up his exchanges with correspondents from the *Adventure* years.[58]

Engel, on the other hand, seems to have had the odd idea that the director of the new archive should actually show up in Washington and run it. Twice in Gordon's first two months of employment by the Library, he wrote and asked what Gordon was doing and what his plans were, and after four months, the Librarian of Congress, Herbert Putnam, sent a telegram to Gordon's wife asking where he was.[59]

Gordon's response to the telegram was to submit a detailed report on his activities in the field and his plans for the future, including the indexing and transcription of his recordings and correspondence, indexing of commercial folksong recordings, efforts to improve recording equipment and to clarify the nature of copyright with regard to folk material, the development of his decentralized collecting network, and the building-up of the archive as a research center.[60]

He would, however, remain in the field, because he believed his material was disappearing before his eyes. Kodish comments:

> He had been a scholar for ten years and had no sustained publications yet; he was never willing to sum up, to conclude. His idea of science provided Gordon with justification for endless collection, for his perfectionist's bent. . . . Even in the fall 1928 with the library beckoning, Gordon still could not turn his back on the rich discoveries he was making in the field. He believed that authentic folksongs were rapidly passing and that timely fieldwork was of the utmost importance.[61]

Gordon also continued his attempts to improve the equipment used for field recording. Working with scientists and equipment manufacturers, he experimented with aluminum disc and wire recorders, and even magnetic tape, fully fifteen years before the first practical tape recorders would be manufactured in Germany.[62]

Relations with his superiors at the Library remained frosty; in April 1929, Engel twice wrote to Gordon in Darien asking his intentions and suggesting, "Mr. Putnam and I would feel a great deal more reassured about the progress of our folk-song project if you would keep us *regularly* informed of your activities. The present method, I am afraid, will not do."[63] He also was late in submitting his first annual report, which provoked Engel to write, "I think I should tell you that, in talking with the Librarian, I gained the impression that he is not pleased with the way things are going. While he has not lost interest in the project, he fears that its future will be seriously endangered . . . unless those, upon whose support we must rely, can be shown a methodical handling of affairs and a substantial progress."[64]

Finally, in the autumn of 1929, over a year after his employment by the Library had begun, Gordon and his family moved to Washington. If anything, his relationship with his employers got worse; eccentricities of personal style, previously noted during his time at Berkeley, seem to have grated on his associates. Perhaps more important, he seems to have continued to have viewed himself as an independent researcher receiving funding from the Library, rather than an employee working within the structure of an enduring institution: "He looked at the archive as his laboratory and demanded control over his materials from the first. He seemed to squirrel things away and to maintain a paternal attitude toward his work. He was reluctant to open up his collection as yet. This ran counter to the philosophy of a national library."[65]

In the summer of 1930, Gordon sought and received a grant from the American Council of Learned Societies (ACLS) for the dual purposes of a pilot recording project in Charleston, South Carolina, and research into the improvement of field recording equipment. Gordon would spend the next two years fussing over the equipment; he collected nothing in Charleston, although he had indicated to the ACLS that the material was rapidly disappearing and that therefore the project took on some urgency.[66]

He did, however, produce an article on "The Negro Spiritual."[67] In it he took a more expansive view of black and white traditions and their interactions with secular and popular song forms than was common at the time. He also made occasional forays back into the field, including a brief fieldtrip to West Virginia to collect more black religious and secular songs—from an elderly white woman who had learned them from blacks in her childhood.[68]

By the end of 1931, the Archive of American Folk Song, as Gordon had christened it, was out of money. The Carnegie Corporation provided funds to keep it running until mid-June 1932, but in the desperate days of the early Depression no further support could be found. The Library told Gordon in March of 1932 that he would no longer be employed after the end of the 1932 fiscal year—30 June.[69] In late May of 1932, Donald Goodchild of the ACLS wrote to executive board member Edward Armstrong in evident frustration:

> He has nothing to show in the way of songs collected, or even in the way of equipment. I have periodically called on him to find out what progress has been made, but the report is always the same: there is no perfect recording machine. It is my impression that Mr. Gordon has a preternaturally keen eye for flies in ointment; at any rate, he has expended much time and some money (though not a great deal) in a series of experiments without positive result.[70]

With the cessation of Gordon's employment, the Library was left with a large collection of raw material and no way to organize it; although Engel had asked Gordon to index the material as it was collected, he had not done so. Faced with a mess, and realizing that Gordon was the only person who could make sense of it, the Library asked the ACLS to use the remainder of its grant to provide a stipend for him to index the material. He was given a clerical assistant and a strict six-month deadline, and, perhaps to the surprise of his superiors, he met it.[71]

In his final report before his formal employment ended, submitted in March of 1932, Gordon gave an indication of what had been accomplished in the creation of the AAFS. It now contained, along with material from independent collectors: eight thousand song texts, seven hundred with tunes; nine hundred songsters; 1,500 volumes of pulp magazines containing old-song columns; 350 commercial recordings (donated by the Victor company); and about one thousand cylinders recorded by Gordon himself. However, Gordon in his final report and Kodish in her biography both suggest that his greatest accomplishments were intangible, in providing bases for and development of his theories of folk song evolution, and his attempt to synthesize the communal and individual models of folk song creation. Kodish also suggests that his independent work, on "Old 97" and "Mademoiselle from Armentières," was intertwined with his institutional work, and should have been considered among his accomplishments during his tenure at the AAFS, even though it was not performed under the Library's auspices.[72]

Once he had delivered the final report on the indexing project in 1932, Gordon was at loose ends. He offered his continued services to the AAFS on a volunteer basis, intending to support himself through freelance writing projects, including several prospective books. Only one, *Mademoiselle from Armentières* (1935), would ever be published; the manuscript of a wide-ranging book on American folk song, written in collaboration with John Strachan and Paul Chancellor, was rejected by Macmillan, which had tentatively accepted the book when it was first proposed. He spent some of his time assisting John A. and Alan Lomax in compiling *American Ballads and Folk Songs*.[73]

In September of 1933 the final blow fell: with John A. Lomax now running the AAFS (for a dollar a year), Librarian of Congress Putnam told Gordon that his services would no longer be needed, even as a volunteer. Gordon broke down. Unable to work, unable to function, he locked himself in his room while his nineteen-year-old daughter worked to support the family. Gordon had always been a two-fisted drinker, but his drinking now increased to the point of acute alcoholism.[74]

After a year of incapacitation, Gordon began pulling himself together toward the end of 1934. He took a short-term job with the Works Progress Administration compiling a bibliography on diamonds and other precious stones, ironically working at the Library again. When that ran out, he taught English composition to night students at George Washington University, then found a permanent position as a junior clerk in the Department of the Interior. He maintained an avocational interest in folksong, speaking to private groups and participating as a lecturer in some of the first folk festivals, and he continued working with Melbert Cary on the *Mademoiselle from Armentières* book, which would be published in 1935.[75]

When funding was finally secured for the reactivation of the AAFS in 1937, then-director of the Music Division, Harold Spivacke, did not consider rehiring Gordon, but instead turned to John A. Lomax and later to his son, Alan. Gordon's cylinder recordings remained in legal limbo and unused (he had taken steps to retain legal ownership of the material he had collected before his tenure at the Library, although it remained on deposit there). Not until 1978, the fiftieth anniversary of the Archive's founding (and the ninetieth anniversary of Gordon's birth), would any of them be made available to the general public.[76] In Kodish's words, "Stored in boxes, tucked away eventually, the Gordon manuscripts and recordings remained a touchy secret, and Gordon himself remained an embarrassment."[77]

While many of his colleagues in the folklore community marginalized him, or pretended he didn't exist, the attitude was not universal. He served as toastmaster for the 1937 meeting of the American Folklore Society; in 1938 his *New York Times* articles were compiled into a book, and published to a good reception.[78] In 1941 he reprised his work on "Old 97" by advising the publisher Shapiro, Bernstein and Co. on a lawsuit concerning the copyright of "Casey Jones."[79]

In that same year he began working on contract for the Naval Research Laboratories' Sound Division, acting as a technical editor for papers relating to their secret work on sonar and the detection of submarines by undersea microphones; in 1945, he would become a full-time employee. Kodish, quoting Spivacke, suggests that this employment provided a further excuse, if one was needed, for the marginalization of Gordon in the world of folklore, although she points out that all of his longer publications came after his employment at the Library had ended.[80]

After his separation from the Library, he drew farther into his shell. In 1942, William Doerflinger and Douglas Bement proposed that Gordon write a popular book on "The Stories behind Your Songs" for E. P. Dutton and Co., where Doerflinger was an associate editor. Gordon does not seem to have replied. Sometime in the mid-1940s, his old friend and colleague at Berkeley, Arthur Brodeur, proposed that Gordon give a series of lectures on folklore; Gordon replied informally that he would be glad to do so, but when the university made the proposal in a formal letter, once again he failed to reply.[81]

Although Gordon gradually withdrew from the world of folklore, his work at the Naval Research Laboratory went well, and he seems to have been well liked and respected by his colleagues. As the years passed, however, his continued eccentricities of style and difficulty meeting deadlines became more noticeable: "His clothing was frequently stained with food; he appeared at work unshaven and disheveled. He fell asleep at his desk."[82] His wife developed a neurological disorder, and in response Gordon deteriorated further. Eventually, after she suffered a severe auto accident, she was institutionalized.[83]

He was not totally forgotten; in 1955, the president of the American Folklore Society arranged for him to be made an honorary life member. But his life was now out of control, and so was his drinking. He began missing work on a regular basis, and despite the attempted interventions of friends, colleagues, and family, he went downhill rapidly. He retired from the Naval Research Laboratory in 1958, at the age of 70, and moved into a garage apartment behind his daughter's house in McLean, Virginia. On 29 March 1961, Gordon died; his death was not marked by an obituary in the *New York Times*, nor by any notice in the *Journal of American Folklore*. In accordance with his wishes, he was buried in Darien—the place where he had done his best work.[84]

EPILOGUE

Robert Winslow Gordon was a walking box of contradictions. Far ahead of his time in recognizing the value of recording actual performances rather than taking them down on paper, he got too tangled in the technology to continue collecting. He saw the unity of black and white folk culture in America, but discounted evidence of African influence that was plain to other researchers. He created dynamic, radical decentralized mechanisms for folklore collection, but failed to understand their limitations. He was interested in the material culture of his informants, but was remarkably insensitive to the daily experiences and social structures that shaped their lives. He valued authenticity, but collected an unusual amount of secondhand material, most notably he persistently obtained a great deal of his African American material from secondhand white informants.

In many ways, Gordon's life was a tragedy. His achievements however, were quite substantial. He created and shaped the Archive of American Folk Song, now the Archive of Folk Culture in the American Folklife Center. His *New York Times* articles provided the first comprehensive introduction to traditional folk songs in the mass media. His *Adventure* columns were a creative, mass-based solution to the dilemma of collecting material from a broad sample of the public in a huge and diverse nation, and his continued use of decentralized, mass-media-based collecting methods was innovative and productive. He was among the first Americans to recognize the importance and promise of sound recording and photography in folklore collection and analysis. He was an early practitioner of the "historic-geographic" method of analyzing folk song evolution, first in his *Adventure* columns, then in his work on "Old 97" and "Mademoiselle from Armentières." He collected a tremendous amount of raw material (over one thousand recordings and eight thousand song texts), from the docks of the San Francisco Bay area to the Georgia Sea Islands. He was documenting material culture well before most of his contemporaries. He was a pioneer in studying bawdy material as folklore and publishing it in unexpurgated form. At the Archive of American Folk Song, he "innovated policies that are still in effect, such as lending equipment, giving technical assistance, and providing for the storage of folksong collections."[85]

Gordon received minimal recognition after his crashing failure at the Library of Congress. That the core of his ideas was fundamentally sound, however, is made evident by the fact that virtually every plan he made, every goal he set for the Archive would eventually be accomplished—by other people.

NOTES

1. Robert Winslow Gordon, "Introduction," in Melbert B. Cary, Jr., ed., *Mademoiselle from Armentières*, vol. 2 (New York: Press of the Woolly Whale, 1935).
2. Debora Kodish, *Good Friends and Bad Enemies: Robert Winsolw Gordon and the Study of American Folksong* (Urbana: University of Illinois Press, 1986).
3. Kodish, *Good Friends*, 14–15.
4. Kodish, *Good Friends*, 16; 22.
5. Kodish, *Good Friends*, 17–19.
6. Kodish, *Good Friends*, 21.
7. Kodish, *Good Friends*, 21.
8. David King Dunaway, *How Can I Keep from Singing: Pete Seeger* (New York: McGraw-Hill, 1981), 36.
9. Kodish, *Good Friends*, 28.
10. Kodish, *Good Friends*, 43.

11. Ron Goulart, *Cheap Thrills: A Popular History of the Pulp Magazines* (New Rochelle, NY: Arlington House, 1972); quoted in Kodish, *Good Friends*, 43.
12. Kodish, *Good Friends*, 30; 46.
13. Kodish, *Good Friends*, 30–31.
14. Kodish, *Good Friends*, 32–33.
15. Quoted in Kodish, *Good Friends*, 36.
16. A scientific method of folklore analysis developed by Julius Leopold Fredrik Krohn, a professor of Finnish literature, in which a researcher distills a piece of folklore into a hypothetical archetype and geographic starting place, and then traces instances across historic travel routes.
17. Kodish, *Good Friends*, 33–42; 88–118.
18. Kodish, *Good Friends*, 43–45.
19. James Hardin, "The Archive of Folk Culture at 75: A National Project with Many Workers," *Folklife Center News* 25:2 (Spring 2003): 3–13; 4.
20. Kodish, *Good Friends*, 46–47.
21. Duncan Emrich, ed.; various artists, *American Sea Songs and Shanties*, Library of Congress Archive of Folk Song LP, 2 vols, AFS L26/27 (1950s); *American Sea Shanties and Songs* Rounder, 1519 (2004).
22. Kodish, *Good Friends*, 48–49.
23. Kodish, *Good Friends*, 56–58.
24. Quoted in Kodish, *Good Friends*, 57.
25. Kodish, *Good Friends*, 58.
26. Kodish, *Good Friends*, 58–61.
27. Kodish, *Good Friends*, 60–63.
28. Kodish, *Good Friends*, 62–65.
29. Kodish, *Good Friends*, 65–66.
30. Kodish, *Good Friends*, 65–68, 72.
31. Kodish, *Good Friends*, 68–74.
32. Quoted in Kodish, *Good Friends*, 95.
33. Robert Winslow Gordon, "The Folk-Songs of America: Negro 'Shouts,'" *New York Times Magazine* (24 April 1927); Robert Winslow Gordon, "The Folk-Songs of America: The Spirituals," *New York Times Magazine* (20 February 1927).
34. Kodish, *Good Friends*, 123–127.
35. Robert Winslow Gordon, "The Folk-Songs of America: Negro Chants," *New York Times Magazine*, 8 May 1927.
36. Gordon, "Spirituals."
37. Robert Winslow Gordon, "The Folk-Songs of America: In the Hills Our Folk Songs Thrive," *New York Times Magazine* (9 January 1927).
38. Gordon, "Negro 'Shouts.'" With this evidence of how Gordon viewed his informants, it's a pity we have no records of how they viewed him!
39. Quoted in Kodish, *Good Friends*, 140.
40. Kodish, *Good Friends*, 143.
41. Victor 19427-A (1924).
42. Norm Cohen, *Long Steel Rail: The Railroad in American Folksong* (Urbana: University of Illinois Press, 2000), 198–202.
43. Henry Whitter, "Wreck on the Southern Old 97," OKeh 40015 (1923).
44. Cohen, *Long Steel Rail*, 199–201; 209–210; 222–223.
45. Cohen, *Long Steel Rail*, 203–204.
46. Cohen, *Long Steel Rail*, 212–215.
47. Kodish, *Good Friends*, 108.
48. Kodish, *Good Friends*, 210; Cary, *Mademoiselle*.
49. Kodish, *Good Friends*, 135.
50. Robert Winslow Gordon, "A Hunt on Hidden Trails," *New York Times Magazine* (2 January 1927).
51. Gordon, "Hidden Trails." The practice of using masculine pronouns as default, standard at the time Gordon was writing, makes it impossible to tell whether he was

dismissing the contribution of women to the process or merely following linguistic convention.
52. Gordon, "Hidden Trails."
53. Gordon, "Hidden Trails."
54. Gordon, "Hidden Trails."
55. Quoted in Kodish, *Good Friends*, 143.
56. Kodish, *Good Friends*, 154–156.
57. Kodish, *Good Friends*, 156–157.
58. Kodish, *Good Friends*, 160–161.
59. Kodish, *Good Friends*, 165; 168.
60. Kodish, *Good Friends*, 165; 169–170.
61. Kodish, *Good Friends*, 164–165.
62. Kodish, *Good Friends*, 174.
63. Quoted in Kodish, *Good Friends*, 175.
64. Quoted in Kodish, *Good Friends*, 177–178.
65. Quoted in Kodish, *Good Friends*, 176–177.
66. Kodish, *Good Friends*, 182–184; 187.
67. Robert Winslow Gordon, "The Negro Spiritual," *The Carolina Low Country*, ed. Augustine Smythe, et al. (New York: Macmillan, 1931), 191–222.
68. Kodish, *Good Friends*, 184; 186.
69. Kodish, *Good Friends*, 187.
70. Quoted in Kodish, *Good Friends*, 187.
71. Kodish, *Good Friends*, 188–189.
72. Kodish, *Good Friends*, 189–191.
73. Kodish, *Good Friends*, 192–193; John A. Lomax and Alan Lomax, *American Ballads and Folk Songs* (New York: Macmillan, 1934).
74. Kodish, *Good Friends*, 193; 195–196.
75. Kodish, *Good Friends*, 204–205.
76. Neil V. Rosenberg and Debora G. Kodish, eds., *Folk Songs of America: The Robert Winslow Gordon Collection, 1922–1932* LP, cassette: Library of Congress, AFS L68 (1978).
77. Kodish, *Good Friends*, 195.
78. Robert Winslow Gordon, *Folk-Songs of America* (New York: National Service Bureau, 1938).
79. Kodish, *Good Friends*, 219–220.
80. Kodish, *Good Friends*, 220–221.
81. Kodish, *Good Friends*, 221–222.
82. Kodish, *Good Friends*, 223–224.
83. Kodish, *Good Friends*, 225.
84. Kodish, *Good Friends*, 225–226.
85. Henrietta Yurchenko, untitled review of *Good Friends* and *Bad Enemies in American Music* 6:3 (Autumn 1988), 333–336.

ELEVEN
Collecting Occupational Songs

Dan Milner

Most people today have never sung occupational songs in a work setting; the few who have probably learned them in a military boot camp where drill instructors used parade ground choreography to mold their platoons into tight teams. Sergeants still teach ditties like this one to help unify the heavy heel beat of their troops and to sooth the *ennui*:

> Cock-a-roaches dance and play in our mess hall every day.
> Sound off. *One, two.*
> Sound off. *Three, four.*
> Bring 'em on down. *One, two, three, four. One, two . . . three, four.*[1]

But there was a time when occupational songs were a mainstay of life in North America. Carters crooned to their horses. Fishermen raised sails and hauled nets to the rhythm of shanties. Prisoners sang as they chopped wood or stamped license plates to the sharp impact of their tools. In the days before broadcast and recorded media, people in isolated working conditions produced their own precursors to *The Ed Sullivan Show* and *Saturday Night Live!*

> Beside the lowest bunks on the two long sides, ran the so-called "deacon seats," made of rough planks or split logs. . . . After supper, if they weren't too worn out, and every Sunday, the men sat along the deacon seat. . . . Someone would have a fiddle to accompany the dancing of jigs, hornpipes, and "breakdowns." And there was usually singing — mostly by individuals rather than the group . . . singing was so welcome that many men built up big repertoires of lumber-woods ballads and of other folk songs. . . . "I could entertain the boys all evening till lights out at nine," one shantyboy told me, "and not repeat myself once."[2]

Those words were written by William Main Doerflinger, a courtly graduate of Princeton and Harvard who edited books for a living and who collected folk songs and performed magic tricks for kicks. Bill Doerflinger was one of a band of enthusiasts who only rarely were actually employed to gather occupational folk songs. Their own professions were diverse: sailors and social workers, bartenders and teachers, mothers and many things more.[3] Nevertheless, they preserved vast stretches of our oral history and, most often, they did it to a remarkably high standard.

The distinct forces that shaped North America into separate regions with different climates, varying fertility and characteristic industries also shaped our occupational music. Whalers out of New Bedford, gold miners in California and farm laborers in the Cotton Belt did not all leave their homes chanting the same, "Hi-ho, hi-ho, it's off to work we go." In the same way, North American folk song collectors living in different parts of Canada and the United States found unique occupational songs attuned to the characteristic geography and regional life of their areas. What these women and men had in common was an abiding love for the regions they called "home" and a fascination with true popular songs — that is, the songs people made for themselves, not the songs that were made for them by others. The musical lore these enthusiasts found and preserved is important because it tells us firsthand what it was like to change the landscape of North America, how people coped with adversity and what happened when they did not.

The books these songcatchers produced first began to appear in the 1920s, save those dedicated to cowboy songs (as detailed by Guy Logsdon in chapter 4). The principal early compilations of collectors who worked with the musical poetry of the northern forests were Roland Palmer Gray's *Songs and Ballads of the Maine Lumberjacks* (1924), Fannie Hardy Eckstorm and Mary Winslow Smyth's *Minstrelsy of Maine* (1927), and Franz Rickaby's *Ballads and Songs of the Shanty-Boy* (1926), a collection of songs found in Michigan, Wisconsin, and Minnesota.[4] Phillips Barry's *The Maine Woods Songster* was published in 1939, followed by Earl C. Beck's *Songs of the Michigan Lumberjacks* (1941).[5] William Main Doerflinger's *Shantymen and Shantyboys* appeared in 1951.[6] Canadian books came to print later, notably Louise Manny and James Reginald Wilson's *Songs of Miramichi* (1968) and Edith Fowke's *Lumbering Songs from the Northern Woods* (1970).[7] Edward D. "Sandy" Ives produced a number of more recent collections including *Folksongs of New Brunswick* (1989).[8] Ronald Cohen has covered the wide range of work songs in his recent *Work and Sing* (2010),[9] as well as Ted Gioia's *Work Songs* (2006).[10] Edith Fowke also prepared a valuable long-playing record, *Lumbering Songs from the Ontario Shanties*.[11]

What strikes one immediately about the songs these collectors found and preserved is that they pay virtually no regard to the U.S.–Canada border. So close was the cultural commonality among American and Canadian men of the forest that songs rarely lost currency as lumbermen crossed the international boundary in search of work. Good songs found a welcome wherever they traveled—and not just among Anglo-Saxons. French-Canadian, Irish, and Scots lumberman worked side-by-side with Anglo-Saxons, and the characteristic songs and performance style of each found their way to the deacon seat. One such song is the Irish-Canadian vision poem, "Lost Jimmy Whalen." It was written following the death of a log driver who perished freeing a jam on Ontario's Mississippi River in 1878. "Lost Jimmy Whalen" was known from Maine to Minnesota, and even traveled back "home" to Ireland.

> As lonely I strayed by the banks of a river
> Watching the sunbeams as evening grew near,
> As onward I rambled, I spied a fair damsel
> Weeping and wailing with many a tear.
>
> "Jimmy" she cried, "won't you come me darling?
> Come to me love from your cold, silent tomb.
> You promised to meet me this evening, my darling,
> But death's cruel angel has sealed your sad doom
>
> "You promised to meet me by the banks of this river
> And give me fond kisses as oft times you gave,
> To hold me once in strong, willing arms
> And to see me again, Jimmy, come from your grave."
>
> Slowly there rose from the depths of the river
> A vision of beauty more bright than the sun,
> In the robes of bright crimson around him a-wavering
> As unto this female to speak he began.[12]

Logging was dangerous work so collectors of the lumber camp repertoire found plenty of tragic songs. They found plenty of humorous ones too. Like the crowds in Broadway theaters, the boys of the timber woods shanties appreciated comedy as well as tragedy. Bosses and cooks typically caught the worst of the flak.

> Then there's a compound of raw cabbage they make,
> Sure it would physic old Satan till his two sides would ache.
> They ferment it and boil it and keep it for kraut,
> And the stink it would reach you a mile from the house.[13]

Other songs tell clearly how to operate an efficient nineteenth century logging operation and, like "The Shanty Boys," are quite specific about the division of labor in these enterprises.

> The choppers and the sawyers, they lay the lumber low;
> The skidders and the swampers, they haul it to and fro.
> In come the loaders with their teams just at the break of day:

"Hurray, me boys, get on your loads, and haste to clear away."[14]

Many people picking up William Main Doerflinger's *Songs of the Sailor and Lumbermen* for the first time are surprised that songs of these two occupational groups should be dealt with in the same volume.[15] Actually, Fannie Hardy Eckstrom and Mary Winslow Smyth's earlier collection, *Minstrelsy of Maine*, also focused on the songs of the forest and sea.[16] Geography is the key. Bill Doerflinger explained it this way:

> In the early days and well into the nineteenth century in many districts, rivers and lakes served as the main arteries of travel and transportation between the coastal settlements and the interior. Down those rivers, as the lumber industry reached major proportions early in the last century, and for many decades thereafter, logs cut in inland forests were floated down to the sawmills and shipping points at tidewater. In seaports such as Bangor and Calais in Maine, and Saint John and the ports of the lower Miramichi in New Brunswick; in Nova Scotian towns and at the big lumber exporting center of Quebec, seamen, woodsmen, and rivermen came into close mutual contact.... The young man hankering after a free and active life could respond either to the call of the salt wind or the shaking white sails, or to the no less alluring ring of the chopper's ax and the roar of the white water in the rapids. Many ambitious fellows followed, at various stages in their careers, both the sea and the lumbering, some of them "shipping out" in the summer months and working in the woods in the winter. It is not surprising, therefore, that many ballads ranked as favorites with both groups of men.[17]

The performance of "big" ballads was a true test of a singer's ability. "The Flying Cloud" was well known on the sea and in lumber camps.

The very next day we sailed away with our cargo of slaves,
'Twould have been much better for those poor slaves had they been in their graves,
For the plague and fever came on board, swept half of them away.
We dragged the dead upon the deck and threw them in the sea.

We sailed away without delay till we came to the Cuban shore
And sold them to the planter there to be slaves forevermore.
The rice and coffee fields to hoe beneath a burning sun,
To lead a long and wretched life till their career was run.

And when our money it was gone, we put to sea again.
Then Captain Moore, he came on board, and said to us his men,
"There's gold and silver to be had, if with me you'll remain;
We will hoist aloft a pirate's flag and scour the raging main."[18]

Occupational folk songs are divided into two groups: songs that were sung while working and that were intrinsic to the work process; and songs that were related to a trade but which usually were sung off duty for relaxation. Laborers sang purely for entertainment purposes in the woods. But, on deep-water sailing ships, singing seamen were highly valued for their ability to rally work parties. The lead singer chose the appropriate work song or *shanty* (also spelled *chantey*)—a tool really—to provide the common rhythm needed to coordinate sailors' efforts for the accomplishment of specific tasks such as tightening sail, raising anchor, pumping bilge, etc.

> Haul on the bowline, our bully ship's a rolling.
> Haul on the bowline, the bowline. *Haul!*

One of the earliest books devoted to American sea songs was Joanna C. Colcord's *Roll and Go*, which first appeared in 1924.[19] It is also one of the finest of its kind and Miss Colcord's unique perspective on maritime life adds a great deal to her work. Coming from an old Maine maritime family, she was born at sea in 1882 on the bark *Charlotte A. Littlefield*, captained by her father. She wrote in the introduction to *Songs of American Sailormen*:

> These work-songs of the sea are drawn in part from my own memories of the years spent on blue water under sail from 1890 to 1899, mostly on voyages between New York and various ports in the China Sea. In part, they are songs learned from my father, who loved them and sang them well, and whose seagoing began about the year 1874.[20]

The story is often told that Queen Victoria was so enamored of Lewis Carroll's *Alice in Wonderland* that she asked a courtier to obtain a copy of his next book as soon as it was published. As it happened, Lewis Carroll was only the pen name of Charles Dodgson, an Oxford mathematics lecturer so, in due course, the queen was presented with an autographed text of *An Elementary Treatise on Determinants with Their Application to Simultaneous Linear Equations and Algebraic Geometry*.[21] Joanna Colcord was, like many songcatchers (and Charles Dodgson), an accomplished person of varied interests. She received an MS in chemistry but spent virtually all her adult life as a social worker. Someone (royal or otherwise) enamored with *Roll and Go* and wanting her next book on a maritime topic, *Sea Language Comes Ashore* (1945), would have had to wait for *Emergency Work Relief* (1933) and *Your Community* (1939) to be published first.[22]

Maritime songs were the first "world music." Some ships hired crews of men from the same area while others hired sailors from anywhere and everywhere. Because the United States in particular was a diverse immigrant nation, there was an increased likelihood that its ships' crews would be cosmopolitan. Furthermore, it was the very nature of a vessel to collect people, as well as cargoes, and to take them to new places. As a generalization, it can be said that for reasons like these a basic repertoire embracing elements of Anglo, American, Canadian, Caribbean, Irish, and other cultures built up amongst deep-water sailors. But deep-water sailors, coastal fishermen, sealers, bay men, whalers, and others did different work and, most often sang unique songs illustrative of their distinctive labor. This specialization is apparent in reading the books of the collectors who gathered maritime songs for preservation and later published them for analysis or popularization.

In addition to the Colcord, Doerflinger, and Eckstorm and Smyth books, some important collections of North American maritime song are Frank Shay's *Iron Men and Wooden Ships* (1924), Roy Mackenzie's *Ballads and Sea Songs from Nova Scotia* (1928), David Bone's *Capstan Bars* (1932), Helen Creighton's *Songs and Ballads from Nova Scotia* (1932) and *Maritime Folk Songs* (1961), Elizabeth Greenleaf and Grace Mansfield's *Ballads and Sea Songs from Newfoundland* (1933), Frederick Pease Harlow's *Chanteying Aboard American Ships* (1962), MacEdward Leach's *Folk Ballads and Songs of the Lower Labrador Coast* (1965), Ken Peacock's *Songs of the Newfoundland Outports* (1965), and Genevieve Lehr and Anita Best's *Come and I Will Sing You* (1985).[23] In 2002, *Windjammers: Songs of the Great Lakes Sailors* was published with the help of Joe Grimm, making available for the first time the maritime songs collected by Ivan H. Walton before his death in 1968.[24] But so numerous and so well traveled were seamen from the great wind powered sailing ships of old that traces of their ballads and songs were strewn across the continent and can be found in almost every collection of North American folk songs. Lastly, Mary Wheeler's *Steamboatin' Days* (1944) is a collection of African-American roustabout songs from the Mississippi River system steam packets.[25] A valuable compact disc of maritime field recordings from the Library of Congress is *American Sea Shanties and Songs*.[26] Two long-playing records are Helen Creighton's *Maritime Folk Songs* and Edith Fowke's *Songs of the Great Lakes*.[27]

Women, equally with men, have been major collectors of folk songs. In the area of occupational song, which connotes sweat, swearing, and all the excesses that make men the less fair sex, one might wonder how women could have been successful or, rather, what they might have missed because their access to certain songs and certain situations was blocked. Fannie Eckstorm and Mary Smyth addressed this issue in the first paragraph of *Minstrelsy of Maine*, "collecting these songs was a man's job . . . we could not go into lumber camps and the forecastles of coasting schooners, nor frequent mill boarding houses . . . and even jails, where the unprinted, and too often unprintable, songs of the kind we must seek originate and flourish."[28] However, just before we dismiss Eckstorm and Smith as Victorian ladies, they present themselves as prototype Rosie-the-Riveters and continue, "But no man appeared steeped in balladry and versed in folk-music, understanding the hearts of the people and wise enough to interpret what he found in them."[29] Joanna Colcord, fearing gender prejudice, first thought to author *Roll and Go* as "J. J.

Colcord" but was dissuaded by her brother. She addressed the tender issue of profanity this way:

> Much has been written about the obscenity of shanties. Gross some of the words undoubtedly were, when the shantyman chose to improvise them; but it was a jovial, forthright, almost wholesome obscenity, with no suggestiveness or *double entendre* such as disfigures our music-hall compositions; and it served its turn. The shantyman who could surprise a laugh from the crowd on the rope made the work lighter.[30]

In truth, while songcatchers generally collected where they lived, they were not often "of the trade"; they were not usually lumberjacks, sailors, etc., themselves. So, with her unique experience as a young woman growing up at sea, Joanna Colcord had heard as much as anyone would by the time she was eighteen and that put her at considerable advantage to virtually all other collectors. One man who admired her work was David Bone, a merchant marine officer who wrote evocatively and sensitively in 1932 in *Capstan Bars*, his book on sailors' work songs:

> Their need for use on board a modern ship has gone.... The hurricane shout that inspired generations of seamen will not again be heard to its fitting accompaniment of storm, and canvas thrashing free in the wind, and the thunder of cleft seas under the bows, or to the musical *clank* of an anchor cable riding home in some far harbor.... As part of radio programs broadcast they have become popular. In the process of adapting them to the requirements of professional singers they are in danger of becoming polished and shiny. In a few years their purpose will be forgotten and, transferred to the motley book of popular song, they will doubtless linger only as entertainment.[31]

The words of Joanna Colcord and David Bone are good guides for modern day "nightingales" who would perform traditional maritime songs.

Frank Shay was another interesting collector of maritime song. Best known as a writer and book merchant, Shay was earlier a sailor, a lumberman and a WWI infantry sergeant. In 1929, he produced the premiere of Eugene O'Neill's *S.S. Glencairn*, a cycle of three maritime-themed plays: *Bound East for Cardiff*, *Moon of the Caribbees*, and *The Long Voyage Home* at his barn-based Provincetown Playhouse. Shay wrote in *American Sea Songs and Shanties* about his introduction to maritime song:

> I heard my first chantey in 1915 while serving as a foremast hand aboard the tanker Standard. She took fire off Yucatan and her entire power plant was burned out; all subsequent work had to be done by hand. Another ship stood by to take us in tow, and heavy hause lines were passed, only to part, and repassed, all handled by the small crew. Work was going poorly until a shipmate sounded off with "Whiskey for My Johnny." The song brought immediate results and others were broken out, mostly in fragments. By the time the Standard made port I had a small collection of the old chanteys.[32]

About 1800, New York surpassed Philadelphia as America's greatest port and preeminent urban center. This assumption of leadership by New York was clear recognition of the geographic reality that it possessed a superior harbor that is closer to Europe. But New York is also situated at the mouth of the Hudson River, eminently navigable 154 miles upstream and part of a viable route to the interior of the continent that veered west at Troy through the Mohawk River valley and onwards to Buffalo. It is no accident that Philadelphia today is a city of roughly a million and half inhabitants while New York has a population in excess of eight million.[33] Beyond physical geography, the most important factor in the rise of New York City was the construction of the Erie Canal (1817–1825), the 363-mile long ditch that connects the head of navigation on the Hudson with the Great Lakes.

No American field collectors devoted their attention solely to canal songs. The best we have is one chapter in Harold W. Thompson's *Body, Boots and Britches* (1940), a fine work that looks at New York State folk songs and lore through twenty topics including "Canawlers," "Lumbermen and Rafters" and "Whalers."[34] Thompson drafted his Cornell University students—250 or more at a time—to collect the material. Another state collection, *Pennsylvania Songs and Legends* (1960), edited by George Korson, contains a chapter written by Louis Edwin Theiss that gives some background on "Canallers" and their lore as well as information on other occupations but not much in the way of songs.[35] Some general folk song collections such as Carl Sandburg's *The American Songbag* (1927) contain canal songs, however, we need to remember many of the canal songs that were recovered from tradition during the twentieth century were actually early vaudeville songs.[36] In what is a true "chicken and egg" conundrum, it may never be known definitively whether "The E-ri-e" from Sandburg's *Songbag*—

> We were forty miles from Albany,
> Forget it I never shall,
> What a terrible storm we had one night
> On the E-ri-e Canal.
>
> Oh, the E-ri-e was rising
> The gin was getting low
> And I scarcely think
> We'll get a drink
> Till we get to Buffalo,
> Till we get to Buffalo. [37]

—is the forerunner of "Buffalo," attributed to Edward Harrigan in Harrigan and Hart's *Isle de Blackwell Songster* of 1878—

> From Buffalo I've just come down
> On the good boat Danger;

> A long, long trip on the Erie, boys,
> I feel just like a stranger.
> We'd heavy fogs, [and windy] storms,
> Forget 'em I never shall;
> I'm every inch a sailor boy,
> On the E-ri-a Canal.
>
> For the Erie is a rising,
> And the gin is getting low;
> I hardly think you'll get a drink,
> Till we get back to Buffalo.[38]

—or vice versa. Early vaudeville singers, including Harrigan of the immensely popular Harrigan and Hart team, traveled extensively and it was through their performances and the sale of their songsters that compositions which can be documented through sheet music, such as "Get Up, Jack, Let John Sit Down" and "McNally's Row of Flats," passed into folk culture and were later taken down as traditional pieces by some of America's foremost songcatchers.

In the eastern United States, railroads followed canals by a couple of generations but canal boats continued moving cargo on viable routes for many years afterwards because, all things being equal, transportation is cheaper by water than by rail or road. But slow-moving canal boats pulled along by mules did not grab public imagination the way that loud, sleek railroad trains could. For over one hundred years, nothing in our North American culture excited us like the big black glistening steam engine, roaring fire and spitting cinders, smoking hot on a summer's day, steaming walls of fog on a winter's night. More than the car or the airplane, it was the train that took us somewhere we dearly longed to go or delivered us from a place we desperately wished to leave.

The railroad so grabbed our consciousness that we tend to forget most railroad songs were composed not by employees but by passengers, not all of whom bought tickets prior to departure. For much of the twentieth century, including all the Great Depression years, huge numbers of people, hoboes young and old, were inextricably bound to life on the cold steel rail as they roamed the United States in search of work.

> All around the water tank, waitin' for a train,
> A thousand miles away from home sleeping in the rain;
> I walked up to a brakeman to give him a line of talk,
> He says, "If you got money, I'll see that you don't walk."
> "I haven't got a penny, not a nickel can I show."
> "Get off, get off you railroad bum" and he slammed the boxcar do'.[39]

The occupational songs of railroad workers most often speak about specialized jobs—engineer, fireman, conductor, brakemen, and the like. Many come originally from African- and Irish-Americans and display considerable occupational pride. "Jerry, Go An' Ile That Car," stems from crews that maintained their own specific sections of railroad track:

> Come all ye railroad section men
> An' listen to my song;
> It is of Larry O'Sullivan
> Who is now dead and gone.
> For twinty years a section boss,
> He niver hired a tar–
> Oh, its j'int ahead and cinter back,
> An' "Jerry, go an' ile that car-r-r!"
>
> For twinty years a section boss
> He worked upon the track,
> And be it to his cred-I-it
> He niver had a wrack,
> For he kept every jint right up to the p'int
> Wid the tap of the tampin'-bar-r;
> And while the byes was a-shimmin' up the ties,
> It's "Jerry, wud yez ile that car-r-r!"[40]

Likewise, Eddie "Son" House, one of America's greatest blues artists, was employed as a porter on the New York Central Railroad later in his life and he displayed in song his pride of working on the crack Empire State Express

> The Empire State she runs on Eastern time.
> She's the rolling-ist baby on the New York Central line.
>
> If you want get over to Chicago and you want get over there quick,
> Catch that Empire State and you can soon get your business straight.[41]

The best single book on American railroad songs is Norm Cohen's authoritative *Long Steel Rail* (1981), but it is a different kind of book than those mentioned above because it includes popular as well as traditional songs, and it is the work of a compiler and an historian more than a field collector.[42] General collections such as John A. and Alan Lomax's *American Ballads and Folk Songs* (1934), Alan Lomax's *The Folk Songs of North America* (1960), and Carl Sandburg's *The American Songbag* (1927) contain chapters on railroad songs and are worthwhile.[43] There are numerous compilations of railroad songs on recorded media too. Field recordings from the Archive of Folk Culture at the Library of Congress previously issued as long-playing records are now available as compact discs in conjunction with Rounder Records. *Railroad Songs and Ballads* contains twenty-two examples of railroad songs and music recorded by sixteen different field collectors between 1936 and 1959.[44]

The steam engines that pulled railroad trains almost always burned coal. They themselves were made of steel, which required vast quantities of coal to produce—so much coal that it was considerably more cost effective to transport the iron ore to the edge of the coalfields rather than vice versa. Coal also once heated our homes and powered our factories. The Appalachian Mountain region was once the world's greatest source of coal. Today, the United States still possesses more coal than all other energy sources combined. The problem always has been how to extract it safely and use it cleanly.

The great collector of American mining songs was George Korson. He was brought from the Ukraine as a boy, grew to manhood in a northeastern Pennsylvania coal town and became steeped in the culture of the coalfields as he worked as a journalist for the *Record* of Wilkes-Barre and the *Republican* of Pottsville. Korson began collecting in 1929 out of respect for the people with whom he spent so much of his time, and his great love of singing miners is etched in most of his work. He is said to have felt "the proper stance of folklorist to folksinger to be that of devoted scribe rather than austere analyst" or, to put it another way, he knew instinctively that folk songs exist because of folk singers and that the songs are more important than scholars' opinions of them.[45] His books include *Minstrels of the Mine Patch* (1938) and *Coal Dust on the Fiddle* (1943), but his first collection of mining songs appeared in the *United Mine Workers Journal*, thought to be the first folklore study to be published in an American trade union periodical.[46] Sound selections from George Korson's fieldwork are available on compact disc: selections from his 1946–1947 recordings have been issued as *Songs and Ballads of the Anthracite Miners* and selections from his 1940 recordings have been issued as *Songs and Ballads of the Bituminous Miners*.[47]

One of Korson's informants was Patrick J. "Giant" O'Neill. O'Neill was actually diminutive in stature but his vertical shortcomings were more than made up by his dancing agility. At one point, O'Neill left the coalfields to join *Howorth's Grand Hibernica*, a vaudeville company that reportedly made an around-the-world tour and was certainly "world famous" in the United States by the late 1870s. They performed variety shows and comedic plays such as *Muldoon's Meanderings, or an Irish American's Troubles in Ireland* and, about 1880, published a songster including "The Man You Don't Meet Every Day." When the *Grand Hibernica* disbanded in 1894, O'Neill returned to his previous occupation as a coalmine blacksmith, and he used that piece which he had learned with Howorth's as the nucleus of the tender, yet powerful, song, "The Hard Working Miner." Collected in 1925, it appears in *Minstrels of the Mine Patch*.

> I'm a hard working man, you can see by my hands,
> Although I am friendly and free.
> A dollar a day is very small pay
> For a man with a large family.

> I didn't come here, boys, to boast or to brag,
> But just for to tell you my troubles,
> I work day and night and the world I must fight
> And load coal with my pick and shovel.
>
> I work in the mines where the sun never shines
> Nor daylight does ever appear;
> With my lamp blazing red on the top of my head,
> And in danger I never know fear.
>
> Just think of the poor man who works in the mines
> With the mules and the rats underground;
> Where the smoke is so thick you can cut it with a stick,
> And can weigh it on scales by the pound.
> My face it is black from the dust of the coal,
> Tough my heart it is open and free;
> I would share my last loaf with the man that's in want,
> Though I earn it quite hard you can see.
>
> Now my kind friends, I will bid you good-bye;
> I cannot stay here any longer,
> I'll pick up my pack, throw it o'er my back,
> And I think I will make my road shorter,
> I have a wife and small family at home in the house,
> And to meet me I'm sure they'll be glad,
> They will stand in the door when I'm on my way home,
> And they'll say to their mama, "Here's Dad."[48]

Those keenly interested in mining songs should also look for Green's excellent *Only a Miner* (1972) with the understanding that it is discussion of the song genre rather than the presentation of an individual collector's fieldwork, and is limited to recordings.[49]

What is not included in this brief survey is nearly as important as what is. Obviously, there are many more occupational settings and songs than can be discussed here. First, some genres, cowboy songs for example, are dealt with in other sections of this book. Second, not all North American songcatchers had their work published and, in all likelihood, no field collector has ever had his or her entire collection made available in print or on sound recordings. Just as an example, nine books were published of songs from the Flanders Ballad Collection but the treasure trove assembled by Helen Hartness Flanders and her colleagues totals more than four thousand musical items. The nine books would have to have been very big indeed to contain it all. Third, not every occupation produced folk songs and some major pursuits like farming produced inordinately few. The likely explanation is that folk songs are the product of the working class, not just of people who work. Farmers are entrepreneurs almost by definition, and it seems to hold true that farm laborers composed many more songs about their toil than did farmers. Fourth and most obvious, these are songs only in the English language; our great North American cultural panorama is much broader than that.

In closing, two areas of occupational song surge to mind: prison songs and union songs. Those interested in the stark, electric songs of confinement sung in the prisons of America's Deep South should seek out the field recordings made at the Louisiana State Penitentiary in Angola by Harry Oster. Some of these are currently available on compact discs from Arhoolie Records as *Prison Work Songs* and *Angola Prisoners' Blues*.[50] Those who want to look into the songs of organized labor—remember, it was the unions that gave us all the forty-hour workweek—should seek out John Greenway's *American Folksongs of Protest* (1953).[51] Greenway's book is a great catchall of labor songs from a broad variety of occupations including textile workers, longshoremen, migrant farm workers, steelworkers and automobile assemblers, and it includes this one last image, a picture as vivid today as the hour it was written:

> Across the board sat Henry Ford
> And his face was full of woe;
> Oh, he bit his nails and his face grew pale,
> But he talked with the CIO.[52]

NOTES

1. Learned by the author from Staff Sergeant Halbert C. Barrix (USAF) at Lackland AFB Training Center, November 1965.

2. William Main Doerflinger, *Songs of the Sailor and Lumberman* (Glenwood, IL: Meyerbooks, 1990), 205–207.

3. Likewise in Britain and Ireland, folk song collector Alfred Williams was a railroad factory worker, Sabine Baring-Gould a parson, Sam Henry a revenue taxman, Joseph Ranson a priest, etc.

4. Roland Palmer Gray, *Songs and Ballads of the Maine Lumberjacks* (Cambridge, MA: Harvard University Press, 1924); Fannie Hardy Eckstorm and Mary Winslow Smyth, *Minstrelsy of Maine: Folk-songs and Ballads of the Woods and the Coast* (Boston: Houghton Mifflin, 1927); Franz Rickaby, *Ballads and Songs of the Shanty-Boy* (Cambridge, MA: Harvard University Press, 1926).

5. Barry Phillips, ed., *The Maine Woods Songster* (Cambridge, MA: Powell Printing Co., 1939); Earl C. Beck, *Songs of the Michigan Lumberjacks* (Ann Arbor: University of Michigan Press, 1941).

6. William Main Doerflinger, *Shantymen and Shantyboys: Songs of the Sailor and Lumberman* (New York: Macmillan, 1951).

7. Louise Manny and James Reginald Wilson, *Songs of Miramichi* (Fredericton, New Brunswick: Brunswick, 1968); and Edith Fowke, ed., *Lumbering Songs from the Northern Woods* (Publications of the American Folklore Society, Memoir Series 55, Austin: University of Texas Press, 1970).

8. Edward D. "Sandy" Ives, *Folksongs of New Brunswick* (Fredericton, New Brunswick: Goose Lane Editions, 1989).

9. Ronald Cohen, *Work and Sing: A History of Occupational and Labor Union Songs in the United States* (Crockett, CA: Carquinez Press, 2010).

10. Ted Gioia, *Work Songs* (Durham: Duke University Press, 2006).

11. *Lumbering Songs from the Ontario Shanties*, Folkways (FM 4052, 1961).
12. Flanders Ballad Collection, Middlebury College, Middlebury, VT. Item 2299, "Lost Jimmy Whalen" as sung by Sidney Luther, Pittsburg, NH.
13. Fowke, *Lumbering Songs*, 179. "I Went to the Woods" as sung by Stanley Botting, Naramata, British Columbia.
14. Fowke, *Lumbering Songs*, 36. "The Shantyboys in the Pine" as sung by Jim Harrington, Ennismore, Ontario.
15. William Main Doerflinger, *Songs of the Sailor and Lumberman* (New York: Macmillan, 1972) is a revised version of Doerflinger's *Shantymen and Shantyboys* (1951), reprinted in 1990 by Meyerbooks.
16. Fannie Hardy Eckstorm and Mary Winslow Smyth, *Minstrelsy of Maine* (Boston: Houghton Mifflin, 1927).
17. Doerflinger, *Songs of the Sailor*, 1990.
18. Flanders Ballad Collection, Middlebury College, Middlebury, VT. Items 1184 – 1187, "The *Flying Cloud*" sung by Lena Bourne Fish, East Jaffrey, NH.
19. Joanna C. Colcord, *Roll and Go* (Boston: Charles E. Lauriat Co., 1924). Republished in an enlarged and revised edition as Joanna C. Colcord, *Songs of American Sailormen* (New York: Norton, 1938).
20. Colcord, *Songs*, 35.
21. Charles Dodgson, *An Elementary Treatise on Determinants with their Application to Simultaneous Linear Equations and Algebraic Geometry* (London: Macmillan, 1867).
22. Joanna Carver Colcord, *Sea Language Comes Ashore* (New York: Cornell Maritime Press, 1945); Joanna Carver Colcord, *Emergency Work Relief as Carried Out in Twenty-six American Communities, 1930–1931* (New York: Russell Sage Foundation, 1932); Joanna Carver Colcord, *Your Community* (New York: Russell Sage Foundation, 1932).
23. Frank Shay, *Iron Men and Wooden Ships* (New York: Doubleday Page, 1924); W. Roy Mackenzie, *Ballads and Sea Songs from Nova Scotia* (Hatboro, PA: Folklore Associates, 1963); David W. Bone, *Capstan Bars* (New York: Harcourt Brace, 1932); Helen Creighton, Songs and Ballads from Nova Scotia (New York: Dover, 1966); Helen Creighton, Maritime Folk Songs (Toronto: Ryerson Press, 1962); Elizabeth Bristol Greenleaf and Grace Yarrow Mansfield, Ballads and Sea Songs of Newfoundland (Cambridge, MA: Harvard University Press, 1933); Frederick Pease Harlow, Chanteying Aboard American Ships (Barre, MA: Barre Gazette, 1962); MacEdward Leach, *Folk Ballads and Songs of the Lower Labrador Coast* (Ottawa: National Museum of Canada, 1965); Kenneth Peacock, *Songs of the Newfoundland Outports*, 3 vols. (Ottawa: National Museum of Canada, 1965); Genevieve Lehr and Anita Best, *Come and I Will Sing You* (Toronto: University of Toronto Press, 1985).
24. Ivan H. Walton and Joe Grimm, eds., *Windjammers: Songs of the Great Lakes Sailors* (Detroit: Wayne State University Press, 2002).
25. Mary Wheeler, *Steamboatin' Days* (Salem, NH: Ayer Publishing Co., 1984).
26. *American Sea Shanties and Songs* (Rounder CD 1519, 2004).
27. Helen Creighton, ed., *Maritime Folk Songs* (Folkways FE 4307, 1962); Edith Fowke, ed., *Songs of the Great Lakes* (Folkways FE 4018, 1964).
28. Eckstorm and Smyth, *Minstrelsy*, vii.
29. Eckstorm and Smyth, *Minstrelsy*, vii.
30. Colcord, *Songs of American Sailormen*, 26.
31. Bone, *Capstan Bars*.
32. Frank Shay, *American Sea Songs and Chanteys* (New York: Norton, 1948), 15.
33. U.S. Census Bureau 2000 statistics were New York: 8,008,278 and Philadelphia: 1,517,550.
34. Harold W. Thompson, *Body, Boots and Britches* (Philadelphia: J. Lippincott, 1940). See especially pages 220–254.
35. Lewis Edwin Theiss, "Canallers" in George Korson, ed., *Pennsylvania Songs and Legends* (Baltimore: Johns Hopkins Press, 1960), 258–288.
36. Carl Sandburg. *The American Songbag* (New York: Harcourt Brace, 1927).
37. Sandburg, *American Songbag*, 180.

38. *Harrigan and Hart's Isle de Blackwell Songster* (New York: A. J. Fisher, 1878), 16–17. The publisher attributes the song as "Written by Ned Harrigan."

39. Norm Cohen, *Long Steel Rail* (Urbana: University of Illinois Press, 1981), 357.

40. Sandburg, *American Songbag*, 360.

41. Son House, "Empire State Express," *Father of the Delta Blues*, Sony/Legacy CD48867.

42. Cohen, *Long Steel Rail*, 1981.

43. John A. Lomax and Alan Lomax, *American Ballads and Folk Songs* (New York: Macmillan, 1934); Alan Lomax, *The Folk Songs of North America* (Garden City, NY: Doubleday, 1960); Sandburg, *American Songbag*, 1927.

44. *Railroad Songs and Ballads* (Rounder CD 1508, 1997).

45. Archie Green, *Only A Miner* (Urbana: University of Illinois Press, 1972), 24.

46. George Korson, Minstrels of the Mine Patch: *Songs and Stories of the Anthracite Industry* (Philadelphia: University of Pennsylvania Press, 1938; reprinted in 1964); George Korson, *Coal Dust on the Fiddle: Songs and Stories of the Bituminous Industry* (Philadelphia: University of Pennsylvania Press, 1943); George Korson, "Songs and Ballads of the Anthracite Miner," *United Mine Workers Journal* (serialized, 1926–1927).

47. George Korson, ed., *Songs and Ballads of the Anthracite Miners* (Rounder CD 1502); George Korson, ed., *Songs and Ballads of the Bituminous Miners* (Rounder CD 1522).

48. Korson, *Minstrels*, 226–227.

49. Green, *Only A Miner*.

50. *Prison Work Songs* (Arhoolie CD 448); *Angola Prisoners' Blues* (Arhoolie CD 419).

51. John Greenway, *American Folksongs of Protest* (Philadelphia: University of Pennsylvania Press, 1953).

52. Greenway, *American Folksongs*, 228.

TWELVE

Commodification and Revival

Paul J. Stamler

Making a living from traditional music has always been a notoriously dubious enterprise. Well before the Folk Scare of the 1960s, however, a few intrepid souls tried their hands in the marketplace and succeeded. This chapter covers two of the era's major actors, Loraine Wyman and Carl Sandburg, performer/collectors who combined the concert stage with field collecting, and who published songbooks for mass consumption.

LORAINE WYMAN (1885–1937)

Loraine Wyman, one of the pioneer collectors of Appalachian music, remains a shadowy figure in many ways. Apart from the short introductions to her two books—*Lonesome Tunes: Folksongs from the Kentucky Mountains* (1917) and *Twenty Kentucky Mountain Songs* (1920)—and an article by her musical collaborator Howard Brockway, "The Quest of the Lonesome Tunes" (1917), we have little firsthand information about her fieldwork.[1] Her life story is also not well documented; as of this writing the only published source of information is Ralph Lee Smith's brief biography contained in a songbook, *Folk Songs of Old Kentucky* (2003).[2] At the time he wrote, even her date and place of death were not known.

Wyman was born about 1885 in Evanston, Illinois; her mother, Julie, was a professional singer in recitals and oratorios. Not long after Loraine was born, the family seems to have broken up; Julie moved to Paris along with Loraine and her sister Florence, while a third sister remained behind with their father, Walter.[3] While in Paris, Loraine took voice lessons from cafe singer Yvette Guilbert, from whom she acquired a taste for French and British folk songs. Returning to the United States, she became a popular touring concert artist, performing French and British songs in peasant costume and charming audiences and critics across the country.[4] In 1914, the *New York Times* reported that she had achieved critical success as a performer in London, and in January 1916 she stood in for an ailing Guilbert in a concert at the Metropolitan Opera, to rave notices.[5]

Her regular accompanist was pianist-composer Howard Brockway (1870–1951). In June of 1916, looking for American material to perform, Wyman and Brockway went on a folksong collecting trip to Kentucky, using the Pine Mountain Settlement School as a base of operations. Wyman noted the words, while Brockway took down the melodies, often struggling to capture the complexities of mountain singing. In Smith's words,

> In six weeks [they] walked 300 miles through the mountains searching for and finding ballads and songs. Loraine's vitality and good humor undoubtedly stood them in good stead in the delicate task of establishing communication and building trust. So did her rejection of the passive style of many folklorists, who say and do as little as possible to avoid polluting the environment they are studying. When mountain children taught her songs in English, Loraine taught them songs in French! They adored it.[6]

In an article published in *The Art World*, Brockway recounted:

> When we reached small towns which were in communication by stage with the nearest railroad, we found banjos and guitars. We soon realized, however, that the banjo pickers and guitar pickers were never conversant with the real object of our quest. They played a type of song which had no interest for us whatever, with little or no relationship to the song-ballet.[7]

He follows with a lament for the predicted destruction of mountain traditional song as the outside world impinged on such isolated areas. In ignoring songs accompanied by guitar and banjo, it appears that Wyman and Brockway missed the chance to document a transitional phase from the tradition of singing unaccompanied or with dulcimer or fiddle to the songs accompanied by guitar and banjo chronicled in the hillbilly records of the 1920s. Brockway's comment belies a popular myth: that the guitar was not part of the mountain tradition until performers like Riley Puckett and Henry Whitter introduced it at the beginning of the hillbilly record era. The existence of well-defined accompaniment styles from the beginning of recording provides further evidence that guitars were part of the story well before they were first recorded.

From Brockway's article in *The Art World*, one might conclude that the only goal of the Wyman/Brockway expedition was to collect the British-derived ballads that many collectors of the era considered the crown jewels of tradition. In fact, this was not the case; both of the resulting books contain examples of lyric songs: "Kitty Alone";[8] "Fair and Tender Ladies";[9] "On Top of Old Smokey";[10] as well as one dance/play-party tune, "Sourwood Mountain."[11] In addition to publishing, Wyman and Brockway also brought their finds to the concert stage, beginning with New York's Cort Theatre in October 1916 and continuing for the next decade to uniformly enthusiastic reviews.[12] Arguably, they could be described as the first urban folk-revival performers in America; certainly they seem to have been the first to present Appalachian music on the concert stage.

Wyman's charm and beauty seem to have been widely appreciated; in 1917 she was even pictured in an issue of *Vogue*, holding a mountain dulcimer.[13] Brockway's arrangements were popular; Australian-English composer Percy Grainger performed them, and dedicated his own setting of "Knight and Shepherd's Daughter" to Brockway. Wyman also had more scholarly folklore interests. She submitted several of her unedited manuscripts to Kittredge at Harvard, who published fourteen of them as part of a large article in the *Journal of American Folk-Lore*.[14] In these songs, unlike those in her books, she directly identified her individual informants. She also undertook a collecting trip to the town of Perce in the Gaspe region of Quebec, publishing the results in 1920 in the *Journal of American Folk-Lore*.[15] Keeping her toe in the world of classical music, she translated an article on the now obscure French composer Prunières for *Musical Quarterly*.[16]

Wyman and Brockway's song collections seem to have been quite popular. According to the International Union Catalog, eighty-nine years after its publication, *Lonesome Tunes* (either in its original edition or a reprint published in 1944) is held in 194 libraries worldwide, while *Twenty Kentucky Mountain Songs* is held in 118 libraries. Wyman herself, however, slipped out of the public eye. Sometime in the 1920s, she married Henry McMahon Painter, M.D., a prominent obstetrician some twenty-two years her senior, and they moved to the French town of Grez-sur-Loin.[17] They must have returned to the United States a few years later, however, for Dr. Painter died in their New York apartment on 11 March 1934.[18] Only three years later, Loraine Wyman Painter died at New York's Doctor's Hospital on 11 September 1937.[19]

Wyman and Brockway's books were intended for singers, not folklorists. She wrote, "In publishing this collection of Folk Songs we wish it to be primarily an impression of Kentucky music—that is to say, songs reproduced as nearly as possible as we heard them sung by the people, regardless of their extraneous origin or defect. To correct these melodies and to perfect the poetic versions would give them a totally different character."[20]

D. K. Wilgus, in comparing the published versions with the unedited material she sent to Kittredge, found that while the tunes appear to have been presented as gathered, the texts were not. Of the forty-five songs printed, twenty-five—more than half—had their texts changed in minor or major ways.[21] (Wyman's papers are deposited in the libraries of Connecticut College and Brown University; it would probably be instructive to perform a more thorough comparison of published and unpublished material.) Wilgus also notes that while the books include the names of Wyman and Brockway's informants, they are listed in the introductions, without indications of which singer furnished which song.[22] Speaking of Wyman and Brockway's work alongside that of Josephine McGill, he concludes in frustration, "They also illustrate one of the prime difficulties of early folksong collection in the United States. As it was once phrased: the scholars were not musicians and the musicians were not scholars."[23]

Somewhat surprisingly, in view of her popularity, Loraine Wyman seems never to have made any recordings, so we have no idea what her performances might have sounded like. Brockway's arrangements are squarely in the modern European art-song tradition; Wilgus dismissed them by saying that they "fall below the British standard" as presumably set by Vaughan Williams, Grainger, and their colleagues.[24] To my knowledge, only one of the settings has ever made it onto a sound recording; in 1944, Nelson Eddy recorded "Frog Went a-Courtin'" with the Robert Armbruster Orchestra for Columbia records, with the arrangement credited to Wyman-Brockway.[25] It is a record whose transcendent awfulness must be heard to be believed.

Notwithstanding these considerations, Loraine Wyman's work demands respect. She shone a popular light on Appalachian culture, and she presented the material in concert and in books in a way that, according to all available accounts, was designed to both inform and delight her readers and listeners while treating her sources with dignity and respect. For the first real practitioner of the urban folk revival, that is no small accomplishment.

CARL SANDBURG (1878–1967)

If Loraine Wyman lived the last years of her life in quiet obscurity, Carl Sandburg spent some fifty years in the limelight as one of America's most admired writers and poets. The story of his life has been told in multiple biographies over the years; most of them are literary in focus, giving short shrift to his collecting and performance of folk songs. Not until *Carl Sandburg: A Biography* was published in 1991 by Penelope Niven—the first biographer to have complete access to Sandburg's papers—did his work in collecting and performance and his compilation of the influential *American Songbag* (1927), receive the attention they deserve.[26]

Carl Sandburg was born into a respectable working-class family, the second of seven children, on 6 January 1878 in Galesburg, Illinois. His parents were Swedish immigrants; his father, a blacksmith's helper in the shops of the Chicago, Burlington and Quincy railroad, worked ten hours a day for fourteen cents per hour.[27] "We're not rich, but we're not poor," Sandburg's mother would tell him; it was an event when his father purchased a stereoscope and a dozen views.[28] Carl (who in his youth went by the Americanized name of Charlie) was often in conflict with his father over a fascination with books and the world beyond Galesburg, a conflict in which his mother often took Carl's side.[29]

His upbringing did not seem to have been notable for traditional songs, either American or Swedish. In Sandburg's autobiographical *Always the Young Strangers* (1953), he remarked:

> Some peasants sing and some don't. The nearest to a folk song I heard my father and mother sing was the one and only "Gubbah Noah" (Old Man Noah), the verses written by the poet Bellmann. Of the many fine old-time Swedish folk songs, I heard none from the Swedes I grew up with. Nor did I hear of any Swede in Knox County who was supposed to know Swedish folk songs, the sort of a fellow that ballad hunters seek. My mother would hum vague tunes gently at her housework occasionally but no songs, and the father neither sang nor hummed at any time except in church joining in the hymns. Yet he loved music. He bought a cheap accordion and worked out one tune that he played over and over.... His accordion was a private affair. He would play it alone, and if Mama or the children came near and listened he would give a happy smile to them as if to say, "Of course I'm not a musician, but what little I can coax out of this box is interesting and somewhat sweet to me and I hope you find it the same."[30]

Most of the tunes Sandburg mentions in *Always the Young Strangers* were mainstream popular songs, hymns, and minstrel-show pieces rather than folk songs.[31] Typical is the Salvation Army song he quotes:

> As we roll along we all are record-makers
> Records black or white,
> In the wrong or right.
> As we roll along we all are record-makers
> Oh be ready when the train comes in.[32]

There are a few exceptions; he mentions a recognizable version of "The Great American Bum,"[33] and there is a bittersweet story of his father:

> For three or four years a blind Negro with an accordion came to town for a few days and gave out with music at the corner of Main and Kellogg, near a poolroom. He had ballads, sad songs and glad, and always my father had time for this fellow. One payday night he listened a half-hour, turning to me once in a while with smiles to see if I likewise appreciated good music and songs. The Jesse James song my father had heard the previous year and wanted it again. His hand went into his pocket and came out with a nickel. He looked with real respect at the nickel, then walked up, dropped it into the tin cup, and asked if

we could have "de Yesse Yames song." Again the next year I saw him drop into the tin cup five cents in United States coin of the realm in payment for a sheer personal delight of no practical and material use whatsoever. Later when I learned the song and brought it home and sang it for him, he was only mildly interested, didn't ask me to sing it twice. I tried to figure it out and the nearest I could come to it was that if I had been blind and a Negro instead of a Swede and sung it with an accordion he would have given me a nickel and had me sing it twice a week. Also, of course, my voice was still a tender boy soprano while the blind man sang in a gravel baritone.[34]

Young Charlie experimented with homemade musical instruments such as a willow whistle, a comb wrapped in tissue paper, and a cigar box banjo; a "slightly disabled concertina" gave way to a two-dollar banjo from Mr. Gumbiner's New York Pawnshop.[35] Sandburg said later, "I had three banjo lessons at twenty-five cents a lesson. I should have gone on but it was Hard Times."[36] His real fascination with traditional music may have begun when, at the age of nineteen, he spent four months as an itinerant worker and hobo: harvesting wheat, hay, and broom corn in Kansas, blacking stoves, working on a section gang, "washing dishes in Denver, where he got paid for it, and in Omaha, where he did not because the hotel went under before he left."[37] At any rate, when he began keeping a journal during those months, he included songs he'd learned on the road.[38]

In 1898, like many others, Sandburg was swept up in the fervor of the Spanish-American War; he enlisted in the Illinois state militia, serving in Puerto Rico without participating directly in combat (he was the cook's assistant).[39] Discharged, he discovered that his military service had left him unexpectedly eligible for free tuition at Galesburg's Lombard College, a Universalist institution that would considerably broaden his horizons. On campus, he began to write serious poetry, learn the art of oratory in the Erosophian Society, edit the school yearbook and literary magazine, and discover the poetry of Walt Whitman, perhaps his most important literary influence. In the summers, he hit the road with a pal as an itinerant salesman of stereoscopic views.[40]

Sandburg continued his oratorical career as well. He gave lectures on Whitman and in 1907 became a speaker and organizer for the Socialist Party in Wisconsin.[41] In the course of this work, he met, courted and married Lilian "Paula" Steichen.[42] Following the 1908 presidential campaign of Socialist Party candidate Eugene V. Debs, Carl had stints as advertising copywriter, court reporter and editorial writer for the *Milwaukee Journal*, and private secretary to Milwaukee's Socialist mayor, Emil Seidel. In 1912 he landed in Chicago.[43] There he would write for several newspapers, finally coming to rest at the great incubator of American literary talent that was the *Chicago Daily News* under Henry Justin Smith.[44]

The Sandburgs quickly made the acquaintance of a literary circle centering on the newly founded *Poetry: A Magazine of Verse*, edited by Harriet Monroe. *Poetry* was host to a new generation of modernist poets that would shake the world of American poetry to its foundations. The new magazine would introduce to the nation such giants as Rabindranath Tagore, Vachel Lindsay, Robert Frost, William Carlos Williams—and Carl Sandburg. His "Chicago Poems," published in *Poetry*'s March 1914 issue, would catapult Sandburg into the public eye.[45] The money he earned from them—$70, the equivalent of three weeks' newspaper salary—was welcome.[46] The poem "Chicago," one of the group of poems published, would also be awarded *Poetry*'s 1914 Levinson Prize for the best American poem to appear in the magazine that year. In 1916 Sandburg would expand the nine poems that appeared in the magazine into a book; primarily on the strength of this work, Sandburg became recognized as one of the most promising and vital modernist poets of an age undergoing the cultural earthquake of World War I and its aftermath.[47]

With his newfound national reputation, Sandburg in 1919 returned to the lecture circuit, reading his poems before audiences that ranged from literary societies to college social clubs. Crucially, he would close each reading with some folk songs, accompanied on guitar. Often, after the formal program was over, he would use the occasion to collect songs from his audiences.[48] His songs might include "Frankie and Albert," "The Boll Weevil," or "Jesse James"—perhaps the same version his father had paid an itinerant musician to sing decades earlier.[49]

In those post–World War I years, Sandburg branched out into new territory. He became the movie editor for the *Daily News*, a job that allowed him to concentrate his newspaper work into one or two days a week, freeing the rest of his time for his other writing projects.[50] Those projects included children's books: *Rootabaga Stories* (1922), *Rootabaga Pigeons* (1923); more poetry books: *Cornhuskers* (1918), *Smoke and Steel* (1920); and investigative journalism: *The Chicago Race Riots, July 1919* (1919).[51] Most important, he began the massive research that would produce the first part of his Lincoln biography, *Abraham Lincoln: The Prairie Years* (1926).[52]

The Sandburg family needed money. Their oldest daughter, Margaret, was sickly; when she was finally diagnosed as epileptic in 1921 (at a time when effective treatments did not exist), the Sandburgs faced escalating costs for her care, including private schooling, occasional stays in sanatoria, and exotic treatment regimens that provided little or no relief.[53] Their second daughter, Janet, would struggle with learning disabilities (aggravated by vision problems which would eventually be corrected by surgery) and would also require special schooling.[54] Both Margaret and Janet would live with their parents until Carl's death in 1967.[55]

The family continued to scrape by; Sandburg combined his salary on the *Daily News* with the modest earnings from his books and his income from readings. As his reputation grew, his bookings became more numerous and prestigious.[56] Only when *Abraham Lincoln: The Prairie Years* (1926) was finally completed in 1925 did Sandburg achieve financial security. His publisher, Alfred Harcourt, sold the serial rights for the almost unprecedented amount of $27,000, of which $21,600 would go to Sandburg.[57] The book would be released in early 1926, achieving broad (although not universal) critical acclaim and excellent sales.[58]

Sandburg might have been ready for a breather from Lincoln, realizing that his labors on *Abraham Lincoln: The Prairie Years* (1926) would be dwarfed by the work required to complete the four-volume *Abraham Lincoln: The War Years* (1939).[59] Instead, while still correcting page proofs, he proposed a very different sort of project to Harcourt: a book of the folk songs he had collected and absorbed in his years of travel and performance.[60] Perhaps as an aural prologue, he cut several disks for the Victor label, and in early 1926, after promotional work for the Lincoln biography, he dove headlong into the compilation of the folk song book, while continuing to write for the *Daily News*, even adding the labor of a new column.[61]

Preparing the folk song book would prove as strenuous as the Lincoln book had been, and the death of Sandburg's mother in 1926 added an additional burden of grief.[62] Partway through the job, Harcourt suggested that the tunes be presented in harmonizations for piano, rather than in raw form, to make the book more accessible to singers. Reluctantly, Sandburg agreed, to the eventual horror of his musical editor, Alfred Frankenstein, who was abroad when the decision was made.[63] Returning, Frankenstein wrote, "Who in hell is the flat head that got the brilliant idea to harmonize these songs? There isn't the slightest reason for publishing them so, and there are a million reasons against it."[64] Sandburg, meanwhile, had recruited sixteen pianists and contemporary composers to create the arrangements, including Ruth Crawford, who would later marry folklorist Charles Seeger and raise a family of distinguished performers and collectors.[65]

Through 1927, Sandburg's health grew more precarious as the songbook work dragged on. Paula, always supportive, had purchased the vacation cottage in Michigan where he did much of the work and herself spent a great deal of time in correspondence with editor Howard Clark and various printers over the page proofs and the difficult job of engraving the plates properly.[66] In June, Sandburg wrote to a friend, "Sometimes I think the reason that kind of book has not been done before is because so many tackle it and die on the job."[67] And in July, he suffered a nervous breakdown, derailing his labors for two months.[68]

With help from friends and family, he rested through the rest of the summer, and took up his burden again in late September, after a brief trip to Chicago to see the Dempsey-Tunney prize fight which ended with the infamous "long count." *The American Songbag* (1927) was finally put to bed in October and published in November, to excellent reviews and brisk sales.[69] It would remain in print, essentially without revision, for nearly a quarter century, and would be issued in several subsequent editions, including a 1990 reprint with an introduction by the celebrated entertainer and writer Garrison Keillor.[70]

After the songbook, Sandburg entered a long period of intense and productive work. He produced more books for children, a biography of his brother-in-law, the noted photographer Edward Steichen, and another of Mary Todd Lincoln. He finally left the Chicago *Daily News* in 1932, after the publisher had cut staff salaries in response to the Depression;[71] he would return to newspaper writing in 1941 with a weekly column for the Chicago *Times*.[72] In 1936, he created "The People, Yes," a book-length poem that incorporated folk sayings and other folkloric material he'd accumulated over the years alongside his visceral response to the Depression-induced suffering around him, and in 1939 he published the second four-volume installment of his Lincoln biography, *The War Years*.[73] The latter would gain him the Pulitzer Prize for history in 1940[74] while his *Complete Poems* would bring another Pulitzer, this time for poetry, in 1951.[75] In 1955, he wrote the prologue to the landmark photographic exhibition and best-selling book *The Family of Man* (curated by Edward Steichen). One wonders if Steichen's use of folk sayings as epigraphs to the pictures was influenced by Sandburg.[76]

In his later years Sandburg retained his fascination with folk song and folklore. On at least two occasions he recorded songs from the *Songbag*,[77] and he frequently appeared as a singer on television programs hosted by the likes of Milton Berle and Ed Sullivan. He collected (and occasionally composed) scatological folk verses[78] and served as consultant on a collection edited by folklorist Duncan Emrich and composer Ruth Crawford Seeger, who had contributed arrangements to Sandburg's own collection.[79]

Sandburg's final decade was a mixture of triumph and sorrow; honored and beloved as an American icon, he addressed a joint session of Congress in 1959 on the 150th anniversary of Lincoln's birth (the first private citizen to do so since 1874), gave numerous commencement addresses, and appeared as narrator in Aaron Copland's *A Lincoln Portrait*.[80] Amid the honor and affection, however, was unyielding pain, caused by the longtime estrangement of daughter Helga, struggling to make her own career as a writer (they would finally reconcile in 1960).[81] Throughout his last years, he continued to work feverishly, with the intent of providing for Margaret and Janet (both still living with their parents) when he and Paula would be gone, even spending eighteen months working with film director George Stevens on the script for *The Greatest Story Ever Told*.[82]

Slowly, his strength ebbed, and he seldom left the farm in Flat Rock, North Carolina, to which the family had moved in 1945. Sandburg died there, speaking his wife's name, on 22 July 1967; at his request, his ashes were buried in Galesburg.[83]

How to evaluate *The American Songbag*? Academic folklorists have given it short shrift; it was never reviewed in the *Journal of American Folklore*, and D. K. Wilgus dismissed it in a single paragraph:

> [T]o those [categories] already discussed may be added another type, the portmanteau, a sort of valise stuffed with all sorts of goodies, often chosen with the tastes of a large public in mind. Most of the collections of this type either select their contents from other publications or are on other grounds not worthy of serious consideration. Carl Sandburg's *American Songbag* (1927) is just that sort of book; it might be valuable as a cross section of American tradition if one but knew the extent to which Sandburg's "constructive memory" is involved. And of course we should like better documentation and indication of the songs borrowed from other collectors, such as Edwin Ford Piper. But the "cute" divisions into which Sandburg classifies his collection may have influenced the organization of Lomax's *American Ballads and Folk Songs*.[84]

As I have discussed in chapter 10, the organizational pattern of Lomax's work is more likely to have been derived from Gordon, as indeed is Sandburg's to a great extent.

Certainly Sandburg's presentation was idiosyncratic; his methods of collection were eclectic rather than "scientific" (see the earlier discussion of his song-exchanges with audiences after performances), and a surprising number of the songs were collected secondhand, often from middle-class sources. The *Songbag* abounds with quotations reflecting his approach:

> A North Carolina woman at Purdue University heard this for years as a girl from a negro woman cook in her home.[85]

> Walter P. Webb of the Texas Folk Lore Society sang an early Negro version of this for me one evening in a dormitory at the University of Chicago. . . . Webb sang it in imitation of an old Negro woman he had heard as a boy.[86]

> The text is from Red [Sinclair] Lewis of Sauk Center, Minnesota, who got the last verse from George Sterling of San Francisco, and one or two other verses from an Englishman in Italy returning from a cruise to Bombay.[87]

> This Negro woodchopper's song came up from Arkansas and the Ozarks to Tubman K. Hedrick . . . when he was a newspaperman in Memphis, Tennessee.[88]

> An old man selling charcoal used to proclaim himself to the residents of Springfield, Missouri, with this morning cry . . . I notated it, hazardously, from the singing of a faculty member of the state teachers' college at Greeley, Colorado. She came from Missouri. [ellipsis Sandburg's][89]

> One song [heard from a horse wrangler brought to a hospital in Duluth and treated by Dr. T. L. Chapman] was The Colorado Trail remembered by Dr. Chapman as here set down.[90]

Where did the songs Sandburg printed come from? More to the point, from whom did he get them? It seemed worthwhile to attempt an analysis, working from Sandburg's introductions. Such an analysis is necessarily ambiguous; Sandburg's prose is often colorfully vague, making the analysis a somewhat subjective endeavor. (Indeed, simply deciding how many songs or versions are in the *Songbag* is difficult; I finally settled on 298.5—the fraction represents a fragment. Sandburg, more modestly, counts 280.) Nonetheless, the results may give an instructive insight into Sandburg's sources:

> Folklorists and professional performers: 67.5
> Middle-class sources (students, professionals, newspaper reporters, etc.): 67
> Working-class or rural proletarian source performers: 43.5
> Personal experience (learned while hoboing, etc.): 11.5
> Printed non-folklore sources: 10
> Source not given or cannot be determined: 99

Note that about 23 percent of the material came from arguably middle-class sources—the segment of the public that might be expected to attend Sandburg's poetry readings. The limited but real social mobility of America's class structure, of course, makes this figure suspect: an attorney or judge might have come up from a working-class background; a newspaper reporter probably did, while a college student probably did not. Still, it's a suggestively high number for a book chronicling the music of the American lower classes. (To be fair, it was not uncommon for folklorists and amateur collectors of the early twentieth century to include material learned by middle-class individuals from members of the lower classes, particularly when collecting material of African-American origin.) Given these origins, it's remarkable that Sandburg seems to have gotten authentic versions of these songs with almost unfailing regularity, judging by the corroborative evidence collected by more methodical folklorists. With so many obstacles in his way, the man got it right far more often than not—an impressive achievement.

A word is in order about the harmonized arrangements created for the *Songbag*. Sandburg opposed them, feeling that the songs would be better served by leaving the melodies unadorned. In hindsight, he was certainly correct; the arrangements are period pieces, interesting chiefly for what they tell us about the musical fashions of the era rather than for their appropriateness to the material. One can speculate that had Sandburg's opinion prevailed rather than that of his publisher, perhaps the academic folklore community might have been less dismissive. (On the other hand, any effort that catalyzed Ruth Crawford Seeger's interest in folk music can't be considered a total loss.)

While it's valid to criticize Sandburg for poor and confusing documentation and skewed collection methods, it's important to note that his intent was to provide a singing book to the public rather than a scientific study for folklorists. Indeed, he acknowledges this when he refers, in his introduction, to "the song history of America, when someday it gets written."[91] Later he makes his intention explicit:

> First of all, this is a book of *singable* songs [italics his]. It is for the library, but it belongs in the music corner of the library, or on the piano, or on the back porch, or at the summer cottage, or at the camp, or wherever people sing songs and want new songs to sing. . . . History, we may repeat, runs through this book. Yet it is first of all, we say again, a song-book to be sung rather than read.[92]

Sandburg, like Robert Winslow Gordon, was a proselytizer for folk songs. Did he succeed in his stated intentions? It's hard to argue that he did not. The *Songbag* presents an overview of American English-language traditional song and an introduction to its richness unparalleled in its time and unmatched in its popular impact, even by Gordon's *New York Times* articles which appeared contemporaneously with Sandburg's volume and covered similar ground. Sandburg claims over one hundred songs never before published, and while earlier sources have been found for some, a remarkable number of "Earliest Date" citations in the Traditional Ballad Index read "1927 (Sandburg)."[93]

That the *Songbag* had a substantial impact on the American public, particularly the generation that would give birth to the urban folk revival, seems undeniable. The corporate successors of Sandburg's publisher have regrettably declined a request to provide cumulative circulation figures, but the fact of the book's remarkable survival in print and numerous reprints and new editions testify to its popularity. Its importance to the folk revival that began in the 1940s cannot be denied; indeed, a quarter century after the book's publication, Pete Seeger could humorously attribute a song to "Sandbag's Songbird" with full confidence that his audience will get the joke. Even today, folk-revival performers issue CDs with songs chosen from the *Songbag*, recognizing it as a treasure trove of material worth reintroducing to the listening public, while no less a celebrity than popular radio programmer Garrison Keillor has lent his name and prestige to the most recent reprinting.[94]

In short, despite its scholarly shortcomings, the book succeeds on its own terms, as a source of singable songs and a vehicle for introducing the American public to the richness of its (Anglophone) heritage. Its enduring influence and popularity are of value in themselves, and a testimony to Sandburg's skill. Three quarters of a century after its publication, *The American Songbag* is still a visceral pleasure to read, and continues to influence new generations of American singers; on those grounds, and in consideration of its pioneering role in presenting the breadth and depth of the tradition to a broad audience, Sandburg and the *Songbag* deserve our respect and admiration.

NOTES

1. Loraine Wyman, *Lonesome Tunes: Folk Songs from the Kentucky Mountains* (New York: H. W. Gray Company, 1917); Loraine Wyman, *Twenty Kentucky Mountain Songs* (Boston: Oliver Ditson Company, 1920); Howard Brockway, "The Quest of the Lonesome Tunes," *The Art World* 2:3 (1917): 230.
2. Ralph Lee Smith with Madeline MacNeil, *Folk Songs of Old Kentucky: Two Song Catchers in the Kentucky Mountains* (Pacific, MO: Mel Bay Publications, 2003), 28–30.
3. Smith, *Folk Songs*, 28.
4. Smith, *Folk Songs*, 29.
5. *The New York Times*, 21 June 1914; Smith, *Folk Songs*, 29.
6. Smith, *Folk Songs*, 29.
7. Brockway, "Quest."
8. Wyman, *Lonesome*, 22.
9. Wyman, *Lonesome*, 55.
10. Wyman, *Twenty*, 1.
11. Wyman, *Lonesome*, 94.
12. *New York Times*, 29 January 1917; *New York Times*, 13 March 1921.
13. *Vogue Magazine*, 1 May 1917.
14. Victor Morin, "Facéties et Contes Canadiens," *Journal of American Folklore* 30 (1917): 141–157.
15. Loraine Wyman, "Songs from Percé," *Journal of American Folklore* 33 (1920): 321–335.
16. G. Francesco Malipiero, "Henry Prunières," *Musical Quarterly* 6 (1920).
17. Smith, *Folk Songs*, 30.
18. *New York Times*, 12 March, 1934.
19. *New York Times*, 13 September, 1937.
20. Wyman, *Lonesome*, dedication.
21. D. K. Wilgus, *Anglo-American Folksong Scholarship Since 1898* (New Brunswick: Rutgers University Press, 1959), 168.
22. Wilgus, *Anglo-American*, 168.
23. Wilgus, *Anglo-American*, 169.
24. Wilgus, *Anglo-American*, 168.
25. Nelson Eddy, "Frog Went a-Courtin'," Columbia 4316-M (1941).
26. Penelope Niven, *Carl Sandburg: A Biography* (New York: Scribner, 1991); Carl Sandburg, *The American Songbag* (New York: Harcourt, Brace and Company, 1927).
27. Niven, *Carl Sandburg*, 47.
28. Carl Sandburg, *Always the Young Strangers* (New York: Harcourt Brace, 1953): 57; 147.
29. Niven, *Carl Sandburg*, 12.
30. Sandburg, *Always*, 84–85.
31. Sandburg, *Always*, 43; 56; 159; 193; 194; 205; 311.
32. Sandburg, *Always*, 310.
33. Sandburg, *Always*, 194.
34. Sandburg, *Always*, 85.
35. Sandburg, *Always*, 204.
36. Sandburg, *Always*, 204.
37. Niven, *Carl Sandburg*, 37.

38. Niven, *Carl Sandburg*, 35.
39. Niven, *Carl Sandburg*, 41–42.
40. Niven, *Carl Sandburg*, 45–63.
41. Niven, *Carl Sandburg*, 116–138.
42. Niven, *Carl Sandburg*, 179–180.
43. Niven, *Carl Sandburg*, 203–214.
44. Niven, *Carl Sandburg*, 292.
45. Carl Sandburg, "Chicago Poems," *Poetry* 3 (1914): 191–198.
46. Niven, *Carl Sandburg*, 235–244.
47. Carl Sandburg, *Chicago Poems* (New York: Henry Holt and Company, 1916); Niven, *Carl Sandburg*, 252–254, 270–281.
48. Niven, *Carl Sandburg*, 376.
49. Niven, *Carl Sandburg*, 347–348; Sandburg, *Always*, 85.
50. Harry Golden, *Carl Sandburg* (Cleveland: World Publishing, 1961), 204.
51. Carl Sandburg, *Rootabaga Stories* (New York: Harcourt Brace, 1922); Carl Sandburg, *Rootabaga Pigeons* (New York: Harcourt Brace, 1923); Carl Sandburg, *Cornhuskers* (New York: Henry Holt, 1918); Carl Sandburg, *Smoke and Steel* (New York: Harcourt, Brace and Howe, 1920); Carl Sandburg, *The Chicago Race Riots, July 1919* (New York: Harcourt, Brace and Howe, 1919).
52. Carl Sandburg, *Abraham Lincoln: The Prairie Years* (New York: Harcourt Brace, 1926).
53. Niven, *Carl Sandburg*, 380–385.
54. Niven, *Carl Sandburg*, 464–465; 488–489.
55. Niven, *Carl Sandburg*, 702.
56. Niven, *Carl Sandburg*, 382.
57. Niven, *Carl Sandburg*, 426.
58. Niven, *Carl Sandburg*, 433–440.
59. Carl Sandburg, *Abraham Lincoln: The War Years*, vol. 1–4 (New York: Harcourt Brace, 1939).
60. Niven, *Carl Sandburg*, 429.
61. The 3 March 1926 recording session for Victor Records with Sandburg on voice and guitar yielded Carl Sandburg, "Classical Guitar Song," Victor BE-24945 (1926); Carl Sandburg, "The Boll Weevil," Victor BE-24946 (1926); Carl Sandburg, "Negro Spirituals," Victor BE-24947 (1926); Carl Sandburg, "The Two Old Timers," Victor BE-24948 (1926); Carl Sandburg, "Two Cowboy Songs," Victor BE-24949 (1926); Carl Sandburg, "Two Hobo Songs," Victor BE-24950 (1926); Niven, *Carl Sandburg*, 430; 439; 454.
62. Niven, *Carl Sandburg*, 450.
63. Niven, *Carl Sandburg*, 448.
64. Niven, *Carl Sandburg*, 448–449.
65. Niven, *Carl Sandburg*, 448–449; Carl Sandburg, *The American Songbag* (New York: Harcourt Brace, 1927), xv–xvi.
66. Niven, *Carl Sandburg*, 454; 456–457.
67. Niven, *Carl Sandburg*, 453.
68. Niven, *Carl Sandburg*, 458–461.
69. Niven, *Carl Sandburg*, 460–463.
70. Carl Sandburg, *The American Songbag* (New York: Mariner Books, 1990).
71. Niven, *Carl Sandburg*, 487.
72. Niven, *Carl Sandburg*, 544–545.
73. Carl Sandburg, *The People, Yes* (New York: Harcourt Brace, 1936). Sandburg, *War Years*.
74. Niven, *Carl Sandburg*, 475; 502–513; 535.
75. Carl Sandburg, *Complete Poems* (New York: Harcourt Brace, 1950); Niven, *Carl Sandburg*, 600.
76. Edward Steichen, *The Family of Man* (New York: Metropolitan Museum of Art, 1955), 2–3.

77. Carl Sandburg, *The American Songbag*, Musicraft 207–210 (1927); Carl Sandburg, *New Songs from the American Songbag*, Lyrichord LL4 (1950); Niven, *Carl Sandburg*, 680; Carl Sandburg, *Cowboy Songs and Negro Spirituals*, Decca A-356 (1945), produced by Alan Lomax.

78. Niven, *Carl Sandburg*, 659.

79. Ruth Crawford Seeger, Larry Polansky, and Judith Tick, *The Music of American Folk Song* (Rochester: University of Rochester Press, 2001). This project was not finished during Seeger's lifetime, but assembled by Polansky and Tick with permission of the Seeger estate; Niven, *Carl Sandburg*, 597.

80. Niven, *Carl Sandburg*, 679–681.

81. Niven, *Carl Sandburg*, 685.

82. George Stevens, director, *The Greatest Story Ever Told*, United Artists (1965).

83. Niven, *Carl Sandburg*, 699–704.

84. Wilgus, *Anglo-American*, 215–216.

85. Sandburg, *The American Songbag*, 248.

86. Sandburg, *The American Songbag*, 322.

87. Sandburg, *The American Songbag*, 340.

88. Sandburg, *The American Songbag*, 377.

89. Sandburg, *The American Songbag*, 459.

90. Sandburg, *The American Songbag*, 462.

91. Sandburg, *The American Songbag*, vii.

92. Sandburg, *The American Songbag*, viii.

93. The Traditional Ballad Index is a collaborative online index edited by Robert Waltz and David G. Engle, hosted by the Department of Folklore at California State University, Fresno. http://www.csufresno.edu/folklore/BalladSearch.html

94. Sandburg, *The American Songbag*, 1990.

Index

AAFS, see Archive of American Folksong
ACLS, see American Council of Learned Societies
Adams, Samuel, 165
Addison, E. Sheldon, 87
Alabama, 166
Allen, Billy, 93
Allen, Col. DeWitt Clinton, 44
Allen, Jules Verne, 62
Alta, S. Fife, 74–75
Altrurian's Club, 108
American Academy of Arts and Sciences, 5, 15n4
American collective consciousness, 13
American Council of Learned Societies, 183
American Dialect Society, 86
American Folk-Lore Society, 8, 31, 39, 77, 79, 185
American Guide Series (WPA), 100n49
American identity, 2
American School of the Air, 161
Ames, L. D., 40
anthropology, 11, 12, 18
Appalachia, 3, 8
Appalachians, 37
Archive of American Folk Song, see also Archive of Folk Culture
Archive of American Folk Song, 11, 70–73, 151, 157, 183–185
Archive of American Folk Song and John Avery Lomax, 56
Archive of American Folk Song and Todd and Sonkin, 69
Archive of Folk Culture, 22, 73, 69
Archive of Folk Culture and the Fife collection, 75
Arkansas, 37, 154
Arvin camp, 69

Ashton, John W., 90
Austin, E. Fife, 74–75
authenticity in song, 3, 7, 8, 12, 14
Autry, Gene, 52
Averill, Gage, 15n1

Bacon, Alice Mabel, 30
BAE, see Bureau of American Ethnology
Bureau of American Ethnology and fieldworker training, 25
Baffin islands, 23
ballad collection and amateur/professional divide, 24
ballad collection and gender roles, 2, 35n51, 132–133
ballad collection and recording technology, 11, 141, 146n4, 151–152, 164, 174–175, 183
ballad collection and texts, 19
ballad collection and transcription, 141
ballad collection, oral and written forms, 22, 23
ballad collectors and amateur status, 38
ballad collectors and broadcast media, 140, 143, 161–163, 168n30
ballad collectors and gender roles, 31–32, 196
ballad transcription, 10, 122
ballad transmission, 8, 10, 11, 12
ballad wars, 8, 12
ballads and archives, 10
ballads and commodification, 13
ballads and context, 10–11
ballads and impact of radio, 109
ballads and individual interpretation, 11
ballads and melodies, 9–10
ballads and migration, 105–106
ballads and oral tradition, 85

223

ballads and print, 85
ballads and the ur-ballad, 10
ballads and variation, 10, 11
ballads in other languages, 85
ballads, text and melody, 2, 4, 11, 30
Barbeau, Marius, 31, 139
Barnicle, Mary Elisabeth, 156
Barry, Phillips, 8, 88, 105, 116, 192
Bartók, Béla, 26
Barton, Matthew, 15n1
Bayard, Samuel Preston, 8
Beck, E. C., 92–94, 161, 192
Beck, Helen, 60
Beckwith, Martha, 18
Belden, H. M., 38, 84–86, 88
Belden, H. M. and Child ballads, 84–85
Belden, H. M. and collection technique, 85
Belden, H. M., and *Adventure*, 173
Belden, H. M., and Louise Pound, 86
Bemet, Douglas, 186
Benedict, Ruth, 18
Boas, Franz, 17–31
Boas, Franz and ballad texts, 34n26
Boas, Franz and Belden, 39
Boas, Franz and collection practices, 19, 33n9
Boas, Franz and gender roles among collectors, 31
Boas, Franz and influence on ethnography, 23
Boas, Franz and non-evolutionary past, 34n26
Boas, Franz and organizing field recordings, 20
Boas, Franz and pedagogy, 21
Boas, Franz and reluctance to finish collecting, 33n9
Bogart, Barbara Allen, 13, 16n40
Bogtrotters, 162
Bone, David, 197
border of U. S. and Canada, 192
Botkin, Benjamin Albert, 111, 70
Botkin, Benjamin Albert and education, 70
Boulton, Laura, 31
Bowditch, Jonathan, 5
Brewster, Paul G., 83, 86, 91

Bristol, Elisabeth, *see* Elisabeth Bristol Greenleaf
Broadside, 1.49
Broadwood, Lucy, 28
Brockway, Howard, 207
Brodeur, Arthur, 186
Bronner, Simon, 22
Bronson, Bertrand Harris, 8, 9, 11, 16n30–16n35
Brown, George, 108, 111
Brown, Willie, 165
Buchan, Peter, 172
Bureau of American Ethnology (BAE), 17, 23–25
Bureau of American Ethnology and the use of the phonograph, 25–26
Bureau of Ethnology, *see* Bureau of American Ethnology
Burger, Charlie, 91
Burlin, Natalie Curtis, 31
Burnett, Frank, 177
Bynum, David E., 6, 15n17

California, 17, 22, 192
California and economic migrants, 68
California Folk Music Project, 71
Camp Fire Club, 174
Campbell, Olive Dame, 8, 134
Canadian Authors Association, 141
canal songs, 198–199
Cansler, Loman, 47
Cantwell, Robert S., 14, 16n44
Carlisle, Irene Jones, 42
Carpenter, James Madison, 116
Carroll, Lewis, 195
Carson, Fiddlin' John, 177
Cary, Melbert, 179, 185
Cather, Willa, 87
Chancellor, Paul, 184
Cheesman, Tom, 15n7, 16n19
Cheney, Thomas E., 75–77
Chicago Democratic National Convention of 1968, 14
Chicago World Columbian Exposition
Chickering, Geraldine, 86, 92
Child ballads in Mormon communities, 76–77
Child ballads in Ozarks, 38

Index

Child, Francis James and ballad research, 5–7
Child, Francis James and British Poetry editions, 6
Child, Francis James and cannonization of his texts, 5–12
Child, Francis James and challenges to his authority, 8–9
Child, Francis James and education, 5
Child, Francis James and "oral literature," 6–7, 9
Child, Francis James at Harvard, 5
Chippewa (Ojibwe), 94
Chisolm Trail, 62
Civil War, 37, 41, 54
Clark, Charles Badger, Jr., 56
Clark, Howard, 214
Clark, Neil M., 54
Coffin, Tristram, 10, 113
Cohen, Norm, 200
Cohen, Phillip, 163
Cohen, Ronald D., 13, 14, 15, 15n1, 16n43, 16n45, 192
Colcord, Joanna C., 195, 196
collection of ballads and agendas, 2
Colorado, 6.21
Columbia school of ballad collectors, 21
Columbia University and anthropology, 18, 21
Committee on Traditions and Ideals, 107
Communist Party in America, 13
Connecticut, 38
Cooke, Alistair, 159
Coolidge, Dane, 59
Copland, Aaron, 215
cowboy poetry, 52
cowboy song and the radio, 62
cowboys and development of "singing cowboy" idea, 51–52, 62
Cowell, Sidney Robertson, 1, 70–71
Cowell, Sidney Robertson and the Archive of Folksong, 158
Cowell, Sidney Robertson and the Lomaxes, 161
Crawford, Ruth, *see also* Ruth Crawford Seeger
Crawford, Ruth, 214, 215

Cray, Ed, 15
Creighton, Helen, 138–144
Creighton, Helen and broadcast media, 138
Creighton, Helen and Cecil Sharp, 143
Creighton, Helen and education, 140
Creighton, Helen and reputation, 139
Creighton, Helen and transcription methods, 141
critical positivism, 21
Cruickshank, Earl, 40
Cultural Anthropology, 17
cultural relativism, 20
cummings, e. e., 172
Curtis Institute of Music, 181
Cushing, Frank Hamilton, 18
Cylinder Project, 1

Dalhart, Vernon, 177–178
Davis, Arthur Kyle, 111
Davis, Asa, 113
Dean, Michael Cassius, 92, 94
Debs, Eugene V., 212
Delaware, 163
Dennisoff, serge R., 13, 16n38
Densmore, Frances and transcription, 1, 34n14, 111
Densmore, Frances, And the phonograph, 31
Dixwell, Epes Sargent, 5
Dobie, J. Frank, 57–59
Dobie, J. Frank and education, 57
Dobie, J. Frank and Nathan Howard "Jack" Thorp, 54
Dobie, J. Frank and publications, 57–59
Dobie, J. Frank and the Texas Folk-Lore Society, 57
Dodgson, Charles, *see* Lewis Carroll
Doerflinger, William, 186, 192, 194
Dos Passos, John, 172
DuBois, Constance Goddard, 31
Dust Bowl and migration, 3, 67

Eckstorm, Fannie Hardy, 8, 103–106, 196
Eckstorm, Fannie Hardy and education, 104
Eckstorm, Fannie Hardy and Helen Hartness Flanders, 106

Eckstorm, Fannie Hardy and Mary Winslow Smyth, 104–106
Eckstorm, Fannie Hardy and Phillips Barry, 105–106
economic migrants, 3
Eddy, Mary O., 83, 86, 88, 89
Eddy, Nelson, 210
Edison, Thomas Alva, 22, 26
Edwards, David Honeyboy, 165
Eliot, T. S., 172
Elliot, Ruth, 69
Emrich, Duncan, 215
Endacott, Uncle Dan 131
Engel, Carl, 151, 153, 157, 181
English Club of University of Missouri in Columbia, 38–40
English Folk Dance Society, 134, 137, 142
Erie Canal, 198
ethnography, 3
ethnologists and theory, 22
ethnomusicology, 10, 12

Fahy, Fergus, 15
Farm Securities Administration, 68, 95, 158
farming sounds, 202
Federal Music Project, 158
Federal Theatre Project, 158
Fewkes, Jesse Walter, 18, 22, 26–27, 28
Fife Folklore Archives, 74–75
Fife, Austin E. and Alta S., 3, 15n3
Filene, Benjamin, 13, 16n42
Finger, Charles J., 77–78
Fisher, Dorothy Canfield, 107
Flanders Ballad Collection, 109, 112–114, 202
Flanders, Helen Hartness, 8, 30, 31, 107–114
Flanders, H. H., 30
Flanders, Helen Hartness and collection practices, 107–109
Flanders, Helen Hartness and John and Alan Lomax, 112
Flanders, Helen Hartness and Phillips Barry, 110
Flanders, Helen Hartness and the phonograph, 31
Fletcher, Alice Cunningham, 31–32, 94

Fletcher, Curley, 52
Florida, 156
Folger Library, 106
folk revival, 2, 4
Folk Song Society of the Northeast, 106, 110
Folk-Song Society, English, 28, 29–30
Folklore and Language Archives at Memorial University, 131
Folklore Society of Utah, 77
folklore, 18
folklorists, 26
Fowke, Edith, 192
Frank C. Brown collection, 39
Frankenstein, Alfred, 214
Frothingham, Robert, And *Adventure*, 173

Gardner, Emelyn Elizabeth, 86, 92
Garrison, Theodore, 43
Gay, Jane, 31
George, David Graves, 178
George, Elmer, 113, 162
Georgia, 156
Gibbon, J. Murray, 141
Gilchrist, Anne Geddes, 28–29
Gilman, Benjamin Ives, 26, 28
Gilman, Daniel, 5
Gioia, Ted, 192
Goldenweiser, Alexander, 21
Gordon, Robert Winslow, 4, 73–74, 171–187
Gordon, Robert Winslow and Old 97, 177–178, 180, 184, 185
Gordon, Robert Winslow and *Adventure*, 173, 181–182
Gordon, Robert Winslow and bawdy songs, 178–179
Gordon, Robert Winslow and collection practices, 173–174, 174–175
Gordon, Robert Winslow and education, 171–172
Gordon, Robert Winslow and Helen Hartness Flanders, 108
Gordon, Robert Winslow and Library of Congress, 181–183, 185
Gordon, Robert Winslow and recording equipment, 183

Gordon, Robert Winslow and recording technology, 174–175
Gordon, Robert Winslow and the Archive of American Folksong, 151, 183, 185, 187
Gordon, Robert Winslow and the Lomaxes, 184–185
Gordon, Robert Winslow and UC Berkeley, 172, 174
Gordon, Robert Winslow and views on race, 176–177, 186
Gordon, Robert Winslow and WPA, 185
Graff, Bennett, 15
Grainger, Percy, 28, 29, 209
Gray, Roland Palmer, 192
Great Lakes songs, 92–94
Green, J. W. ("Johnie"), 94, 100n48
Greenleaf, Elisabeth Bristol, 121–122, 127–133
Greenleaf, Elisabeth Bristol and collection practices, 128–131
Greenleaf, Elisabeth Bristol and education, 127
Greenough, Mrs. Dennis, 142
Greenway, John, 203
Gresham, Mary E., 156
Grimm brothers, 5
Grover, Carrie B., 115
Gummere, Francis and Robert Winslow Gordon, 172
Guthrie, Woody and Dust Bowl, 67

Haffer, Charles, 165
Hall, sharlot M., 54
Hamilton, Goldy Mitchell, 40
Hampton Folk-Lore Society of Virginia, 30–31
Hand, Wayland, 79
Harrell, Kelly, 177
Harrigan and Hart, 198–199
Harrington, John Peabody, 17, 26
Harris, Marvin, 24
Hart, Walter Morris, 16n18
Hartlan, Enos, 140
Harvard school of ballad collection, 8
Hawkins, Sidney William, *see* Sidney Robertson Cowell
Hemenway, Mary, 26, 27

Hemphill, Sid, 166
Henneberry, Ben, 140
Henry Francis duPont Winterthur Museum and Gardens, 44
Henry Street Settlement, 70
Herskovitz, 21
Herzog, George, 156
Hickerson, Joseph C., 81n22
High, Fred, 37, 47–48
historic-geographic method, 173, 187, 188n16
hobo songs, 79–80
Hoffman, Arthur Sullivan, 172
Hollywood Ten, 60
Holmes, W. H., 24–25
Hoosier Folklore Society, 91
Hoot!, 13
Hootenanny, 13
horse opera, 52
House Committee on Un-American Activities, 60
House, Eddie Son, 165, 200
Hubbard, Lester A., 75–77
Hudson River, 198
Hudson, Arthur Palmer, 39
Hummel, Lynn Ellis, 42
Hunter, Max, 37, 46
Hurston, Zora Neale, 111, 156

Idaho, 75–77
Illinois, 37, 88, 91
Indiana Folklore Institute, 144
Indiana, 88, 91, 158
International Union Catalog, 209
Iowa, 88
Ives, Edward D. ("Sandy"), 192

Jackson, Aunt Molly, 162
Jackson, George Pullen, 111
Jackson, Irene V., 16n36
Jackson, Ulysses, 165
Jacques, Mary J., 54
James, William, 20, 33n9
Javanese music, 27
Jenkins, Gregory, 81n22
Johns Hopkins University, 38
Johnson, Charles S., 164, 165
Johnson, Robert, 165
Johnson, Turner Junior, 165

Johnson, W. S., 40
Joint Committee on Folk Arts, 73
Jones, Lewis Wade, 164–166
Journal of American Folk-Lore, 18

Kahn, Ed, 15n1
Kansas, 37, 40, 88
Karok music, 22
Karpeles, Maud, 29, 133–138
Karpeles, Maud and Cecil Sharp, 136–134
Karpeles, Maud and collection practices, 133–137
Karpeles, Maud and education, 134
Kaye, Andrew L., 15n1
Keillor, Garrison, 214, 218
Kentucky Folklore Record, 78
Kentucky, 37, 134, 157
Kester, Frank, 174
Kittredge, 30
Kittredge, George L., 7–10, 15n16, 16n22, 30, 40, 55, 73, 111
Kittredge, George L. and John Avery Lomax, 55
Kittredge, George Lyman and Robert Winslow Gordon, 172
Kittredge, George Lyman and Robert Winslow Gordon, 73
Knott, Gertrude, 117
Koehn, Willa Mae Kelly, 72
Kolinski, Mieczyslaw, 8
Konomihu music, 22
Korson, George, 111, 201
Krehbiel, H. E., 28
Kroeber, Alfred L., 17–19
Kroeber, Theodora, 19, 31
Kwakiutl, 21, 27

Lancaster, Theodore, 181
Lange, Dorothea, 68
Langenegger, John, 163
Langille, Old Bob, 125
Langille, Easter Ann, 125
Langille, Maggie, 125
Langley, Samuel, 23
Larkin, Margaret, 40, 60
Larkin, Margaret and songs of social protest, 60
Latter-day Saints, *see* Mormon.

LDS, *see* Latter-day Saints
Lead Belly, *see* Huddie Ledbetter
Ledbetter, Huddie ("Lead Belly"), 67, 152, 154, 162
Lewey, Fred, 177–178
Lewis, Meriwether, 24
Library of Congress Music Division, *see* Archive of American Folksong
Library of Congress Archive of Folk Song and Vance Randolph, 41
Linscott, Eloise Hubbard, 114–117
Linscott, Eloise Hubbard and collection practices, 114–115
Linscott, Eloise Hubbard Collection, 117
Liss, Joseph, 163
Little Sandy Review, 13
Lochtenberg, J. S., 40
Lomax, Alan and John Avery Lomax see *also* Lomaxes
Lomax, Alan and the Archive of American Folksong, 157, 11
Lomax, Alan and ballad collection, 51–56, 151–166
Lomax, Alan and Eloise Hubbard Linscott, 117
Lomax, Alan and John Avery Lomax and publications, 56
Lomax, Alan and the Natchez proposal, 168n41
Lomax, Alan and politics, 4
Lomax, Alan and Sidney Robertson, 95–96
Lomax, Alan and Vance Randolph, 41
Lomax, Alan in Wisconsin, 95–97
Lomax, Alan, 1, 11, 15n1
Lomax, Elizabeth, 158–159, 165
Lomax, John Avery and Alan Lomax see *also* Lomaxes
Lomax, John Avery and *Adventure*, 173
Lomax, John Avery and Alan Lomax and publications, 56
Lomax, John and the Archive of American Folksong, 56, 151–152
Lomax, John Avery and ballad collection, 4, 8, 51–56, 151–166
Lomax, John Avery and Barrett Wendell, 55

Lomax, John Avery and collection technique, 55
Lomax, John Avery and editing texts for publication, 56
Lomax, John Avery and education, 55
Lomax, John Avery and field recording, 55
Lomax, John Avery and George L. Kittredge, 55
Lomax, John Avery and Harvard, 30
Lomax, John Avery and Nathan Howard "Jack" Thorp, 56
Lomaxes and African-American song, 157–166
Lomaxes and Archive of American Folksong, 185
Lomaxes and broadcast media, 163, 168n30
Lomaxes and New York City, 162
Lomaxes and politics, 154
Lomaxes and recording in prisons, 152, 154–155
Lomaxes and recording technology, 151–152, 163, 168n41
Lomaxes and Robert Winslow Gordon, 184–185
Lomaxes in the Bahamas, 156
Long-Wilgus, Eleanor, 79
Louisiana, 152, 154–155
Lowie, Robert H., 18, 20, 21
Lowry, Ethel, 40
Lunsford, Bascom Lamar, 111, 163

Macdonald, Sandy, 124
Mach, Ernst, 20, 21
MacKenzie, W. Roy, 40, 122–127, 140
Mackenzie, W. Roy and collection practices, 123–126
Mackenzie, W. Roy and education, 122–123
Mackenzie, W. Roy and Helen Creighton, 127
MacLeish, Archibald, 163
MacMillan, Sir Ernest, 141
Maine, 195
Maitland, Capt. Richard, 162
Major Powell, *see* John Wesley Powell
Maltz, Albert, 60
Mandan, 94

Manny, Louise, 192
Mansfield, Grace Yarrow, 129
maritime songs, 195–198
Maryland, 163
Matthews, Mike, 140
Maynard, Ken, 52
McBride, Bill, 93–94
McCord, May K., 44, 45
McCoy, Joseph G., 51
McDonald, Grant, 42
McGee, William John, 23
McGill, Josephine, 209
McInnes, Campbell, 141
McKay, Ian, 13, 16n41
McNeil, William K., 38
Mead, George Herbert, 33n9
Meeks family murder, 40
Menominee, 94
Merriam, C. Hart, 17
Michigan, 92, 160, 192
Milburn, George, 80
Millar, Branford, 41
Mills Music Library, University of Wisconsin, 100n53
Milman Parry Collection of Oral Literature, 9
mining songs, 3, 79–80
Minnesota, 92, 192
Minnesota Historical Society, 95
Mississippi, 152, 154, 164, 166
Missouri, 37–40, 83–88
Missouri folk songs, 39
Missouri Folk-Lore Society, 38, 39, 40, 84
Missouri Historical Society, 44
Mitchell, Gillian, 14, 16n46
Mitchell, Merlin, 46
Modern Language Association of America, 39, 86
Monroe, Harriet, 213
Monroe, Henry, 142
Montana, 79
Morgan, Lewis, 24
Morganfield, McKinley, *see* "Muddy Waters"
Mormon lore and song, 3, 74–75, 75–77
Morton, Jelly Roll, 159–160
"Mr. Texas," *see* J. Frank Dobie.

230 Index

Music Division, Library of Congress, see Archive of American Folksong
musical instruments and religion, 88
Musick, Ruth Ann, 45
Musick, Ruth Ann and Vance Randolph, 45

National Folk Festival, 70
National Service Bureau, WPA, 73
Nebraska Academy of Sciences, 87
Nebraska, 87
Neely, Charles, 86, 90
Nettl, Bruno, 12, 16n36
New Hampshire, 110, 115
New Mexico, 53, 62, 63
New York, 198
Newell, Colquitt, 40
Newell, William Wells, 8
Newfoundland, 121, 127–138
Nez Perce, 31
Ní Chonghaile, Deirdre, 15n2
Niven, Penelope, 210
Noell, Charles, 177–178
North Carolina, 37, 134, 163, 175
Norton, C. E., 5, 15n1–15n11
notation and performance, 27
Nova Scotia, 123

O'Neill, Patrick J. ("Giant"), 201
Ohio, 37, 83, 89, 158
Oklahoma, 37–40, 53, 60, 67–70, 163
Oklahoma Folk-Lore Society, 70
Oklahoma State Folklore Society, 58
Oklahoma Writers, 70
Old Put, see John A. Stone
Old Sturbridge Village, 44
Olney, Marguerite, 112
Omaha Indians, 94
Ong, Walter, 8, 23
Oral History of Texas Oil Pioneers, 73
oral literature, 6
oral tradition, 8
Osborne, Mrs. Thomas, 140
Oster, Harry, 203
Owens, Jessie Ann, 72
Owens, William A., 72–73
Ozark Folk Center, 38
Ozark mountains, 3, 37–48, 85

Papa Franz, see Franz Boas
Parks, Oscar, 158–159
Parler, Mary Celestia, 37, 41–46
Parler, Mary Celestia and Vance Randolph, 41
Parsons, Elise Clews, 18, 20, 31
participant observation, 19
Pawlowska, Harriet, 92
Pawnee, 87
Payne, Leonidos Warren, Jr., 71
Pearson Circle, 21, 34n15
Peirce, Charles Sanders, 20
Peters, Harry, 97
phonograph and ambivalence of fieldworkers, 22, 23, 28
phonograph and American versus British attitudes, 29–30
phonograph and audio fidelity, 28
phonograph and early field recording efforts, 24, 26
phonograph and gender, 31–32
phonograph and government-sponsored fieldwork, 23
phonograph and impractical employment of it in the field, 2, 22, 25
phonograph and transcription, 26–27, 29–30, 32
phonograph and value in the field, 17–26, 29–30
phonograph as a distraction, 21
phonograph use and attitudes toward it, 21
Pierce, Charles, 153
Pierce, Shanghai, 62
Pine Mountain Settlement School, 208
Pinkerton Detective Agency, 62
play party, 89
Pound, Louise, 86, 88, 93
Pound, Louise and American Folklore Society, 86
Pound, Louise and H. M., 86
Powell, John Wesley, 23–25
prison songs, 203
Puckett, Riley, 177, 208
Pueblo music, 27
Putnam, Herbert, 152

Quarterman, Wallace, 156

Index

Radin, Paul, 18, 20, 23
radio and its role in sustaining folksong, 92
Radio Research Project, 163, 168n33
ranching songs, 3
Randolph, Vance, 37–41, 111
Randolph, Vance and Alan Lomax, 41
Randolph, Vance and amateur status, 41
Randolph, Vance and Charles Seeger, 41
Randolph, Vance and collection efforts, 41
Randolph, Vance and documentation, 49n16
Randolph, Vance and education, 40
Randolph, Vance and Mary Celestia Parler, 41
Randolph, Vance and recording technology, 41
Randolph, Vance and Ruth Ann Musick, 45
Randolph, Vance, and weekly columns, 40
Rayburn, Otto Ernest, 44
Recording technology and field techniques, 69
Reichard, Gladys, 18, 31
Reneau, George, 177
Resettlement Administration, 158, 161
Rickaby, Franz, 92
Riddle, Almeda, 47
Rieuwerts, Sigrid, 15n7–15n15, 16n19
Riggs, Lynn, 60
Roberts, E. C., 94
Roberts, Helen Heffron, 18, 22–23, 31
Roberts, Helen Heffron, and the phonograph, 31
Roberts, Manuel, 130
Robertson, Sidney, 95–96
Robertson, Sidney, *see also* Sidney Robertson Cowell
Robins, John, 141
Robinson, Leighton, 174
Rosenberg, Neil, 13, 16n37
Rosie the Riveter, 42
Roy, Carmen, 139

Sacred Harp singing, 166
sailing songs, 4
Samoan music, 27
Sandburg, Carl, 13, 40, 198, 210–218
Sandburg, Carl and childhood, 210–212
Sandburg, Carl and collection practices, 216–217
Sandburg, Carl and outside academe, 43
Sandburg, Carl and performing, 213, 220n61
Sandburg, Carl and writing, 212–214
Sanovic, Ilija, 156
Saussure, 10
Schmidt, Harold C., 164
Schwab, Mary Jo, 74
secondary orality, 23
Sedgwick, Elizabeth Ellery, 6
Seeger, Charles and Sidney Robertson Cowell, 70
Seeger, Charles and UC Berkeley, 172
Seeger, Charles, and Vance Randolph, 41
Seeger, Ruth Crawford, 156
Seidel, Emil, 212
Senior, Doreen, 142, 143
sensorium, 23
Sharp, Cecil J., 8
Sharp, Cecil and objections to phonograph use, 29
Shay, Frank, 197
Shearin, Hubert G., 88
Sherrard, William J., 115
Sing Out!, 13
singing cowboy, *see* Joseph G. McCoy and Jules Verne Allen
Sires, Ina, 61
Siringo, Charles Angelo, 62–63
Slave Narrative Project (WPA), 157
Smith, Carleton Sprague, 119n36
Smith, Dennis, 143
Smith, Henry Justin, 212
Smith, Hobart, 166
Smith, Marion, 33n9
Smithsonian Institution, 1, 23
Smyth, Mary, 196
Social Music Program, 70
Songcatcher, Who is?, 37
Sonkin, Robert, 68–69

South Carolina, 183
South Dakota, 88
Special Skills Division of the Resettlement Administration, 70
Spivacke, Harold, 157, 159, 185
Steichen, Edward, 215
Steichen, Lilian ("Paula"), 212, 220n42
Steinbeck, John, 68
Stevens, George, 215
Stevenson, Matilda Coxe, 31
Stilley, John, 43
Stone, John A., 79
Stoneman, Ernest, 177
Stout, Earl J., 86, 90–91
Strachan, John, 184
Stratman-Thomas, Helene, 96–98
Stringtown Clodhoppers, 91
Strong, W. H., 44, 45
Szwed, John, 15n1

Tarleton, Fiswoode, 177
Taylor, Mart, 80
Tennessee, 37, 134
Texas, 58, 62, 71, 152–153, 160–161
Texas Folk-Lore Society, 57
Texas Folklore Society, 56
Texas Folklore Society, 71
Theiss, Louis Edwin, 198
Thompson River Indians, 21
Thompson, Ann, 124
Thompson, Ernest, 177
Thompson, Harold W., 198
Thompson, stith, 83
Thorp, Jack, *see* Nathan Howard ("Jack") Thorp.
Thorp, Nathan Howard ("Jack"), 53–56
Thorp, Nathan Howard ("Jack") and editing cowboy songs for publication, 53–54
Thorp, Nathan Howard ("Jack") and horses, 53
Thorp, Nathan Howard ("Jack") and John Avery Lomax, 56
Thorp, Nathan Howard ("Jack") and song collection technique, 53–54
Todd, Charles L., 68–69
Todd, Charles L. and Robert Sonkin and collection techniques, 69
Tolman, Albert H., 88, 89

Turkish music, 27
Turner, James C., 15n9

Underhill, Ruth, 18
union songs, 203
University of Arkansas, 41
University of Missouri in Columbia, 38, 39, 40
University of Nebraska, 38
University of Newfoundland Folklore and Language Archive, 147n36
University of Strasbourg, 38
Utah, 75–77

van Ravenswaay, Charles, 44
Vassar Folklore Foundation, 129
Vermont, 107, 110–112, 115
Vermont Commission on Country Life, 107
Virginia, 37, 134, 162, 166
von Hornbostel, Erich Moritz, 26

Walton, Ivan H., 196
Walton, Ivan, 92, 94
Ward, Grace B., 54
Waters, Muddy, 163, 165
Watson, Ivan and Inez, 91
wax cylinder recording in the field, 1, 18–19
Weeks, Governor John E., 107
Weisner, Jerome, 163
Welty, Lois, 40
Wendell, Barrett, 30, 55, 172
Wendell, Barrett and John Avery Lomax, 55
Wendell, Barrett and Robert Winslow Gordon, 172
West, John O., 56
Western Historical Manuscript Collection at University of Missouri-Columbia, 44
Wheelwright, Mary Cabot, 105
Whisnant, David, 13, 16n39
Whitman, Walt, 212
Whitter, Henry, 177–178, 208
Wiggins, Ella May, 60
Wilgus, D. K., 8, 10, 56, 78–79, 92, 209
Wilgus, D. K. and Michael Cassius Dean, 92

Wilgus, D. K., And John Avery Lomax, 56
Wilgus, D. K., And Loraine Wyman, 209
Willan, Healey, 141
Williams, C. H., 40
Williams, George, 40
Williams, Maude, 38, 40
Williams, Ralph Vaughan, 29, 133
Wilson, James Reginald, 192
Winnebago (Ho-Chunk), 94
Wisconsin, 92, 192
Wissler, Carl, 18
Wolf, John Quincy Jr., 47
Wolford, Leah Jackson, 86, 88–89
Wolford, Leo T., 88
Wood, Ray, 45
Woodward, Judy, 101n61
Woolcott, Alexander, 163
Work, Henry Clay, 177

Work, John W. III, 164–165
Works Progress Administration, 71
Works Progress Administration California Folk Music Project, 70
Works Progress Administration Federal Writers Project, 70
WPA, *see* Works Progress Administration
Wright, Maude, 42
Wyman, Loraine, 13, 207–210
Wyman, Loraine and education, 207
Wyman, Loraine and performance career, 207–208
Wyoming, 88

Yoffie, Leah, 40

Zumwalt, Rosemary Levy, 26
Zuni music, 26, 27, 28

About the Contributors

Matthew Barton is curator of recorded sound at the Library of Congress. He worked as an assistant to Alan Lomax in the 1980s and from 1996 to 2003, and he was production coordinator of the Alan Lomax Collection CD series released by Rounder Records. He has worked at the Library of Congress since 2003, where he became curator of recorded sound in 2008. Barton has contributed essays to *Alan Lomax: Selected Writings, 1934–1997* (2003).

Erika Brady spent more than a decade working with ethnographic cylinder collections at the Library of Congress, and was the principal preservation specialist for the Federal Cylinder Project. Educated at Harvard-Radcliffe, UCLA, and Indiana University, she has a longstanding research interest in ballad and folksong. She has been a professor in the Department of Folk Studies and Anthropology at Western Kentucky University since 1989.

Norm Cohen is the author of several books on American folk and folk-derived music, including *All This For a Song?: Folksong Case Studies* (2009); *American Folk Song: A Regional Encyclopedia*, 2 vols. (2008); *American Folk Music: A Regional Exploration* (2005); *Long Steel Rail: The Railroad in American Folksong* (2nd ed., 2001); and *A Finding List of American Secular Songsters Published between 1860 and 1899* (2002). He has edited and/or annotated more than three dozen albums of folk and country music, and has written numerous articles, book chapters, and book reviews on various aspects of folk, country, and popular music. He divides his time between Portland, Oregon, and Green Valley, Arizona, with his wife and son.

James P. Leary is professor of folklore and Scandinavian studies at the University of Wisconsin–Madison, where he directs the Center for the Study of Upper Midwestern Cultures and coedits the *Journal of American Folklore* with Thomas A. DuBois. His field and archival research on the folklore of diverse peoples in America's Upper Midwest, undertaken since the mid-1970s, has resulted in numerous museum exhibitions, media productions, and publications—including the 20 CD/book package, *Down Home Dairyland* (1996), coproduced with Richard March, concerning traditional and ethnic music of the Upper Midwest; and *Polkabilly:*

How the Goose Island Ramblers Redefined American Folk Music (2006), winner of the American Folklore Society's annual Chicago Folklore Prize for the best book in the field. He is currently at work on a multi-CD/DVD/book project, *Folksongs of the Other America: Field Recordings from the Upper Midwest, 1937–1946.*

Guy Logsdon became interested in fellow Oklahoman Woody Guthrie in 1955 and acquired his first tape recorder in 1957; his first taped recording was his cowboy brother-in-law singing a traditional cowboy song. He has been recording, collecting and writing about Woody Guthrie, western folk music and folk musicians ever since.

Dan Milner comes from a long line of Irish traditional singers. He is a cultural geographer and historian, a folk song collector and researcher, a writer for *Voices: The Journal of New York Folklore* and other publications, a former National Park Ranger at Ellis Island and the Statue of Liberty, and an instructor in New York University's freshman honors program. His recordings include *Civil War Naval Songs* and *Irish Pirate Ballads* (Smithsonian Folkways), and *Irish Ballads & Songs of the Sea* (Folk-Legacy). Dan sings with Robbie O'Connell, The Washington Square Harp & Shamrock Orchestra, and The New York Packet maritime song group.

Canadian folklorist **I. Sheldon Posen** has conducted scholarly research and published on a wide variety of song and music topics including traditional song in the Ottawa Valley; the Canadian children's folk music industry; Jewish cantorial song; singing at children's summer camps; hockey star Maurice "The Rocket" Richard in popular song; shape note singing; English village carols; and highly decorated musical instruments. For several years he wrote the "Songfinder" column in the popular American folksong quarterly *Sing Out!* Posen is director of the Ethnology and Cultural Studies division at the Canadian Museum of Civilization. He lives in Ottawa, Canada.

Nancy-Jean Ballard Seigel, a Vermonter now living in Maryland, is the granddaughter of the New England folksong collector, Helen Hartness Flanders. Currently working on a biography of her grandmother, she has published articles and given presentations about the Flanders Ballad Collection, its singers and songs. Nancy-Jean, a former French teacher, has also worked at the American Folklife Center of the Library of Congress. In 2001, she received an award from the Parsons Fund for Ethnography to support researching, organizing, and adding to the files of the Helen Hartness Flanders Ballad Collection in the Archive of Folk Culture.

Scott B. Spencer is currently the National University of Ireland, Galway/American Irish Cultural Institute Visiting Research Scholar. He has published articles on Irish music and sonic studies in a variety of journals, most recently the *Journal of the Society for American Music*. He teaches music and Irish studies courses at Drew and Villanova Universities and has run the Center for Traditional Irish-American Music at the City University of New York's Institute for Irish-American Studies in the Bronx. He plays flute with the Washington Square Harp and Shamrock Orchestra, and he lives with his family in Swarthmore, Pennsylvania.

Paul J. Stamler was born into a family of folk-revival participants in 1950 and attended his first performances of folk music (by Pete Seeger and Frank Hamilton) when he was five years old. In the years since, he has been a performer of traditional songs and dance music; helped found the major folk venue St. Louis's Focal Point; recorded folk-revival performers such as Martin Carthy and Dave Swarbrick and the Buckhannon Bros.; presented concerts; remastered 78s; called dances; and written for *Come for to Sing* and *Sing Out!* magazines. For twenty-four years he has hosted "No Time to Tarry Here" on KDHX-St. Louis. He was part of the group that created the Traditional Ballad Index, and he is currently an adjunct faculty member of the Department of Audio Aesthetics and Technology at Webster University.